About Island Press

Since 1984, the nonprofit organization Island Press has been stimulating, shaping, and communicating ideas that are essential for solving environmental problems worldwide. With more than 1,000 titles in print and some 30 new releases each year, we are the nation's leading publisher on environmental issues. We identify innovative thinkers and emerging trends in the environmental field. We work with world-renowned experts and authors to develop cross-disciplinary solutions to environmental challenges.

Island Press designs and executes educational campaigns in conjunction with our authors to communicate their critical messages in print, in person, and online using the latest technologies, innovative programs, and the media. Our goal is to reach targeted audiences—scientists, policymakers, environmental advocates, urban planners, the media, and concerned citizens—with information that can be used to create the framework for long-term ecological health and human well-being.

Island Press gratefully acknowledges major support of our work by The Agua Fund, The Andrew W. Mellon Foundation, The Bobolink Foundation, The Curtis and Edith Munson Foundation, Forrest C. and Frances H. Lattner Foundation, The JPB Foundation, The Kresge Foundation, The Oram Foundation, Inc., The Overbrook Foundation, The S.D. Bechtel, Jr. Foundation, The Summit Charitable Foundation, Inc., and many other generous supporters.

The opinions expressed in this book are those of the author(s) and do not necessarily reflect the views of our supporters.

What Makes a Great City

What Makes
a Great City

ISLANDPRESS Washington | Covelo | London

Keywords: beach, Bilbao, boulevard, business improvement district (BID), habitability, livability, park, pedestrian, plaza, promenade, public realm, public square, public transit, rectilinear grid, remediation, resilience, street, urbanization, walkability

Library of Congress Control Number: 2015960067

♻ Printed on recycled, acid-free paper

Manufactured in the United States of America
10 9 8 7 6 5 4 3 2 1

Contents

Chapter 5: Attracting and Retaining Market Demand . 91

Chapter 6: Providing a
Framework for Successful Urbanization 125

Chapter 7: Sustaining a Habitable Environment . . 159

Chicago lakeshore (2008).
(Alexander Garvin)

PREFACE

What Makes a Great City

A few years ago a friend asked me, "What makes a great city?" Despite having studied cities for more than half a century, I had no ready answer to this question. All that evening I found myself coming back to it: What makes a great city? Not a good city, or a functional city, but a *great city*. A city that other cities' inhabitants feel obliged to admire, emulate, and learn from. I thought about the Chicago lakeshore, with thousands of people on the beach enjoying the sun in front of a backdrop of stupendous office towers and apartment buildings. I remembered the first time I strolled down the Champs Elysées in Paris. I even reread a passage from F. Scott Fitzgerald's essay "My Lost City," in which he described the skyline of Manhattan as "the white glacier of lower New York swooping down like a strand of a bridge to rise into uptown."¹ No matter how I tried, I was still unable to answer the question.

I thought about the reasons people come to a city in the first place. The reasons are as numerous as the residents of the city. They come for work, for intellectual stimulation, to do business, to shop or sightsee, and sometimes even to start a new life. They come to visit a department store, attend a college, sample a hotel, consult a library, be treated in a hospital, browse a museum, see a show, or visit one of the thousands of other useful and interesting destinations that all great cities provide. Yet, whether people come to a city for a day or to live there permanently, a city must do more than contain the stores, schools, libraries, museums, residences, places of employment, and other facilities for them to use, either alone or with others.

A great city also must be easily accessible, safe, and friendly. It also must include a wide array of well-maintained amenities that are open to anyone and provide something for everybody. And, most important, it must offer people a chance to achieve their dreams. These were certainly characteristics of a great city. They did not, however, answer the question, What makes a great city?

As a professor of urban planning and management at Yale University, for most of my adult life I have been observing and writing about the major municipal centers of the world. And yet, that night, and the next day, and the day after that, I simply could not come up with a satisfactory answer to my friend's seemingly simple query. This fact bothered me—a lot.

So, gradually, an idea began to take root in my mind: Why not take advantage of the time and opportunities that come my way during the next year or so to travel to some great cities to answer this important yet elusive question? I had already traveled to most countries in Europe and to all the major cities of the United States, but never with the intent of answering this particular question. With the question in mind, I'd make a special visit to Paris, which I knew well from working there as a young architect and which I believed had for centuries set the standard for a brilliantly designed and managed urban realm. I'd go back to American cities that were thought to be examples of good planning, such as Portland, Oregon, and Minneapolis, and cities, such as Houston and Atlanta, that many experts criticized as examples of terrible planning. I'd spend time in Madrid, which in the past few years has bootstrapped itself up from urban anarchy to one of the most well-run cities in Europe. I'd even revisit places in New York City, which has always been my home and where I had worked in different capacities within five different city administrations.

I decided that I would not go to cities outside North America and Europe for three reasons. First, I have a rule that I have followed for nearly half a century: I neither speak about nor write about places to which I have not been. Second, I would not have the time I needed to learn about the many cultures of Africa, the Middle East, or South Asia. And third, although I had been to some cities in East Asia, as well as to Turkey, Australia, and South America, I had only a superficial understanding of their centuries-old cultures, and I knew better than to try to develop the deep understanding that would be required to write knowingly about cities that I did not know well.

In all, I planned to visit the cities in Europe and North America that my respected colleagues and I considered among the great cities of the world and some that experts thought illustrated mediocrity or worse. Once there, I'd observe them close-up. I'd wander their streets, browse their shops and museums, eat at their sidewalk cafés, study their traffic patterns and pedestrian zones, sit in their parks, cycle their bike lanes, talk to their people, and breathe their air, and in the process keep posing the question, What makes this city so special? What makes a great city?

For the next two years I did just that. I traveled to some of the great cities of the Western World and while there dedicated myself to determining why these cities were so great. This book is my answer. It is neither a textbook nor a travelogue. It is the story of my quest to determine *what makes a great city* and a presentation of my conclusions.

The question What makes a great city? is not about the most beautiful, convenient, or well-managed city; it isn't even about any "city." For me it is about what we can *do* to *make* a city great. To my surprise I found the answer in Bilbao, Spain.

I was familiar with the "Bilbao Effect," in which the opening of a branch of the Guggenheim Museum, I had been told, reversed years of economic decline and transformed Bilbao into an urban celebrity. To be fair from the outset, I thought that the notion that showpiece attractions, like the Bilbao Guggenheim, could by themselves make a city great was highly unlikely, but not impossible. After all, when people think of London, they remember St. Paul's Cathedral, Westminster, and London Bridge, just as they recall the Statue of Liberty, Times Square, and the United Nations when they think of New York. Identifying a city with its special attractions is a widespread phenomenon, but ascribing that city's greatness to the presence of one special attraction seemed to me a bit of a stretch.

Bilbao Guggenheim Museum (2013). (Alexander Garvin)

I became aware of Bilbao thirty years ago when the city had become a well-known economic basket case. At that time, there was no reason for me to go there. That reason came later with the opening of a branch of the Guggenheim Museum in 1997. I wanted to see Frank Gehry's extraordinary new building, so in 2013, I traveled to Bilbao to discover what had happened and to learn why.

When I arrived in Bilbao, I found a thriving metropolis whose residents had little involvement with the Guggenheim Museum. They jammed stores and restaurants. Children, parents, and dog walkers filled the parks. Unlike me, they were not visitors who had come to see the Guggenheim. Certainly, the museum had enhanced the life of the city, made Bilbao a tourist destination, and generated substantial additional economic activity. How, I wondered, could a museum solve fundamental economic problems?

As I soon discovered, the museum alone had not transformed the city. Bilbao's transformation was the product of major investments in environmental decontamination, flood protection, and riverfront redevelopment, as well as its significant expansion of the public transportation system, and perhaps most

The city moved shipping, warehousing, and manufacturing from the Nervión River to the Bay of Biscay, redeveloped the newly available sites along the river, and invested in a transit system to connect them. One of these sites came to house the Guggenheim. (Owen Howlett, Alexander Garvin)

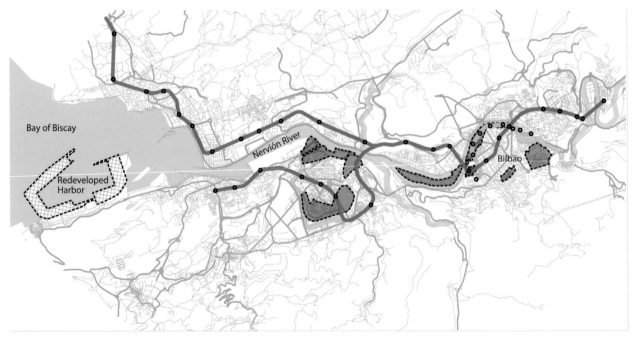

 Urban Redevelopment Areas
Redeveloped Harbor
Bilbao Metro System
Bilbao Light Rail

important, major improvements to its streets, squares, and parks. Indeed, collectively, these initiatives were the reason that the city was full of satisfied shoppers, ordinary grandmothers, international business leaders, curious teenagers, talented workers, and everybody else.

When the municipality of Bilbao reached its peak population of 433,000 in 1980, it was famous for the filthy buildings and foul air "from the blast furnaces along a stinking river that trafficked in floating objects."[2] At that time, the city's industrial base (steel, machine engineering, and shipyards) was already in decline. Unemployment was close to 25 percent. Between 1975 and 1995, Bilbao lost 60,000 industrial jobs, cutting industrial employment in half.[3] The accompanying flight of population from Bilbao resulted in a population decline of 81,000 people (19 percent) by 2010.[4]

Disaster hit on August 26, 1983, when the Nervión River, which runs through Bilbao, flooded, rising as much as ten feet (3 m) in some places. The flooding caused parts of two bridges to collapse and resulted in the death of thirty-seven people in that region of Spain. Local, regional, and national leaders responded to the crisis with a program that dramatized the devastation caused by flooding as a way of galvanizing public support for actions that addressed fundamental economic and environmental problems.[5]

The redevelopment program that emerged over the next eight years included:

- eliminating pollution from the Nervión River;
- decontaminating and physically reconstructing large areas of land along the river;
- expanding port facilities at the mouth of the river in the Bay of Biscay, relocating shipping activity from the river to the bay, and redeveloping riverfront property previously used for shipping or manufacturing;
- investing in public transportation that included Metro, a new underground system that connects the communities along the river with those along the bay, restructuring and expanding the existing urban railway, creating a light rail system connecting in-town neighborhoods, and interconnecting all of them;
- creating a 4.7-mile (7.5-km) riverfront promenade.

These actions were embodied in the Strategic Plan for the Revitalization of Metropolitan Bilbao that was agreed to in 1991. They would be promoted and implemented by two agencies created with the specific purpose of carrying out the plan: Bilbao Ría 2000 and Bilbao Metrópoli-30.[6]

Plaza Moyua, Bilbao (2013). The city's subway, designed by architect Norman Foster, made travel downtown easier and less expensive. (Alexander Garvin)

Long before the strategic plan was officially adopted, government agencies had decided to invest in the subway system and began assembling properties and decontaminating sites that had redevelopment potential. In 1988 the British architect Norman Foster won a competition for the design of the Metro.

Three years after Foster began work on the Metro, when an art exhibition from the Guggenheim opened at the Reina Sophia Museum in Madrid, the Bank of Bilbao was persuaded to finance a successful effort to convince the Guggenheim Museum to open a branch in Bilbao. It took the leaders of Bilbao another two years to convince the Guggenheim to accept the offer of a site along the Nervión River that was in one of several redevelopment areas.

The new museum was designed by the American architect Frank Gehry. And when it opened in 1997, the Bilbao Guggenheim became the instant icon of the city's revitalization—a beacon announcing its importance to the rest of the world. The spectacular building that Gehry designed made him the most famous American architect since Frank Lloyd Wright, and the publicity that the museum building generated transformed this relatively obscure provincial city (the tenth largest in Spain) into an internationally known tourist destination. It was natural, therefore, to believe that the museum was responsible for Bilbao's revival.

Riverfront promenade and light rail, Bilbao (2013). This 4.7-mile riverfront promenade bears little resemblance to the polluted, chaotic industry that once characterized the area. (Alexander Garvin)

The Bilbao where the Guggenheim Museum now stands bears little resemblance to the city that the Nervión flooded in 1983. In 1996, the year before the museum opened, 169,000 visitors came to Bilbao. Fifteen years later, the number had risen to 726,000, with some of the increase attributable to the opening of the Bilbao Exhibition Centre in 2004, which attracted an additional 100,000 convention participants.[7] The city's population had fallen from 433,000 in 1980, stabilizing in 2010 at just above 350,000. The metropolitan area gained 113,000 jobs between 1995 and 2005.[8] The unemployment rate dropped from 25 percent to 14 percent, four percentage points lower than that of Spain as a whole.[9] Clearly the city had been doing something right, but it would be rash to ascribe such success solely to the opening of a major museum when the story is so much deeper.

Calle Ercilla, Bilbao (2013). Residents of Bilbao now enjoy much improved streets that have been reconfigured for public use. (Alexander Garvin)

Access to the riverfront via a beautiful promenade may be what visitors encounter as soon as they leave their hotel to go to the Guggenheim Museum, but those visitors are only a small portion of the people sitting on benches, or strolling, jogging, and cycling along the promenade. Residents flock to reconfigured and repaved downtown streets. In some areas, such as Calle Ercilla, the street has been re-landscaped, vehicular traffic prohibited, and the roadway reallocated entirely to pedestrians. Many public squares have been redesigned, and if there is a subway stop, such as at Plaza Moyua, outfitted with distinctive entrances to the Metro. Public parks have been updated to provide places for dog owners to congregate, children to play, older people to sit in the shade, and everybody to enjoy.

The riverfront promenade, street improvements, pedestrian precincts, reconceived public squares and parks, light rail and subway lines, and new public buildings were envisioned as ways of retrofitting Bilbao for the twenty-first century. These public realm investments made the city easily accessible to tens of thousands of people for whom reaching the city and getting around in it had been difficult and expensive. Its streets, squares, parks, and once-contaminated sections of the waterfront were transformed into safe, well-maintained, friendly places that provide amenities for everybody, regardless of income, social standing, or proximity to the city center. In addition to making it more livable, this massive public investment throughout the city also transformed perceptions of the city. People began to think of Bilbao as a desirable place to live and do business. Many of them decided to expand existing businesses or open new ventures there. The Guggenheim was not what made the difference, rather the new public realm (of which the Guggenheim is now part) attracted and kept people and businesses in Bilbao. And these people are the ones who are making Bilbao one of the great cities of Spain.

My visit to Bilbao convinced me that people are what make a city great. The public realm may be what initially attracts them. But there comes a time when without adjustments it will no longer keep them there. So they make the changes they need, changes that attract others as well. What I learned in Bilbao underscored what I already believed: that a great city, unlike a great painting or sculpture, is not an exquisite, completed artifact.

To explain what makes a great city, I decided to describe the ways in which the people who use great cities continually change the public realm so that it meets current needs without impairing the ability of future generations to continue doing so. This book takes a markedly different approach from authors who depend on secondary sources. The examples presented are the result of personal observation, usually as a result of numerous visits, only supplemented by other people's writings. It does discuss the history, demographic composition, politics, economy, topography, history, layout, architecture, and planning of great cities, but it is not about those topics. It also examines the design and functioning of the public realm, but it is not about them either.

The first two chapters of this book explain what exactly is meant by the expression "the public realm" and what the characteristics of a great public realm are. The next six chapters describe each of those characteristics in detail, as well as when and how they work or don't work. The book's penultimate chapter discusses how a particular component of the public realm (squares in London, parks in Minneapolis, and streets in Madrid) shapes people's daily lives. At the end of the book I present twenty-first-century initiatives undertaken in Paris, Houston, Atlanta, Brooklyn, and Toronto that are making an already fine public realm even better—initiatives that demonstrate how any city can improve its public realm.

Place de la République, Paris
(2014). (Alexander Garvin)

ACKNOWLEDGMENTS

E ver since I read *Death and Life of Great American Cities* in 1961, I have agreed with Jane Jacobs that "Cities are an immense laboratory of trial and error, failure and success in city building and city design," and followed her advice to study "success and failure in real life."[1] This book is the product of my determined empiricism, but it also reflects the impact of many people, including three important thinkers who have deeply influenced my work and the contents of this book—Edmund Bacon, Frederick Law Olmsted, and Pierre Pinon.

I met Edmund Bacon (executive director of the Philadelphia City Planning Commission from 1949 to 1970, and the "father of modern Philadelphia") twenty years ago, after I had published my first book, *The American City: What Works, What Doesn't*. From then until 2005, when he died, I visited him in Philadelphia five or six times a year. We would walk around the city while he explained to me what he thought about everything we passed, always explaining how a city planner ought to think about it. I already believed in the importance of the public realm. For Bacon, however, it was more than important: it was the very foundation of city planning. So, the Bilbao epiphany that I described in the preface was not really a discovery. It was a confirmation of what Bacon had made explicit during our many visits together: great cities develop around a great public realm.

Frederick Law Olmsted has been a major influence on me for as long as I can remember. I grew up in New York City, across the street from Central Park, which he and Calvert Vaux had designed. As I explain in chapter 4, I began learning about the public realm as a toddler wandering around this extraordinary place. After more than seven decades exploring what makes Central Park the world's greatest public realm and having read all nine volumes of *The Papers of Frederick Law Olmsted*,[2] as well as the two supplementary volumes, there are two elements of the Olmstedian conception of a great public realm that stand out in my mind. First, he convinced me of an inseparable and ongoing relationship between man and nature: that any landscape will affect the lives of human beings who pass through it every bit as much as those human beings also will have an impact on the landscape. Therefore, the design, development, maintenance, and management of any component of the public realm must consider that interaction on an ongoing basis. Second, at all times, the public realm acts as the cradle for a civil society, and democracy, in particular.

I believe you cannot understand any physical landscape—urban, suburban, or rural—without familiarity with how it got to be that way. So, from childhood I have been fascinated with the history of the places I visited. While working on my last book, *The Planning Game*, I came across *The Atlas of Haussmann's Paris* by the architect and historian Pierre Pinon.[3] Pinon's work opened my eyes to the many, many attempts at transforming Paris by countless players, many of whom did not succeed at obtaining the changes they sought, but did inspire later initiatives that were successful. More importantly, by reproducing countless maps, drawings, and photographs, Pinon demonstrated that Paris, and by extension all other cities, is the product of the ongoing exploration of ideas by and the cumulative actions of generations of city dwellers. I am indebted to Pinon's work not just as it applies to the sections of Paris I discuss in this book, but also to his conception of every city as an evolving product of its residents.

I owe a great debt to these intellectual forbears, but just as importantly, this book, and all my books, would not exist were it not for the continuing support of all my friends.

The books would never have been published but for the persistent support of my friend, student, and literary agent, Arthur Klebanoff. He has given me the backbone to persevere in the face of adversity and I am forever grateful to him doing so.

The increasing amount of personal observations in my writing is due entirely to my friend Rick Rubens. He has continued to insist that it is not enough for me to present the facts. With each book he has pushed me further toward expressing my opinions. I hope that with this book I have provided what he has so long argued for.

I wish I could produce prose with one one-hundredth of the evocative beauty of my favorite writer, F. Scott Fitzgerald. He, Ernest Hemingway, and Thomas Wolfe had the benefit of a great editor, Maxwell Perkins. I thought, quite erroneously, that this was standard. I have had some thoughtful editors, Nancy Green and David Carroll in particular. In editing this book, however, Heather Boyer has provided more ongoing challenges, questions, and suggestions than is common to the publishing industry. She, along with the entire production team at Island Press, especially Milan Bozic who designed the book, have helped to create a work that I hope will astonish and fascinate its readers.

This book is as good as it is because of two people: my assistant, J. D. Sagastume, and Owen Howlett. J. D. read every word of multiple versions of the text; corrected errors; questioned ideas and, often, facts; disputed arguments; and discussed every page with me. This book's 252 illustrations are as important as the text, and so I owe a great debt to Owen Howlett, who created some maps and adjusted others initially drafted by Joshua Price, Ryan Salvatore, and Cortes Crosby. Together with the 26 historical images, 2 renderings, and 191 of my photographs, these 33 maps convey what would have required tomes of text to explain.

Ryan Salvatore made suggestions about early versions of the text. David Freeland contributed greatly to my understanding and discussion of both the Plaza Mayor in Salamanca and Times Square. Bob Ethington took me on several excursions around Uptown Houston and helped me better understand Post Oak Boulevard. Chris Glaisek first introduced me to the Toronto waterfront, took me on numerous tours, and adjusted the text. Dan Biederman has been instructing me about the 34th Street and the Bryant Park business improvement districts for years. Without his tutoring the discussion of those places would be far less interesting and convincing. Regina Myer took me on several walking tours of the Brooklyn Bridge Park, without which I would have been unable to explain its smashing success.

Many other people have been generous with their time and thinking about many of the places discussed in the book. You all know who you are. I thank you along with Antti Ahlava, Carolyn Adams and John Meigs, Leslie Beller, Doug Blonsky, David Brownlee, Ricky Burdett, Terry Farrell, David Freeland, Trevor Gardner, Michael Graf, Ken Greenberg, David Haltom, Isaac Kalisvaart, Paul Kelly, Max Musicant, Herman Pettegrove, Alec Purves, Heywood Sanders, Janette Sadik-Khan, James Santana, Jim Schroder, Sam Schwartz, Alfonso Vergara, Rodney Yoder, and Olga Zinovieva.

National Mall in Washington, D.C. (2010). (Alexander Garvin)

The Importance of the Public Realm

Bilbao had become a great city by investing in its streets, squares, parks, and infrastructure. These are the parts of the city that people share in common, occupy together, and use on an everyday basis. They matter to *everybody*. That's why its occupants had devoted their time, money, and efforts to reconfigure them to meet their latest needs.

Any city's infrastructure (its water, sewer, utility, and transportation systems) is what allows people to live there. The more widespread and comprehensive the infrastructure, the greater the number of people who can use it. But is it part of the public realm? Similarly, the more extensive a city's network of streets, squares, and parks, the easier it is to live there. But does the public realm include anything else?

Defining the Public Realm

With the exception of the transportation network, especially subways, infrastructure is not accessible to everybody, so it may seem to be apart from the public realm. This infrastructure has come to be managed everywhere as a public utility paid for on a fee-for-service basis, rather than from general government revenues. Unlike the rest of a city's infrastructure, however, the public is able to come, go, and circulate within the transportation network in the same fashion as it does in streets, squares, and parks. But it does have to pay for using subways, buses, trains, and other components of the transportation network. Thus, although transportation is not usually available for free, it really is part of a city's public realm.

I already understood that the public realm included everything that was accessible but not in private ownership. I also understood that this included sidewalks, public benches, lighting, signage, vehicular roadways, and everything else within city streets, squares, and parks. But I was overly focused on these three main components of the public realm. I understood that only during a visit to Hvar, a small Croatian city on an island in the Adriatic Sea, late in my quest to determine the importance and characteristics of a great public realm.

Promenade, Hvar, Croatia (2015). This combination of street, park, and square is central to life in this small city. (Alexander Garvin)

I was walking along the city's harbor promenade, which is lined on one side by boats of every size and description and on the other side by hotels, bars, cafés, restaurants, and souvenir vendors. In the distance, the hills sloping down to the harbor were covered with charming, red-roofed, limestone buildings that provide residents with places for business, family life, and community activities. Lots of people were out walking along the promenade, having coffee in the cafés, meeting friends, making new acquaintances, sitting on benches, walking along the beach, tying up boats . . . The promenade provided a welcoming part of Hvar's public realm that was easily accessible to all the city's residents. It was not a street with cars and trucks, yet people were using it to get from one place to another; it was not a park, although children were using it to play games and adults were sitting on benches sunning themselves; it was not a square, either, but groups of people were using it as a gathering place.

For me this experience only emphasized that I had to explain the importance of the public realm not just by discussing streets, squares, and parks as the three major components of the public realm, but also by examining the sometimes ordinary, but usually very special places, such as Hvar's waterfront promenade, that are not exactly streets, squares, or parks, but are also very much a part of the public realm.

Streets, Squares, and Parks

Streets, squares, and parks have specific and very different functions. Each component, in turn, complements its core functions with a variety of other activities that make its contributions to the public realm even richer.

As this book will explain, of the three major components, it is a city's streets that contribute most to shaping its character. Their chief function is to provide corridors that allow people, goods, and vehicles to move from points of origin to specific destinations. This may be the core function of streets. But along the way, streets play host to a wide variety of activities, both commercial and recreational, that keep a city energized, interconnected, and socially functional. When streets take the form of limited-access highways, however, they are not entirely "public," as they only are available to motor vehicles and their occupants.

When walking these streets, many people will simply pass through. Others will avail themselves of the streets' special attractions or casually stroll, check out the window displays, and enjoy the buzz. Still others will make their way to destinations located along the street or elsewhere in the city. In fact, the number of people passing through a street usually far exceeds those who are there for a specific reason. Nonetheless, great streets offer passersby the opportunity to stop and shop, rendezvous with friends, sit, or park their bicycle along their way.

City squares, like streets, contribute to the public realm by offering a wide choice of social, political, and business activities designed to attract both individuals and groups. People from all over the city gather in these squares at different times of day, and at different seasons of the year. A myriad of activities take the stage here: celebrations, protests, musical events, political rallies (such as Occupy Wall Street), candlelight vigils, free children's shows, farmers markets, speeches, street performances, art exhibits, and anything else people can think of. But the main function of a city square is to serve as a social and political center that invites participation from all levels of society and that provides a sense of community and unity to those who participate.

Parks offer city dwellers a variety of recreational opportunities, though a great deal more than recreation takes place there. People pass through (and enjoy) public parks on their way to somewhere else, just as they do on city streets. They gather there for public events, just as they do in squares. But because a far greater proportion of the territory occupied by parkland consists of greenery, parks are likely to provide a healthy haven from the surrounding city and contribute to its livability.

Beyond Streets, Squares, and Parks

There are some examples of the public realm that cannot be neatly fit into the category of street, square, or park—places such as the National Mall in Washington, D.C., the Galleria Vittorio Emanuele II in Milan, the greenways in the Society Hill section of Philadelphia, and subways everywhere. People everywhere use open air malls, skylit arcades, and pedestrian walkways.

They function in the exact same way as streets, squares, and parks do. Yet they are not, strictly speaking, any one of the three. Everybody understands that they are part of the public realm, but we often forget that they require funding for the same maintenance and management personnel that are routinely devoted to the streets, squares, and parks that are conventionally thought of as making up the public realm.

The National Mall in Washington, D.C., for example, connects the Capitol with the Washington Monument, the Lincoln Memorial, and a dazzling array of great museums; yet it is not a street. It is a national gathering place that has hosted everything from civil rights protests and antiwar demonstrations to concerts for tens of thousands of Washingtonians and millions of television viewers; yet it is not a public square. It includes 309 acres of grass, trees, plants, and walkways; yet it is not a park. But it serves as the most significant part of the public realm of the United States, which the entire nation shares once a year on Independence Day, every four years when a new president is inaugurated, and whenever events of national importance take place.

National Mall, Washington, D.C. (1993). (Alexander Garvin)

Galleria Vittorio
Emanuele II, Milan (2012).
(Alexander Garvin)

In Milan, the six-story, glass-roofed cruciform public space known as the Galleria Vittorio Emanuele II, which includes stores and restaurants on the lower floors and offices and residential apartments above, is similarly difficult to categorize. Many Milanese gather here to socialize, but the Galleria is not a square. Others pass through on their way to and from the square in front of the Duomo, Milan's cathedral, or from the square in front of the Scala Opera and other destinations; yet, like the National Mall, it not a street. Still others go to the Galleria to have fun and relax; but it is not a park.[1] Everybody who comes to Milan, however, goes to the Galleria, and its contribution to that city's public realm is as great as any park, square, or street.

Similarly, Society Hill's *greenways* were cut through the large blocks of the Philadelphia neighborhood during the 1960s and have become a valuable part of that city's public realm.[2] Previously, residents traveling to a destination at the other end of the neighborhood had to walk the long distances between streets before being able to turn a corner to go in another direction. The greenways provide a more convenient route but have become more than a shortcut in the years since their construction. In some places the greenways have become community gathering places; in others they are where children play; but everywhere the greenways have made neighborhood circulation easier.

Indeed, though few would place a city's transit terminals or metro stations in the same category as its parks, the most frequently ignored component of the public realm is the transportation system. Many are hidden from view as underground

St. Peter's Greenway,
Philadelphia (2009).
(Alexander Garvin)

Bond Street Underground Station, London (2004). (Alexander Garvin)

subways. Smart public officials have long understood that they can be a potential source of revenue from retail rents paid by the stores that cater to the hundreds of thousands of daily riders who pass through places such as Grand Central Terminal, but few recognize their importance as public realm. A great public realm can assist in convincing those riders to do something they had not anticipated when they got there. Indeed, transit stations do not need to be as impressive as Grand Central to be important components of a city's public realm. The London Underground station at Bond Street, for example, presents identifiable displays of merchandize in a space that is easy to use and move around in, inducing people on their way from the subway to the street to purchase items carried by the retailers along their route.

Making Cities Great

All large metropolises start out with an underdeveloped public realm. It takes the work of generations along with wise management and judicious investments to transform that public realm into a place that is convenient, vibrant, attractive, and nurturing. Improvements to the Mall in Washington, D.C., and the Galleria in Milan have been under way since the nineteenth century, when they opened. The twentieth- and twenty-first-century changes to the greenways of Society Hill and many London subway stops are much less obvious. In all four instances, however, the enhancements have strengthened the public realm characteristics introduced in the next chapter. They are what continue to make those cities great.

Boulevard Saint-Michel, Paris (2014). (Alexander Garvin)

The Characteristics
of a Great Public Realm

London, Paris, and Rome have continued to be great cities for centuries. None of these cities were great from the very beginning. What we see when we look at them or any flourishing contemporary metropolis is a cultural artifact of great complexity that reflects generations of evolutionary growth and adjustments made by residents, property owners, businesses, government agencies, and other—sometimes external—forces. It took those people generations to create a public realm that

1. is *open to anybody,*
2. offers *something for everybody,*
3. *attracts and retains market demand,*
4. *provides a framework for successful urbanization,*
5. *sustains a habitable environment,* and
6. *nurtures and supports a civil society.*

I summarize each of these six characteristics in this chapter. The individual chapters that follow discuss each characteristic in detail.

Remaining a great city depends on people continuing to want to be there, to enjoy being there, and to remain there, and that depends on continuing to make improvements to the public realm—improvements that meet the needs of future generations.

Old Town Square, Prague (2012). This square is used as a site for concerts, retailing, meeting friends, sitting at a café, or simply getting from place to place. (Alexander Garvin)

It is a mistake to judge a city's public realm based on the primary purpose of each of its components. Public parks are not just outdoor recreational facilities; public squares are more than places for social interaction; public streets are not mere travel corridors. The activities specifically designed to take place in these parts of the public realm are not the only things that can or should happen, just as cooking is not the only thing that happens in a kitchen. Some activities may take place only at certain times of the day and seasons of the year, just as cooking a turkey is more likely to take place in a kitchen around Thanksgiving than during the middle of summer. For example, on Sundays people pass through Old Town Square in Prague on their way to religious services; on other days they come and go to classical music concerts. During the Christmas season there is a special market in the square. The square does not exist specifically for any of these activities, but rather adapts to each individual use.

Open to Anybody

The public realm of any great city is open to anybody: children and the elderly; residents and visitors; businesses and their customers; pedestrians, bicycles, cars, buses, trucks, and streetcars; revelers and demonstrators; performers and their audience . . . It would not be public if it weren't. But is it open to anyone if only a few people use it?

Jane Jacobs, in her powerful book *The Death and Life of Great American Cities*, argued that "a most intricate and close-grained diversity of uses that give each other constant mutual support, both economically and socially . . ."[1] will "insure the presence of people who go outdoors on different schedules and are in the place for different purposes, but who are able to use many facilities in common."[2] She is, of course, describing the land uses and occupancy of the privately owned buildings that open onto the public realm, rather than the public realm itself. Those were the characteristics of Manhattan's West Village during the 1950s, when Jacobs lived there. After six decades of gentrification, however, many of the people who used Hudson Street and the other busy sections of the West Village no longer go to West Street and other places in the West Village because they are too expensive.

In chapter 3, rather than consider the buildings enclosing the public realm, I focus on what makes the public realm itself open to anyone. My approach is as commonsensical as Jacobs'. It argues that for the widest diversity of people to share the public realm it must be overwhelmingly identifiable, accessible, and easy to use. As important, when they get there, people must feel safe and comfortable enough to remain there.

Heckscher Ballfields, Central Park, Manhattan (2001). This ballfield simultaneously provides room for a wide variety of other uses. (Alexander Garvin)

Something for Everybody

A successful public realm must be more than just open to anybody. Nobody would be there unless there were things for them to do and see. In chapter 4 I explain that there must be enough room for all those activities, that people must be able to have fun there, and for it to remain overwhelmingly welcoming, cities must devote adequate resources to its maintenance and management.

Attracting and Retaining Market Demand

London, Paris, and Rome each were very different cities in 1800, 1900, and 2000. In the nineteenth and early twentieth centuries, their streets were filled with horses, horse-drawn carts and carriages, and horse droppings; by 2000 they were dominated by motor vehicles. We cannot predict what will dominate them in the twenty-second century. As I explain in chapter 5, they are likely to remain great cities, however, because great cities continually alter their public realm to meet the changing demands of their occupants. That is the reason that during the twentieth century Minneapolis reconfigured Nicollet Avenue, its main street, twice for automobiles and twice for pedestrians, and is currently repeating the process in the middle of the second decade of the twenty-first century. Though one could argue that these revisions corrected past mistakes, the reality is that the city adapted to its changing character. Without these changes the public realm would have lost the customers, whether they came on horse, on foot, or in an automobile, bus, or streetcar.

When such changes increase the consumer base, neighboring property owners and real estate developers become the players most likely to renovate or replace nearby buildings and to upgrade surrounding territory. Thus, the public realm is essential in responding to the changes in a city's economy and character.

Left to right: Nicollet Avenue, Minneapolis (1922, 1947, 1979, and 2012). The city's main street has been reconfigured over and over again to accommodate changes in the city's economy and character. (1st and 2nd figures courtesy of Minnesota Historical Society, 3rd and 4th by Alexander Garvin)

Chicago Lakeshore (2005). The city's lakeshore parks provide a framework around which so many of its buildings cluster. (Alexander Garvin)

Providing a Framework for Successful Urbanization

Some locations—waterfronts, for example—are more likely than others to attract market demand. Intelligent investment in the public realm, then, can exploit that market demand to provide a benefit to city dwellers. People in Chicago, for example, have always preferred living and working near Lake Michigan. Once the city began creating its 3,130-acre chain of lakeshore parks, however, people were willing to pay even more to be nearby. Naturally, developers were eager to supply apartments and offices close to those lakeshore parks—as eager as Parisian developers were to supply offices and residences along its broad boulevards, rather than in the sunless neighborhoods with narrow winding streets and alleys. Chapter 6 describes the axial vistas, ring roads, and rectilinear grids that provide a framework around which property owners and developers erect the buildings that make up the city and the importance of ongoing management to the success of that framework. But what elements of that framework are perceived as desirable by property owners and developers? Chapters 7 and 8 explain the importance of a habitable environment and a civil society to retaining the people who have made a city great and to attracting future generations who will make it even greater.

Sustaining a Habitable Environment

The Brundtland Commission, in its 1987 report *Our Common Future*, enunciated the goal of sustaining a habitable environment by satisfying "the needs of the present without compromising the ability of future generations to meet their own needs." It was not clear, however, what exactly were the "needs"[3] of a contemporary city, or the "needs" its inhabitants will face in the future. Nor did the report explain how to meet the needs of the present without "compromising the ability of future generations to meet their own needs." Achieving these objectives is possible only with a clever combination of building and natural environments.

As I explain in chapter 7, a great public realm plays an important role in sustaining a city's habitable environment when it includes prominent natural features, especially when it is designed to provide shelter from the elements and nicely landscaped areas in which people can linger and enjoy their surroundings. From early spring to late fall the trees, bushes, flowers, and grass consume carbon dioxide and water, and release oxygen; capture contaminants from the air; and absorb noise. Living, breathing leafy canopies provide relief from heat in the summer, and after the leaves have fallen in the winter, filter sunlight through tree branches, bringing added warmth. Green spaces also play a primary role in protecting the city from storm surges and soaking up excess rainwater.

Prinsengracht, Amsterdam (2012). A great public realm ought to make people feel safe and comfortable. (Alexander Garvin)

Nurturing and Supporting a Civil Society

Creating an environment in which civil society thrives is probably the most complex and difficult of the functions of the public realm. Although every part of the public realm can contribute to a civil society, public squares play a special role because they are natural locations for public gatherings. To provide fertile ground for people to gather and interact, however, all the different components of the public realm (not just squares) must be designed to provide places where everyone can pursue their activities without interfering with others. But design is not enough to prevent people from intruding on each other's territory, physical and psychological alike. Sharing the public realm requires effort on everybody's part to be sure that nobody acts in a way hostile or harmful to others, while simultaneously allowing them to do as they wish. That is, after all, the very essence of a civil society.

As chapter 8 explains, for the public realm to meet the needs of future generations, people must be able to make alterations that will adapt the public realm that they have received from past generations. Those alterations will inevitably involve the interaction of a wide variety of individuals, civic organizations, businesses, and government agencies—interaction that nurtures civil society.

Similarly, hard-earned experience has proven that busy streets, squares, and parks suffer inevitable damage from heavy use by large numbers of people unconscious of the impact of "normal" activity. If there is no entity responsible for maintaining the public realm and managing the activities that take place there, or if those entities are not provided with the resources to do so, deterioration is inevitable. The deterioration is followed at first, also inevitably, by the abandonment of the public realm by large numbers of people who have better alternatives. The loss of a usable public realm that people once shared in common and mattered to *everybody* usually provokes citizen action to restore cherished public spaces—action that nurtures a civil society.

By now, it should be evident that this book is different from many of the great works that discuss the public realm. It is not just about physical design, finance, political action, history, topography, and climate. It is about all these considerations as they contribute to an ever-evolving public realm. But, most important, it is about how people keep dealing with aspects of the public realm that are unsatisfactory, what they have done to make it better, and how to ensure that they will continue to do whatever is needed to create an ever-greater public realm.

New Bond St., London (2013).
(Alexander Garvin)

Entry to Plaza Mayor, Salamanca, Spain (2013). (Alexander Garvin)

Open to Anybody

My favorite public square is the Plaza Mayor in Salamanca, Spain, although the Plaza Mayor in Madrid is more famous. People come to the Plaza Mayor from all over Salamanca, because it is overwhelmingly identifiable, accessible, safe, and easy to use. It accommodates people of different goals, backgrounds, and reasons to be there. For some it is a shortcut. Others shop at the retail stores inside the building colonnades. Some are tourists, like me, who are there to drink in the passing scene.

I first came to the plaza arounzzd noon. I was so charmed by it that I returned around two in the afternoon, in the evening for tapas and wine, again for a late supper that night, and for a final walk the following morning. As in any public square, most people were there to socialize, standing around chatting, sitting on a bench, or at café or restaurant table.

While I was enjoying my tapas selections, commuters passed through the square on their way home. They walked past groups of teenage girls who sat together on the pavement near the center of the square and adults who sat on the twelve benches in the center of the square. Single men on bicycles glided past groups of gossiping parents with strollers. Near the plaza's center, groups of teenage guys lingered. Despite the activity, many restaurant tables remained empty. For a moment, the arrival of five handsome men in black suits holding black Givenchy umbrellas—even though it was a lovely evening without a chance of rain—captured everybody's attention. One of them pretended to be Gene Kelly singing "Singin' in the Rain." They danced, opened and closed their umbrellas, and after their performance flirted with some of the women in the crowd that they attracted. Ten minutes later they were gone.

Plaza Mayor, Salamanca (2013). Activities in the Plaza Mayor vary greatly depending on the time of day. (Alexander Garvin)

Plaza Mayor at night in Salamancia (2013). (Alexander Garvin)

When I returned at 9:45 that night, the plaza was still well-lit by the waning sunlight. The inhabitants of the space had changed slightly: there were fewer people, no toddlers, and no prams. Adults now congregated at the entrances of bars and restaurants, rather than at nearby tables. Suddenly at 10 p.m. hanging floodlights and store windows illuminated the colonnade. The transformation was magical. Young women in tight miniskirts and spike heels now began passing by on the arms of young men in evening dress. Having finished my supper, I wandered around inspecting the lit-up monuments and soaking in the glittering atmosphere.

Early the next morning, sanitation workers arrived to remove the trash and sweep the pavement. Shortly thereafter, delivery vehicles paraded in with supplies for the retail businesses while café and restaurant personnel cleaned and rearranged tables and chairs. By midday the cycle of activity had started all over again and the Plaza Mayor was peopled by teenagers and commuters, bicyclists and young parents with strollers.

While seated at a table in the Plaza Mayor having a glass of wine, I realized something that should have been obvious: that everybody who was there wanted to be there. That realization was one of the first *AHA!* moments of my quest to determine the characteristics of a great public realm. During my visits to the Plaza Mayor, I had seen every possible city inhabitant and visitor: from babies and old people to waiters and tour guides, and anybody else who might be in Salamanca on that day.

Although we think that every component of the public realm is open to anyone, there are many parts of the public realm that, unlike the Plaza Mayor, are not really open to anyone. Highways, for example, are only open to people in motor vehicles. Parkways exclude trucks, buses, and commercial traffic. Most of the "public" squares of London discussed in chapter 9 are open only to the occupants of surrounding buildings. After the attack on the World Trade Center in Lower Manhattan, bollards and metal detectors were installed in all sorts of "public" places to restrict access.

None of these restrictions apply to the Plaza Mayor. But the wide variety of people whom I saw there were not in the square merely because it was universally accessible; they were there because they *wanted* to be in the Plaza Mayor. For that reason, I concluded that any great public realm had to be a destination where people enjoy spending time. For that to happen it must be overwhelmingly identifiable, accessible, easy to use, safe, and comfortable.

Some people in Salamanca rarely go to the Plaza Mayor. Many of them cannot afford to have a glass of wine in one of the cafés, do not have the money to buy something displayed in one of its stores, or have no business in one of the government offices or apartments upstairs. The same is true of many of the other places discussed in this chapter. Providing something for everybody is an equally important characteristic of a great public realm. But that is the subject of the next chapter.

Overwhelmingly Identifiable, Accessible, and Easy to Use

In Salamanca I identified several characteristics that made people who wanted to be in the Plaza Mayor feel it was open to them whenever they wanted to be there. It was overwhelmingly *identifiable*, overwhelmingly *accessible* (easy to get to from anywhere in the city and easy to move around in when they got there), overwhelmingly *safe*, and overwhelmingly *easy* to use. Those characteristics did not just happen. It took the people of Salamanca generations to perfect those characteristics.

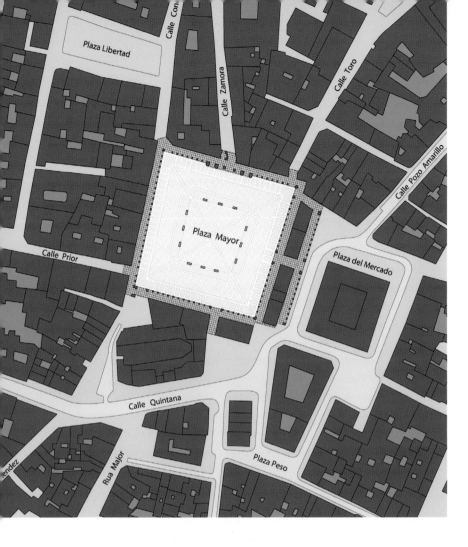

Plan of the district around
Plaza Mayor in Salamancia.
(Owen Howlett,
Alexander Garvin)

Plaza Mayor, Salamanca, Spain—For most of its history the central part of Salamanca has been located within the imprint of the original city walls. Consequently, the Plaza Mayor has occupied essentially the same position within the city for centuries. At the center of everything, it is immediately identifiable and easily accessible from any point along streets that lead to the square.

Although there have been periods in history when the plaza played host to special events such as bullfighting, the tenancy of the buildings enclosing the square also has remained essentially the same: government offices, retailing, residences, cafés, and restaurants intermingle in the Plaza. The design of the central open area, on the other hand, has been altered numerous times during its history. Those changes, however, proved to be the critical factor in continuously improving the space's ability to attract and accommodate increasing amounts of people and the ease with which it could be used. This was particularly true after the invention of motor vehicles, which initially made it easier to get to the square and to operate businesses that received deliveries from vans and trucks. Eventually, however, those vehicles crowded out too many of the people who came by foot, causing the Plaza Mayor to be reconfigured yet again.

At the end of the eighteenth century the square was a fenced-in, tree-lined open space with planted areas and a fountain in the middle occupied more than half the square. This was easier for visitors to use the outer sections.

At the start of the twentieth century, the fountain was still there along with redesigned areas for greenery and flowers, but the tree-lined fence separating the landscaped setting at the center of the square had been removed to make it easier for people to reach the central garden.

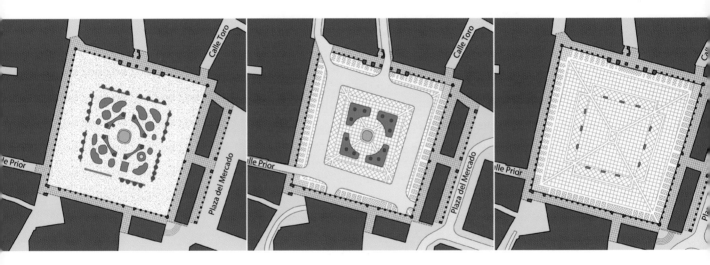

Diagrams of Plaza Mayor in Salamancia 1785, 1901, and 1955. Over time, this central square has contained fountains, gardens, and vehicular roadways but now exists as a single hardscape. (Owen Howlett, Alexander Garvin)

In 1901, the periphery of the central landscaped area was replaced by a broad vehicular roadway exiting through arches that led onto five different streets. The resulting traffic made the entire square less pleasant and more difficult to use.

Finally, in 1973, the city banned all but service vehicles from the square and repaved the entire space as a single hardscape. The open area at its center, which formerly hosted gardens as well as the central fountain, was modestly defined by three benches along each of its four sides. Once trees, fences, and all the other obstacles had been removed, the square was used by more people than ever before.

Any city that wishes for a great public realm would do well to emulate what Salamanca achieved: keep making changes to the public realm until it meets the demands of the people using it at that time and continue making changes thereafter to meet the expectations of future generations.

Creating an Identifiable, Accessible, and Easy-to-Use Public Realm

How does one identify something special about the public realm without a marquee or a prominent placard, especially when the city's public realm is without an abundance of remarkable places? The underground subway system of Paris is such a place. Identifying it is easy because of the many prominent art nouveau Metro entrance structures that announce it. The Federal Center in Chicago, an understated group of public buildings designed by the architect Mies van der Rohe (discussed later in the chapter), provides the best example I know with which to demonstrate how, with an absolute minimum of elements, one can create an exceptionally identifiable public realm. In some cities the centerpiece of the public realm is a *single*, overwhelmingly identifiable square, such as the Plaza Mayor in Salamanca or the Piazza del Campo in Siena (usually called the Campo; also discussed in this chapter). The Campo began before the founding of the city as a gathering place for people from nearby hillside farming communities. It soon became and remains the area's central marketplace, its seat of government, and, with the rise of international tourism, one of Italy's most famous tourist destinations.

Other cities, such as New York, Moscow, and Rome, have several important squares in different parts of town. But only in a small number of cities, such as Savannah (as explained later in this chapter), Edinburgh, and London (see chapter 9), do a city's many squares play as important a role in determining the character of a city's public realm as do streets or parks.

Many prominent city streets are easy to identify. The Champs-Élysées is known as the broadest street in Paris. Pennsylvania Avenue in Washington, D.C., is the location for events of major significance to the entire United States. Michigan Avenue is the location of most of the major retailers in Chicago. But how does one transform an ordinary city street into an overwhelmingly accessible and safe, easy-to-use destination? Denver has done just that by making Sixteenth Street the most accessible street in the metropolitan area. It established garages at critical points along the street, erected suburban bus terminals at either end of the primary downtown section of the street, and built a regional light-rail system connecting Sixteenth Street with the entire metropolitan region. It is easy to get around when you get there because of the free buses that run between the bus terminals, and easy to use because there is no other traffic on the street and there are shaded areas with tables, chairs, and even pianos for people to use. It is one of the safest places in Denver because there are so many people there so much of the time.

The Federal Center and Sixteenth Street are by definition open to anybody. The same is true of any portion of a great public realm. The more popular it is, the more likely people will be willing to pay to be there, whether they are tourists, tenants, or potential customers. So it is not surprising, even if it is open to anyone, that there are more people on the Champs-Élysées sitting in cafés, buying things displayed in store windows, or going to the movies in one of its theaters, than people who are there but are unwilling or unable to spend money there. Like the Champs-Élysées, the Paris Metro, the Federal Center in Chicago, the Campo in Siena, the squares of Savannah, Sixteenth Street in Denver, the other examples of a great public realm that are discussed in this chapter are truly open to everyone.

The Paris Metro—Underground subways, in particular, are generally not overwhelmingly identifiable. Often only residents, workers, and frequent visitors to a city know where to go to get to the subway—*except in Paris*. There, entrances to the subway are overwhelmingly identifiable to everybody: residents, workers, day visitors, and tourists.

From its very inception in 1900, the Metro (Paris's underground rapid transit system), created a powerful brand with its stylish art nouveau stairway markers that lead into its maze of shafts, stairs, and tunnels. Thanks to a common entry stair design, everybody, Parisian or visitor, can quickly identify a Metro entrance and infer how to get to the train platform with a minimum of difficulty. Thereafter, riding the Metro may be confusing.

The Paris Metro (2007).
(Alexander Garvin)

Chicago's Federal Center.
The square consists of several
subsidiary volumes of spaces
that are woven seamlessly into
the fabric of the surrounding
city. (Owen Howlett, Alexander
Garvin)

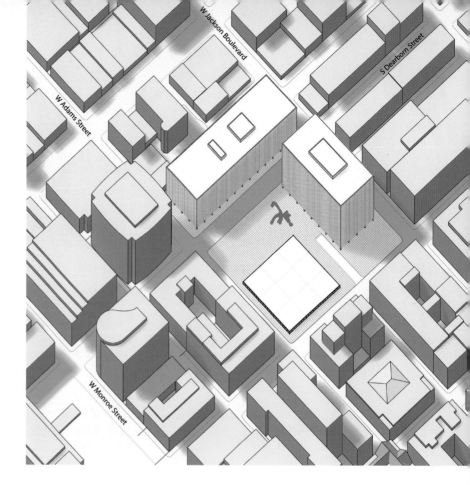

Federal Center, Chicago—Hiding in plain sight, and rarely even appreciated by
its users, the Federal Center has nevertheless become a seamless part of the city.
When asked about it, Chicagoans instantly identify the Federal Center. They tell
you to head for the big red Calder sculpture in front of the one-story post office.

Federal Center, Chicago (2013).
Alexander Calder's painted
steel sculpture, Flamingo,
provides a familiar landmark for
people coming to the Federal
Center or passing by as they go
about their business elsewhere
in the city. (Alexander Garvin)

The design for the 4.6-acre (1.9-ha) Federal Center consists of three structures—two office buildings and a post office—plus a series of public spaces which together constitute a public square. Two of the buildings are located within one city block, and the third is across the street. The area is subject to a high volume of foot traffic during the day. More than 14,000 government employees have offices within this 2.4 million-square-foot (22.3-ha) complex and thousands more come to do business with them.

Despite all the people coming and going to the government offices and the buildings around them, few people who go there think of it as a public square, but it is! Some go to the post office. Some are on their way in or out of the buildings. Others cut across the open space on their way to other parts of the city, walk by on the sidewalks, or drive past on city streets. The Calder sculpture provides all of them with a point of orientation.

Mies seamlessly integrated the Federal Center with the rest of Chicago by using the street walls of older masonry buildings on the north and west sides of the square as well as his mid-twentieth-century glass buildings on the east and south sides to enclose a cubical volume of space. This space contains the one-story glass post office and the Calder sculpture, as well as the streets and sidewalks in front of both buildings. The reflections of the older buildings on the glass surfaces of the newer buildings integrate the modern Federal Center into the fabric of a great city, while providing an identifiable central destination within downtown Chicago.

Federal Center, Chicago (2013). More people pass through the square on their way to somewhere else than enter the Federal Center's buildings. (Alexander Garvin)

Piazza del Campo, Siena, Italy—The large, scallop-shaped public space in the center of Siena, Italy, emerged before the thirteenth century, in a topographical hollow at the center of hillside farming communities that occupied three converging ridges. It was the one place in the region to which the residents of each community could easily travel.[1] In 1347 the Campo was divided into nine brick-paved areas by long, radiating, travertine strips. Each area symbolized a district represented in the Council of the Nine, which governed the city and laid out the piazza. The Palazzo Pubblico (city hall), with its 330-foot-high (100 m) tower, was erected at a lower point to the south of the square, where it could serve as the backdrop for public events. Water carried from distant aqueducts was piped to the high point of the square on its north side, where in 1409 the sculptor Jacopo della Quercia created the Gaia Fountain.

Piazza del Campo, Siena, Italy (2011). (Alexander Garvin)

Residents came to the Campo to get water from the fountain, to meet their friends, do business in the Palazzo Pubblico, learn the latest news, have a meal or a drink, or attend specially staged public spectacles and sporting events. It was not until 1656, however, that the Campo's most famous annual event was staged: the Palio, a race among the representatives of the various districts into which Siena is divided. Twice each summer, to the delight of thousands of visitors, those representatives dress in colorful historical costumes and race horses around the square.

Though the Campo's central location initially attracted local residents, it eventually became an attraction in its own right for visitors interested in its design and history. Even without the Palio, on most days, thousands of people, many of whom are international tourists, go to the Campo. Almost everything in the city is within a fifteen-minute walk of the square, so the square is an ideal place to begin a variety of activities. People leaving the Campo take one of eight streets to go to museums, churches, stores, restaurants, and hotels, all of which profit from the business they get from the people leaving the square. Its popularity arises from not only its centrality but from the huge range of activities it supports.

The Squares of Savannah—Savannah's repetitive sequence of squares immediately distinguishes it from other cities in Georgia or the Old South. Indeed, the city's public squares are so deeply ingrained in its culture that residents identify themselves as living on Madison Square or Lafayette Square, or one of the other squares of Savannah, rather than living in a particular neighborhood or on a particular street.

James Oglethorpe (1696–1785), the man behind the creation of the twenty-member Georgia Trustees that founded the colony of Georgia, was also the designer responsible for the plan of Savannah. His scheme consisted of twenty-four squares, each of which was to be established as the center of a "ward," whose development was timed to absorb market demand.[2] The squares were to be enclosed by streets that separated them from the surrounding eight blocks. These eight blocks were classified in two manners: four "Tything" blocks, bisected by a service alley, were initially set aside for residential lots, and four "Trust" blocks that were, by contrast, initially allocated for religious uses and for other public buildings.

Plan of Savannah. Each square helps to identify its surrounding neighborhood and takes on attributes desired by people there. (Owen Howlett, Alexander Garvin)

Today, each of the squares is slightly different in its dimensions, landscaping, and use. People from all over the city, especially office workers, tend to use those that are within the business district, while the squares in more residential wards are much quieter and primarily attract nearby residents.

Each time Savannah inaugurated a new square, an entire ward grew up around it. By interspersing private lots with the city's unique, high-quality public realm, each square provided the amenity that attracted the ward's initial residents and provided a framework for later development that continued to add value for generations afterward.

Chippewa Square, Savannah
(2013). (Alexander Garvin)

As in the Plaza Mayor, the most ordinary activities take place in the squares of Savannah. On a typical afternoon in Chippewa Square, for example, some people sit on benches in the shade of oak trees, others walk their dogs, cut across the square on their way to work, or linger in the sun. The residents largely ignore the life-size sculpture of James Oglethorpe that is the centerpiece of the square, just as residents of other wards pay scant attention to the special features of its square. What is very special is the sense of belonging those squares generate.

The last time I was in Chippewa Square, residents had arranged several rows of folding chairs on one side of the square. Guests, who sat in those chairs, were waiting for a rabbi to begin a wedding ceremony. On the other side of the square two older ladies seated on a bench were engaged in a heated argument, while a group of young people lay on the grass enjoying the sun. Everybody there knew it was "their" square. Thus, the legacy of James Oglethorpe's plan for Savannah is its immediately identifiable public realm. The fact that residents have come to identify themselves by their local square is a testament to the plan's success.

Place de la Bastille, Paris (2013). Swirling, fast-moving traffic keeps this square from contributing anything to the public realm except the symbolic column at its center. (Alexander Garvin)

How different the Federal Center, the Piazza del Campo, and the squares of Savannah are from the rivers of vehicular traffic encasing Place de la Concorde, Place de l'Etoile, or Place de la Bastille in Paris—all of which are called "public squares" even though the swirling traffic makes them very difficult to use!

Sixteenth Street, Denver—Like so many American cities, post–World War II Denver experienced rapid growth of residential subdivisions surrounding the city. The suburban commuters who moved into those suburbs travelled by car to get to and from work, shopping, and other downtown facilities. Their cars tied up traffic in the morning, at lunch time, and in the evening. When traffic became a problem, some businesses simply followed their workers and moved to suburban office parks, just as some retailers followed their customers to suburban shopping centers.

By 1964 Denver's inventory of downtown office space (3,324,000 square feet; 30.9 ha) was more that 20 percent vacant.[3] Since the early 1950s this suburban exodus had alarmed city property owners and business leaders alike, who feared a loss of customers and a decline in living conditions. Consequently, in 1955, they formed Downtown Denver, Inc. (DDI) to institute changes that would improve the downtown area. Thirty-seven years later in 1982 DDI became a business improvement district (BID) responsible for keeping the entire 120-block Denver downtown area clean, secure, and attractive.[4]

The strategy of privately providing remedial services to commercial streets was not, it should be said, invented for Denver. The first BID had already been established in 1970 to revive West Bloor Street in Toronto, and many other cities had found various ways to improve downtown conditions. Some BIDs, for instance, combined spending on sanitation and security personnel with investment in new paving and street furniture. Others paid for changes that restricted traffic to buses or eliminated vehicular traffic altogether. In cities where tourism was a major component of the local economy, BIDs provided wayfinding and visitor information. When a city needed to attract more customers to its downtown districts, BIDs programmed street fairs, concerts, craft shows, street markets, festivals, and other special events that brought consumers to areas in the central city that they might never have otherwise visited. Though BIDs were in their infancy when the DDI was first formed, by the second decade of the twenty-first century there were more than 1,400 of them in North America.[5]

At first, civic leaders in car-loving Colorado did not want to "pedestrianize." Steeped in car culture, they believed that the city's office space was underused because the 25,300 existing downtown parking spaces were insufficient to meet parking needs. Increasing the number of downtown parking spaces, they thought, would make Denver more accessible. Consequently, in 1958 voters approved a $4 million bond issue to pay for the construction of 1,700 additional parking spaces in three downtown garages. But when these garages opened for business two years later they failed to attract enough paying users to cover the debt service on the bonds that had financed them, eventually causing the city $1.5 million in losses.[6] Obviously, the root of the problem was *not* insufficient parking.

Sixteenth Street, Denver (1938). (Denver Public Library X-23375)

The critical step that finally turned things around took place when Denver planners decided to revamp Sixteenth Street, the city's major commercial artery. Removing private motor vehicles from this central roadway had been under discussion for more than a decade. Fortunately, the city understood that simply eliminating private vehicular traffic would be an insufficient fix. More was needed, so it added a free bus that ran at 70-second intervals along the 1.25 miles of Sixteenth Street between two newly built suburban bus stations at either end.

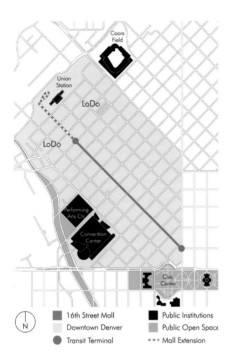

The Sixteenth Street mall is within four blocks of all the major destinations in the city's downtown, Denver. (Ryan Salvatore, Alexander Garvin)

The $76.1 million Sixteenth Street Mall opened in 1982, designed by the architectural firm I. M. Pei and Partners and Hanna/Olin landscape architects. This team redesigned the 80-foot-wide (24-m) right-of-way to include a central 22-foot (6.7-m) tree-lined promenade and a sitting area flanked by 10-foot (3-m) bus lanes and 19-foot (5.8-m) sidewalks.[7]

In addition to pedestrianization and two bus stations, the city made major downtown investments in the Denver Art Museum, Central Library, the 2.2 million-square-foot (20.4-ha) Colorado Convention Center, the nine-theater Performing Arts Center, the 50,000-seat Coors Stadium, Denver Pavilions entertainment center, the 20,000-seat Pepsi Center, and the three-university Auraria educational campus. It also encouraged renovation of the LoDo loft district and the Larimer Square Historical District. By the turn of the twenty-first century every location of significance in this area was in walking distance of Sixteenth Street, including all of Denver's public institutions, plus the State Capitol, City Hall, Union Station, virtually all downtown retail and office space, more than 8,400 hotel rooms, and the new residential district developing at the north end of the street. As a result of the proximity of all these facilities and the convenience of using the free bus, the 90,000 people per day who used Sixteenth Street made it the focus of downtown life and transformed it into Denver's number-one day and night tourist attraction.[8]

Sixteenth Street, Denver (2011). Sixteenth Street carefully sets aside places for the things most people might want to do there: a roadway for a free bus, a tree-shaded walk for promenading, moveable chairs placed among planters containing colorful flowers for people who wish to sit down, even pianos for would-be entertainers to play. (Alexander Garvin)

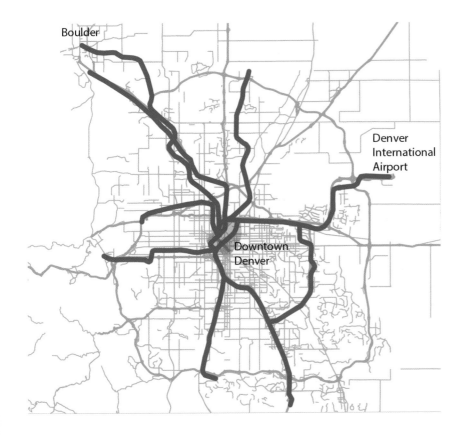

Boulder

Denver
International
Airport

Downtown
Denver

Denver's FasTracks light
rail system. (Owen Howlett,
Alexander Garvin)

Nevertheless, Sixteenth Street still was not easily accessible to much of Denver's increasingly suburban population. So, in 2004, voters in eight counties approved a fourth of a cent sales tax to pay for the 119-mile FasTracks regional light- and commuter rail system, along with eighteen miles of bus rapid transit, all leading to Sixteenth Street, which would connect this popular destination to most of the 600,000 people who lived in the city of Denver plus the 2,540,000 who would live in its metropolitan area by 2010.

Denver, like all cities, continues to evolve and will be making changes to further improve Sixteenth Street. The Downtown Denver Partnership is working on a "security action plan," and the city has hired Gehl Architects, specialists in public realm planning, to propose changes that will make the street even easier to use.[9]

For any part of the public realm, like Sixteenth Street, to succeed it is not enough to be identifiable, accessible, and easy to use. It must continue to be open to anybody. Doing so requires making people feel safe and comfortable while they are there, and feel that they belong there. That is why Denver has continually made improvements to Sixteenth Street.

Keeping the Public Realm Safe

Safety from physical harm is essential to keeping the public realm open to anyone. It is often the little-noticed aids and devices that do the most to ensure citizen safety. For example, streetlights are obviously necessary and essential for the safety of motorists, pedestrians, and cyclists. They illuminate roadways, bike paths, and sidewalks at night, lessen the chance of accidents, and discourage crime. Similarly, the signals provided by red, green, and yellow traffic lights can at times deliver the extra increment of visibility needed to prevent accidents on an otherwise dark roadway.

Another, less obvious example of a safety feature is parked vehicles. Most people pay no attention to parked cars on a street, and almost no one thinks of them as safety devices, yet cars sitting at a curb provide pedestrians with protection from vehicles that might swerve suddenly off the road. Statistically speaking, such accidents are surprisingly common on streets that do not allow parking. Parked cars can also provide safely for bike paths that are located between the cars and the sidewalk. What's more, a parked car offers far less impact potential than hard, flat pavement in instances where cyclists are knocked off their bikes, sometimes even serving as a kind of protective wall to soften the blow of a sideways fall. Clearly, help on a street sometimes comes from strange and unexpected sources. The function of all these design details is particularly evident on the Gran Via de les Cort Catalanes (or Gran Via, as it is popularly known) in Barcelona (discussed below).

Besides preventing traffic accidents, however, street safety also includes protection from pickpockets, muggers, and assorted criminal intrusions. Police patrols discourage these menaces, but the presence of large numbers of people on a street cheerfully going about their business is an even better way to increase safety. Why? Because the very presence of these people is, as it were, its own police force. That is just what happens every day on many of the busier streets of Paris.

Of course, the fact that many engaged people milling about on a street significantly increases its safety begs a principal question: how does a city get enough people *onto* its streets in the first place to eliminate crime? As explained in chapter 4, Jane Jacobs would reply that the more eyes there are on the street, the safer that street will be. This is especially true at night.

Gran Via, Barcelona—Pedestrians, cyclists, and drivers on the Gran Via are able to see far into the distance, identify possible dangers, and avoid impending mishaps. Equally important, the right-of-way on the Gran Via is broad enough to provide room for every wheeled and on-foot activity, thus avoiding a variety of possible collisions and conflicts.

The very configuration and design of a street itself can often eliminate potential hazards. For example, the Gran Via is a 165-foot-wide (50-m) boulevard with a thick row of bushes planted between the trees that line its curbs.[10] This natural hedge makes it difficult for people to enter the roadway except at street intersections and for unattended children to dash suddenly into traffic. The protective hedge likewise ensures that only the upper parts of vehicles moving in the central roadway are visible from flanking service roads and pedestrian precincts, thus preventing automobile headlights from blinding nighttime cyclists and ensuring that trucks or cars do not veer off the roadway into pedestrian or bicycle lanes. Finally, these leafy shrubs improve the look of the roadside landscape and help filter out noise and sprays of water splashed up by vehicles driving through puddles.

Gran Via de les Cort Catalanes, Barcelona (2013). The plantings along the street protect pedestrians from being blinded by headlights, prevent cars from swerving on to the sidewalk, and provide shade during the hot summer. (Alexander Garvin)

Walking under the protection of a tree-lined street like the Grand Via is obviously better for the constitution than facing the hot summer sun or frigid winter winds. Still, to randomly plant trees (palm trees in particular) along a boulevard or highway is not enough to ensure anyone's physical well-being; trees must be positioned in strategic locations and in the proper configurations to maximize their protective value. During the hot Barcelona summers, the thick foliage from Gran Via's majestic trees protects pedestrians from the sun, while in winter these same trees serve as windbreaks to filter the sun and protect walkers from chill breezes. Furthermore, due to the excellent visibility on this boulevard, pedestrians, cyclists, and drivers can look into the distance, identify any dangers that might be awaiting them, and avoid any potential problems.

Piet Heinkade, Amsterdam (2012). The planting along the street is too far away to provide shade for passing pedestrians. (Alexander Garvin)

Piet Heinkade, Amsterdam—For instance, one of Amsterdam's wide streets is lined with numbers of large trees, but all of these are located too far from the street's sidewalks and building entrances to be of any functional or protective use. True, the handsome plantings decorate the edge of the motorway in a graceful way and give it a hint of green, but due to their placement they leave pedestrians to fend for themselves against inclement weather in both summer and winter. To further complicate matters, the monotonous, consistent building heights on Piet Heinkade, its extremely broad sidewalks with nothing of interest to attract pedestrians (except racks to store bicycles), and the paucity of retail stores, cafés, and restaurants make this street anything but pedestrian-friendly. No wonder one sees so few people strolling on its sidewalks.

Rue de la Victoire, Paris (2007). Café-goers, store owners, retail customers, upstairs occupants, and building concierges all provide the eyes on the street that make this one of the safest streets in the city. (Alexander Garvin)

The Streets of Paris—In high-density neighborhoods where there are many mixed-use buildings, plenty of people are likely to be on the street. They keep the street safe and relatively crime-free. Streets such as the Rue de la Victoire in Paris, for example, draw crowds due to a variety of attractions; establishments from bars and restaurants to pharmacies and shoe stores occupy the fringes of the street. In addition, because so many of these visitors are potential consumers, street retailers keep their stores open late into the evening. Consequently, the Rue de la Victoire is self-policed by customers, shop owners, and restaurateurs who occupy the ground-floors of its buildings, and by concierges and upstairs apartment residents who keep an eye on street activity from above.

So many streets of Paris are so busy and lit up that one wonders why the city doesn't save money by turning off the street lights after closing time. Perhaps the caretakers of that city's streets understand that it isn't the prevalence of police patrols that makes them safe. Rather, it is the vast crowds of eager consumers that do the job, providing precisely what Jacobs recommends: plenty of people with plenty of eyes on the street.

Feeling Comfortable

Being identifiable, accessible, easy to use, and safe is not enough to make a successful public realm. One also must feel comfortable. If there is enough room in the public realm to move around, if it is easy to do what you want to do, if you can sit down when you want to, if it isn't too hot or too cold or too loud, and if you are at ease, you will happily go there, stay for a while, and keep coming back. The Palais Royale in Paris, Commonwealth Avenue in Boston, and the Kungstradgarten in Stockholm, for instance (all discussed later in the chapter), are among the places that keep attracting people because they pay attention to these attributes and people feel comfortable when they are there.

People believe that a place is open to them when they feel they belong there. This reaction is more emotional than cerebral, and is difficult to quantify. Yet, its importance is clearly observable when it is absent. Notice, for instance, how little time it takes pedestrians to know they are somewhere they should have avoided, because they feel disoriented, out of place, bored, or in danger.

Many European cities provide the people who live and work there with a sense of rootedness, which is largely the product of the buildings that enclose the public realm. The families living in Italian cities as disparate as Rome (population 2.6 million in 2010) and Gubbio (population 33,000 in 2010), for example (as explained later in this chapter), have maintained homes there for centuries. These longtime denizens have heard interesting tales and accounts of city life from their own families and from other families as well. They have grown up with pride of place, and these stories provide a special sense of local history and connectedness, and of belonging.

The well-being that comes from visiting a street where one feels affinity with that street's cultural heritage is not restricted to older, traditional villages such as Gubbio, however. The same feelings can be inspired virtually overnight by a great designer, such as architect Addison Mizner, who built Worth Avenue in Palm Beach, Florida, during the 1920s. It also can be created by residents who want to overcome the initial mass-produced mediocrity of places such as Levittown, Long Island, where after decades of painting or decorating their houses, they no longer look like their neighbors.'

Jardin du Palais Royale, Paris—The Jardin du Palais Royale is a secluded rectangular space in the middle of the six-story Palais Royale. These two acres (0.8 ha) are not exactly a park or a square. People call it "Jardin," or garden in French, because it was once a pleasure garden for the nobility. It is surrounded by residential buildings with a common arcade at the ground level. People wander in and out of these buildings' ground-floor boutiques, lounge on moveable chairs around the decorative fountain in the middle of the Jardin, stroll under the trees, bring their children to feed the pigeons, invite their friends to play a game of boule, and sit reading, talking, and doing business. Whether they are residents of the surrounding buildings, workers or owners of nearby businesses, or visitors to the area, however, they think of the Palais Royale as a place where they can be comfortable.

Jardin du Palais Royale, Paris (2010). This secluded former royal garden has provided a charming escape from the noise and confusion of the surrounding city for nearly four centuries. (Alexander Garvin)

The Palais Royale, completed in 1639, was designed by architect Jacques Lemercier as a residence for Cardinal Richelieu. Upon Richelieu's death the Palais Royale became crown property that was used as a royal residence. After Richelieu's death the different buildings whose backs opened onto it were given a common façade, designed by architect Victor Louis (1731–1800).

After the revolution of 1789, the Palais Royale was opened to the public. Thereafter, calling this secluded place a "garden" became a misnomer because it had become a public park to which large numbers of people flocked. Building colonnades facing the park were lined with shops, restaurants, and casinos.

For a while the complex deteriorated, but it was repossessed and restored by Napoleon III. After he was forced from office in 1870, however, some of the residences within the Palais Royale were turned into brothels and gambling venues. Nevertheless, lots of people wanted to live around the square. During the early twentieth century, its fortunes began to improve. It even became the residence of such notable Parisians as Colette and Jean Cocteau.[11]

People who come to the Jardin du Palais Royale come because there they are protected from the hustle, bustle, and noise of the surrounding city. They can wander under the shade of carefully manicured trees, listen to birds chirping, supervise the small children they have brought to play with their friends, or simply relax. Those are all among the reasons that people feel comfortable being there.

Back Bay, Boston (2014). (Alexander Garvin)

Commonwealth Avenue, Boston
(2015). (Alexander Garvin)

Commonwealth Avenue, Boston—Just as the Jardin du Palais Royale is more than just a garden, Commonwealth Avenue is more than just an avenue. It is a park and a meeting place, a promenade and a sitting area, a haven for office workers seeking a quiet place to escape from the rush and tumble of Boston, as well as a convenient spot for nearby residents to walk their dogs.

Commonwealth Avenue is the product of a landfill project begun in 1856 by the Commission on Public Lands created by the Commonwealth of Massachusetts four years earlier. Its purpose was to replace the increasingly polluted swampy land of the Back Bay with construction-ready property on which developers would build residences to house Boston's overflowing population.[12] The plan called for five east-west streets, separating blocks of residential buildings, the central artery of which is Commonwealth Avenue. The sixteen-foot-wide (4.9-m) service alleys that bisect the blocks divert delivery and service vehicles from all Back Bay streets. Consequently, there is less commercial traffic on Commonwealth Avenue and the other streets of the Back Bay than in similar neighborhoods.

This reduced commercial traffic is only one reason people feel comfortable on Commonwealth Avenue. The main attraction is that the avenue is an expansive open space, 240 feet (73 m) across, that accommodates two broad sidewalks flanked by row houses. The avenue boasts two one-way streets with enough room for parked cars and three lanes of traffic, and a generous tree-lined park-promenade down the middle. Some people use the park-promenade to walk to work, go shopping, or return home. Others sit on benches reading, chatting with one another, or just watching the world go by. Still others, especially children, go there to play.

Kungstradgarten, Stockholm (2012). Although many royal gardens retain the appearance that was fashionable when they were established, they are often unsuitable for intense public use. Two decades after the Kungstradgarten became city property it was completely redesigned so that it could become an important component in the daily life of Stockholm. (Alexander Garvin)

Kungstradgarten, Stockholm—Like the Jardin du Palais Royale, the Kungstradgarten was royal property. During the Middle Ages it was used as the royal kitchen garden, supplying produce for the king. Later, it was enlarged and transformed in stages into a royal pleasure garden, similar to those being created for royal families throughout Europe at the time. It even had a similar symmetrical Baroque design. But in the early nineteenth century, its walls were demolished and Kungstradgarten was opened to public use, just as the Jardin du Palais Royale was after the French Revolution. In 1970, it became city property. The biggest change came in 1998, when the Stockholm City Planning Administration transformed what masqueraded as a park into a public gathering place that resembles the busy public squares in the rest of Europe.[13] By the early twenty-first century, Kungstradgarten included so many of their favorite activities that people felt comfortable being there and thus it became one of the most popular components of Stockholm's public realm.

So many people feel comfortable when they are in the Kungstradgarten that, unlike the Jardin du Palais Royale or Commonwealth Avenue, it is frequently crowded and often noisy. During the summer it hosts more than 150 special events. Throughout the Taste of Stockholm Festival, for instance, which lasts for a week in June, the Kungstradgarten is jammed with even more people sampling local dishes while they enjoy the music provided by bands that play throughout the day. In winter the pool that people enjoy in the summer converts into a skating rink, and at Christmas a seasonal market goes into operation. It is a destination of choice for toddlers wading in the water, hipsters drinking beer, young men and women sunning themselves, teenagers eating ice cream at the café, older people strolling under the trees, business people rushing to a meeting, vendors selling souvenirs, cyclists on their way home, tourists dragging suitcases on wheels, groups of friends taking photos in front of famous statues, and often all of these at the same time.

Via dei Condotti, Rome (2012). The obelisk on the Spanish Steps provides a visible destination for people on the street and a reminder of the city's historical past. (Alexander Garvin)

Via dei Condotti, Rome—The Via dei Condotti has been in use since prehistoric times, serving as a direct route from the Tiber River to the Pincian Hills, where the Spanish Steps rise to the church of Trinità dei Monti. The street gets its name from underground conduits that once ran beneath it, channeling water throughout the city and ending at the Baths of Agrippa, where the Emperor Augustus Caesar may have made an occasional ablution. Walking this street today with knowledge of such history enhances feelings of belonging, giving strollers a place, if just for a moment, within the life and evolution of this ancient site. A great street like Via dei Condotti makes people feel they are part of its history, even if they are just passing through.

Via Aquilante, Gubbio, Italy—In Italy the sense of kinship that emerges from historical and cultural roots is not restricted to streets such as the Via dei Condotti or even to Rome itself. It belongs to those who live in modest country towns as well, where residents value family roots and traditional practices as much or more than city excitement and financial profit.

The Umbrian hilltown of Gubbio in central Italy, for example, attracts thousands of visitors each year to its picturesque fourteenth- and fifteenth-century churches and monuments. Some town residents profit from the tourists who pay to see these sights, of course, but a majority have little to do with tourism. Rather, most residents of Gubbio draw their civic pride from living and working on the town's local streets like the Via Aquilante, a narrow thoroughfare that today looks very much like it did two, four, or even six centuries ago.

And indeed, when you stand on the Via Aquilante it is clear why the townspeople feel such connections. This intriguing roadway is paved with local cobblestones laid, as elsewhere in Gubbio, with a very slightly sloped central drainage gulley. The buildings lining the street are all constructed of the same stone blocks, and are all laid in the same patterns, giving the street a look of design consistency. The beautiful clay tile roofs that rise above the Via Aquilante are the same as those found on most other streets in the city, providing the town's neighborhoods with structural unity and a sense of harmonious fitting together.

The Via Aquilante may be a little known street in an obscure part of a small town, but it makes a major contribution to the well-being of those lucky enough to be there. Many visitors cannot help but be impressed by the care and thought that residents put into adapting their homes to their personal needs; little things, such as adding window boxes filled with flowers or colorful banners that hang from the walls, are common. These and dozens of other aesthetic and historical markers that characterize their privately owned buildings combine to make residents of Gubbio feel comfortable on the streets where they were raised and where their families have lived for generations—streets that are the product of tried-and-true loyalty to centuries-old building traditions, and that in their own way can be called great.

Via Aquilante, Gubbio (2011).
People who live on this street
have the sense of belonging
here that their families
have had for generations.
(Alexander Garvin)

Worth Avenue, Palm Beach (2012). Addison Mizner and the people who created this street almost overnight have provided visitors with instant roots to a fantasy past. (Alexander Garvin)

Worth Avenue, Palm Beach—The lack of thousands of years of history is not a barrier to fostering a sense of belonging. Worth Avenue in Palm Beach, Florida, for instance, is an exclusive four-block concourse brimming over with chic and expensive retailers. Six decades after these shops opened their doors architect Robert A. M. Stern, who was not yet born when Worth Avenue was built, described how tourists and residents browsing the street's 250 high-fashion boutiques, art galleries, jewelry shops, restaurants, and private clubs so easily made it part of their "resort life-style: leisurely, casual activity by day; formal, frequently extravagant entertaining in the evening."[4]

The many façades that greet Worth Avenue's visitors offer a mélange of Spanish, Romanesque, Gothic, Mediterranean, and Renaissance styles. Present along and behind the street in generous supply are manicured gardens, bougainvillea-covered walls, stone towers, medieval fountains, Baroque stairs, rows of palm trees, arched Saracen windows and doorways, red tile roofs, jutting glass porches, elaborate decorative tile work, and a variety of other design devices, all of which give the seasonal occupants a sense of instant roots in a town that for many of them is simply a temporary residence. Moreover, as shoppers walk down Worth Avenue, they are enticed to veer off the main drag onto one of the rambling, shop-lined pedestrian walkways, known to the veteran Palm Beachers as "Vias," that cut through the block at various junctures. Here too, high design and the swank of exclusive stores combine to make the street's visitors feel somehow at home.

For the thousands of people who frequent Worth Avenue every year its consumer temptations and explosion of contrasting design motifs of the privately owned real estate along the street somehow make them feel grounded and part of something they love—the fantasy world they always hoped they would discover when they finally escaped to their vacation or retirement paradise and found a place in the sun where they really belonged.

Levittown, Long Island (2006). Not a single building on this street looks as it did when the first residents moved in. Property owners' remodeling has transformed it into a street of their own making. (Alexander Garvin)

Levittown, Long Island—More than one thousand miles north of wealthy Palm Beach, Florida, in the suburbs of New York City, there is yet a middle-class variation on the theme of a how street influences the mood, attitude, behavior, and lives of the people who frequent it. It is not the product of an elite designer attempting to provide instant roots for an itinerant population. Among the mass-produced suburban subdivisions, there are lots of places that have been adjusted and remodeled by thousands of inhabitants—people who turned garages into additional rooms, converted attics into bedrooms, added screened-in porches, enlarged kitchens, and planted trees and shrubs, and in the process transformed both their homes and the streets they live on into a reflection of their personal way of life.

Here mass-produced, monotonous rows of inexpensive suburban "Cape Coddages" provided little connection with high-end Colonial New England architecture. Rather, they provided high-quality, affordable housing for the millions of families still reeling from a devastating world war. In these towns, designers focused more on efficiency and scale than aesthetics.

The mother of all such faceless postwar developments, the famous Levittown in Long Island, located just outside of New York City, typifies this pattern. At the time it was built, between 1947 and 1951, this row-upon-row tract of identical single-family homes constituted the first and perhaps most famous large-scale housing development ever built in the United States, a mind-bogglingly large construction project that at one time became an emblem of what the cognoscenti were sure would become an undistinguished cultureless suburbia.

Those who purchased plots in Levittown for its planned 17,747 houses were given only five architectural designs to choose from. Most observers (though not residents) assumed that living in such a canned and cutout community guaranteed a conformist future. As it turned out, however, the residents of Levittown proved far more creative and resourceful than many of their critics had expected.

How so? Unlike their counterparts in Gubbio, the residents of Levittown did not decorate their new homes with fine stonework and colorful banners (except at the Fourth of July). Unlike the stone buildings of Gubbio, Levittown's simple wooden houses were surprisingly malleable and easy to adapt to the individual needs of the people living there. Many added window boxes with flowers, but that's where the similarity ended. From the get-go this new development hummed with creative activity. Doubters watched as residents sometimes completely transformed small houses into large, expensive-looking residences.

Today, sixty years after its construction, it is almost impossible to find one of the original houses on the streets of this landmark development that has not been altered. The result is that many of the streets in contemporary Levittown, originally condemned as the epitome of sameness and lack of imagination, are more user-friendly than many streets at the higher ends of the socioeconomic scale. Levittown's once-monotonous streetscape lined with "little boxes, all the same" has completely vanished.

Forever Welcoming

Being open to anyone means that today, a decade from now, and a century from now, any great example of the public realm will remain, identifiable, accessible, and easy to use, safe, and comfortable. Public squares such as the Plaza Mayor, the Piazza del Campo, the squares of Savannah, and the Federal Center in Chicago are even more welcoming today than they were when they were first created. The same is true of streets such as the Gran Via, Sixteenth Street in Denver, Via dei Condotti, and Commonwealth Avenue and parks such as the Jardin du Palais Royale and Kungstradgarten. Nobody can be kept from entering or passing through these extraordinary components of the public realm. They are, to all intents and purposes, *forever welcoming*.

To be open to anyone a place must be identifiable, accessible, and easy to use. People won't go there, however, unless they feel safe and comfortable there, and believe they belong there. That is what they feel when they are in the Gran Via, Kungstradgarten, the Via dei Condotti, and all the other places discussed in this chapter. That is what attracts and keeps people in the city, and those places make Barcelona, Stockholm, Rome, and cities like them great.

This only underscores the importance of continually adjusting the public realm to meet the changing demands of its user populations.

Esplanadi, Helsinki (2014).
(Alexander Garvin)

4

Something for Everybody

One of my stops during my quest to determine what makes a great public realm was Palace Square in St. Petersburg. On the way I stopped in Helsinki to see how it had changed in the fifty-two years since my last visit. After checking into my downtown hotel, I stepped out for a walk along Esplanadi, a long stretch of lush green space at the heart of the city that hadn't been much used the last time I had been there. To my surprise, it was now jammed with people having fun.

The Esplanadi seemed to be the "cool" place to be, which drew some users. But people were also there for other reasons: older people sitting in the sun, cyclists who had stopped to rest on their way to somewhere else, workers taking a lunch break, children playing games, and countless others, including some who may have had nowhere else to go. Here, I thought, was a public realm that always seemed to cooperate with the goals of those who used it—a place that existed for everyone who was there because it had *something for everybody*.

As I walked around Esplanadi, I asked myself, "Why must a great public realm provide something for everybody?" One reason, of course, is that human beings are social animals who need places where they can be with others. They cannot all be in the same place at the same time. Thus, as this chapter explains, there must be a place for every activity that has brought them there. Manhattan's Central Park, for example, was specifically designed to bring together rich and poor, young and old, "each individual adding by his mere presence to the pleasure of all others."[1] Multifaceted use is possible because it is large enough (843 acres; 341 ha) and was designed to include myriad destinations for everybody to use. Smaller places can easily get overcrowded and cease to function properly. With good management, however, they can accommodate large numbers of people. As explained in the next chapter, proper management is how Kärntner Straße in Vienna and Bryant Park in New York have come to be used by so many more people than were able to do so a century ago.

But how did the Esplanadi come to have something for everybody? It was designed to function simultaneously as a park, a street, and a square. The lush carpet of grass and the rich foliage of the trees give Esplanadi the appearance of a park. Yet, like the Plaza Mayor in Salamanca or Kungstradgarten in Stockholm, it is a popular gathering place. Although it is not exactly a street, the interesting shops and popular restaurants that line the streets on either side of Esplanadi consequently play the role of a place for people to gather and hang out, similar to the major boulevards of Paris, or Kärntner Straße in Vienna.

Every day I was in Helsinki, I came back to Esplanadi several times, just as I had done with the Plaza Mayor in Salamanca. People there were having fun no matter the time of day. While strolling under the trees I also noticed that residents and out-of-towners alike felt they were rubbing shoulders with people who were there for the same reasons they were; they could go about their business without disturbing others or being disturbed themselves. But every time people were having fun there.

Esplanadi, Helsinki (2014). People use this popular part of the public realm simultaneously as they would a street, a square, and a park. (Alexander Garvin)

In 1812, when Czar Alexander I made Helsinki the capital of Finland, it was a small town occupied by just over four thousand people. Development plans for the new capital expanded its rudimentary port and marketplace with imposing government buildings, Russian Orthodox and Lutheran cathedrals, and a long rectangular open space, called Esplanadi, which extended west from the port and south from the proposed public buildings. At that time, Helsinki was essentially a small town, whose residents could easily walk to surrounding open land. So there was little reason to create the large public open space that became Esplanadi. Nevertheless, the development plan called for a large, landscaped gathering place downtown. Social interaction at Esplanadi grew with the city's population, but continued to be quite staid during the next century and a half.

Today, however, when the population of this national capital exceeds 600,000 people, the decision to establish Esplanadi seems both brilliant and obvious, not just because of the increase in Helsinki's population, ongoing careful maintenance of the open space, and a 1998 restoration of the landscaping, but also because of more relaxed contemporary attitudes about social interaction.

Esplanadi is a four-acre (1.6-ha) open space extending westward for nearly 1,300 feet (390 m) from the public market at its eastern edge to the Swedish Theater at its western end. Despite being interrupted by three north-south city streets (one of which does not allow vehicular traffic), Esplanadi functions well as park-promenade sandwiched between two parallel boulevards. Its northern boulevard is one of Helsinki's prime shopping streets and includes the city's oldest and biggest department store and its best bookstore. Two blocks north is the city's railroad station. The city's finest hotels, office buildings, and retail stores are located in the two-block-wide band between Esplanadi and the railroad station.

Without this park-promenade, the center of Helsinki would not have included the recreational space that is now so actively used by many of the people who come downtown. They go to Esplanadi for scheduled jazz concerts, folk dancing, fashion shows, and other popular events that take place in Esplanadi, or to have food and drink in the cafés.

The bench-lined promenade running down the center of Esplanadi has become the place people go to see and be seen. It is enclosed within parallel low hedges. On the other side of each hedge there is a lawn, which on summer evenings is filled with young people making use of the virtual twenty-four hours of daylight Helsinki's northern latitude provides. They camp out on the grass, enjoying themselves into the wee hours of the morning. As a result, Esplanadi has become "Helsinki's summer living room."

During my quest to determine the characteristics of a great public realm, I took two trips to Paris to observe what I believe to be one of the most beautiful cities in the world. Early on my initial visit I decided to walk from the Madeleine to the Bastille. When I got to the Boulevard des Italiens, I sat down on a bench to watch the passing parade. Some pedestrians on the thoroughfare were clearly on their way from point A to point B, but they were the minority. Most men, women, and children on the block were there because they were engaged in various social and business interactions. Scores of tourists and residents indulged in that favorite Parisian diversion, window shopping. Along the way I passed a street magician with a small but spellbound audience and several sidewalk cafés bustling with eaters and drinkers. In short, most of the people I saw that day were not walking to a specific destination. They had come to the boulevard to *be* on the boulevard and to enjoy its rich public and commercial life, all the while safely sequestered from the cars, buses, and trucks that roared by on the street's five broad lanes.

A Reason to Return Again and Again

For any component of the public realm to be successful, people must want to visit, have reasons for staying, and keep returning. It should be busy during the day and at night, in summer and in winter, in good weather and bad, and continue serving people year in and year out. For that to happen there must be things for them to do and places for them to go. Jan Gehl, in *Life Between Buildings: Using Public Space*, discussed just that, dividing them into necessary, optional, and *social activities*.[2] There needs to be enough room for those activities, and places where people can have fun. To remain welcoming, however, cities must devote adequate resources to their maintenance and management.

That cannot happen in a street that provides only a corridor for traveling, a square that is only a gathering place, or a park that is set aside only for a single recreational activity. Thus, it must be a place that can serve all the functions that the different people coming there might desire.

The boulevards of Paris are anything but single-purpose places. Great public squares and parks are not single-purpose places either. From its inception as the private garden of the queen of France, the Jardin du Luxembourg was designed to provide various places of amusement for its occupants. Once it was turned into a public park, these amusements were expanded and space for one activity after another was set aside until it contained most of the activities the residents, students, and workers in the surrounding neighborhoods might want. Washington Park in Chicago, which was initially acquired and designed for recreational activity of whatever variety its users might decide upon, also shares this pattern of development.

Boulevard des Italiens, Paris (2011). (Alexander Garvin)

Boulevard des Italiens, Paris—Like so many other streets in Paris, the Boulevard des Italiens is designed to be a great deal more than a traffic artery for transporting goods and pedestrians; it is an accommodating communal space filled with men, women, and children who are there because they like being there.

People are drawn to the boulevards of Paris for the same reasons that people are drawn to charming, thriving streets everywhere: interesting shops, good restaurants, affable crowds, easy access and walkability, engaging places of entertainment, nearness to public transportation—all the usual suspects. While strolling along these "successful streets" residents and out-of-towners alike feel at home. Pedestrians feel safe on these streets, and welcomed—there is a feeling that one belongs, that one is an insider, not an outsider, and that amusing diversions and social activities are always at hand to keep one pleasurably occupied, sometimes for hours.

Boulevard des Italiens, Paris (c. 1840). (from *Les Grands Boulevards de Paris*, by Patrice de Moncan, Les Editions du Mecene, Biarritz, 1997)

By 1830, when the Boulevard des Italiens was first paved, it had already become a fashionable destination for prominent citizens to visit so that they might be seen and hopefully be talked about. Its name was derived from the nearby location of the Theater des Italiens, an opera house, which opened in 1783. Ladies and gentlemen arranged rendezvous along this bustling promenade, meeting at the city's trendiest cafés, clubs, and restaurants, and browsing the street's high-end stores. Property owners outdid each other in opening the newest and grandest emporiums, catering to this affluent and ever-growing stream of *boulevardiers*, the word used to identify the bon vivants who frequented the most fashionable locales of Paris and other great cities. A boulevardier might have gone there to meet friends, pick up a date, do business, patronize stores, restaurants, bars, and hotels, or do almost anything else.

During the Second Empire, the Boulevard des Italiens was described by the writer Edmond Texier (1815–1887) as "the most French spot in France."[3] In many ways it still is. The difference, however, is that the fancy townhouses of an earlier age have been supplanted by major office buildings and hotels, while the nineteenth-century glitterati have morphed into Parisians of every class, ethnicity, and income, who intermingle with hordes of foreign tourists. Nonetheless, people today still sit in the numerous cafés along the boulevard expecting to see

Boulevard des Italiens (2011). Contemporary boulevardiers stroll, chat, and window shop on the street's ample sidewalks. (Alexander Garvin)

friends walk by or to pick up a date—to see and be seen. They watch as shoppers admire the designer fashions in store windows or gaze at the posters, billboards, and hanging signs advertising everything from the latest action movie to the vacation specials offered by trendy travel agencies.

Boulevard Montmartre (1897). Painting by Camille Pissarro. (State Hermitage Museum, St. Petersburg)

Camille Pissarro skillfully captured the importance of the boulevards to Parisian life at the end of the nineteenth century in a series of paintings of the Boulevard Montmartre, the eastward continuation of the Boulevard des Italiens. His historical masterpieces depict an avenue filled day and night with carriages, gaslights, and elegantly dressed men and women. However, this dreamy vision was not to last long. During the early twentieth century the carriages were replaced by Model T's and Mercedes-Benzes, while gaslights gave way to the ubiquitous neon sign. The Boulevard des Italiens continued to be one of the most fashionable sections of Paris, mostly because it provided residents with access to major Parisian destinations, including the opera, the popular hotels, movie houses, and stylish retailers. As always, it honored its multifunctional history and offered something for everyone.

Jardin du Luxembourg, Paris (2010). (Alexander Garvin)

Jardin du Luxembourg, Paris—Queen Marie de Medici, widow of King Henri IV and regent for her son, King Louis XIII, commissioned the Jardin du Luxembourg in 1611. Following its construction, she kept enlarging the property and entrusted the design of the garden to Jacques Boyceau de la Barauderie, who produced a formal arrangement of pools, fountains, *parterres* with *broderies* of flowers (geometric floral tapestries), *allées* of clipped trees, and rectangular lawns, all designed for the pleasure of a privileged few.

Jardin du Luxembourg, Paris (2013). Contemporary Parisians rearrange moveable chairs to transform this formal seventeenth-century royal garden into an actively used twenty-first-century public park. (Alexander Garvin)

After the French Revolution, however, the palace was appropriated by the new government as a parliamentary assembly and eventually became the home of the French Senate. The garden was then enlarged and opened to the public. Later, other adjustments were made to accommodate arterial improvements made during the Second Empire (see chapter 6). Through all these changes, however, the design conception of the garden has hardly changed—only the people who come to the Jardin du Luxembourg have changed and with them the activities they bring to the park.

Jardin du Luxembourg, Paris (2013). The seventeenth-century decorative fountain became a popular site for small children to play with model sailboats in the twentieth and twenty-first centuries. (Alexander Garvin)

Some children, who rent or bring their own model sailboats, race them in the large octagonal pool that originally was created as decoration. Others pay for a pony ride down the *allées* of clipped trees or a ride on the carousel that was added to the garden along with the marionette theater after the garden became a public facility.

But the Jardin du Luxembourg is not just for children. Students from the nearby Sorbonne sit on the benches (added during the nineteenth century) reading, arguing with their colleagues, or just sunning themselves. They join impromptu soccer games with local teenagers, attend concerts at the band shell, or have a glass of wine at the café, which, like most of the attractions in the garden, was added after its original construction.

People use the many movable chairs, set up picnics, or wander through the park. They come pushing baby carriages, carrying sketchbooks, and bringing tennis rackets to play on courts added during the twentieth century. Others stretch out on *tapis verts* (green carpets) that have been there since the garden was created in the seventeenth century. All of these features, regardless of their date of construction, attract tourists who flock to the park to photograph the artwork, the chateau, and Parisian park-goers. The multifunctional character of the Jardin du Luxembourg is the reason that it is able to provide something for everybody.

Washington Park in Chicago—a place with a very different history from the Jardin du Luxembourg and a completely different appearance—is just as multifunctional.

Washington Park, Chicago—In 1871, Washington Park's designers, Frederick Law Olmsted and Calvert Vaux, included playing fields for the first time in an American public park. Their plan for Chicago's 372-acre (151-ha) park featured flat grasslands that could be used for any of the field sports that were becoming increasingly popular in America. The 100 acres (40 ha) they set aside for active recreation was not designed to accommodate any specific sport, because they recognized that tastes change over time. They could not know what would be the nation's most popular game or whether some other game might surpass its popularity at a later date. Instead of specialized allocation of athletic space, they ensured that the open space would be usable for all "athletic sports, such as baseball, football, cricket . . . running games, and others which are liable to come again much more in fashion."[4]

From 1980 on, whenever I visited Washington Park, there were several baseball games going on in different sections of the meadow. More recently, I saw Japanese-Americans playing baseball while South Indian–Americans were playing cricket. I understood immediately that Olmsted and Vaux had designed a multifunctional public realm that could be adapted at any time to whatever uses people might have in mind.

Washington Park, Chicago (2008). Chicagoans enjoying a game of cricket in the park, where earlier a group had played baseball and later another would play touch football. (Alexander Garvin)

Dilworth Plaza, Philadelphia (2015). Ask any child why they go to Dilworth Plaza in front of Philadelphia City Hall and their answer will be, "I go to there to have fun!" (Alexander Garvin)

Having Fun

Perhaps the single most important characteristic of a great public realm is that it is a place where people can enjoy themselves. Isn't that why so many people spend time in places like Washington Park, the Boulevard des Italiens, or any number of playgrounds? Part of the fun of being in cool places like Esplanadi or Piazza Navona in Rome is to see who is there and what is going on, and to be seen by the others who are there. Other places—playgrounds in particular—are specifically designed as places of amusement. By the middle of the nineteenth century, specially designed amusement destinations like these began to appear in every city with territory specifically set aside for play. As a result there are now more parks and playgrounds in most cities than there are public squares.

Neufeld Playground, Riverside Park, Manhattan (2011). Many of the standardized, mass-produced swings, slides, and sandboxes installed in the 1930s are still in use in the twenty-first century. (Alexander Garvin)

Playgrounds—The playing fields in Washington Park are used primarily by adolescents and adults, but for the youngest city dwellers, playgrounds are the real draw. Rationales for erecting playgrounds in densely packed city neighborhoods include providing space for physical activity where children can develop muscle control, use up their abundant energy, and spend time that would otherwise be spent in antisocial activity.[5] Playgrounds also provide jobs and patronage. They can be created quickly without large expenditures or major dislocation, so civic leaders often propose playgrounds as a neighborhood improvement.

Kolomenskoye Park, Moscow (2014). Twenty-first-century designers have invented a much wider variety of fantasy playground environments. (Alexander Garvin)

During the first half of the twentieth century most playgrounds consisted of swings, slides, seesaws, sand boxes, and other standardized equipment. This made financial sense, because playground equipment was mass-produced and available at inexpensive prices. After World War II many children, parents, designers, and public officials thought bare bones equipment was no longer enough to really "have fun." And so new types of playgrounds began springing up with different recreational equipment, often in bright colors. By the twenty-first century very few cities still had old-fashioned, Spartan playgrounds. One of the playgrounds in Moscow's Kolomenskoye Park, for example, is an inflated, bright-colored fantasy cityscape on which children can jump up and down, climb, slide, and play peekaboo.

Piazza Navona, Rome—As Michael Webb, writer and chronicler of public squares, explained, "At their best, squares are microcosms of urban life offering excitement . . . and public ceremonies, a place to meet friends and watch the world go by."[6] The better the entertainment, the more enthusiastic people are about being there. Indeed, this is not a recent phenomenon. Residents of Rome during the first century AD, for instance, attended sporting events and other spectacles in the stadium built by the Emperor Domitian (AD 81–96). Today that spot is known as the Piazza Navona. In fact, this square, which occupies the elongated oval area used for the stadium's athletic competitions, has become one of the most popular tourist destinations in Rome. For four centuries starting in 1477, the piazza has been the site of a city market that also provided room for jugglers, actors, singers, and other performers.[7]

Piazza Navona, Rome (2012).
(Alexander Garvin)

Over time, a number of people have left an indelible mark on the square, including Pope Innocent X (1574–1655), Girolamo Rainaldi (1570–1655) and his son Carlo Rainaldi (1611–1691), Francesco Borromini (1599–1667), and Gian Lorenzo Bernini (1598–1680). Pope Innocent built his family residence, the Palazzo Pamphilj-Doria, at one end of the square. He was also responsible for the church of Sant'Agnese in Agona (which is largely the work of the Rainaldis with changes by Borromini) and for Bernini's work on the three fountains in the square, including its stunning centerpiece, the Fountain of Four Rivers (1651).

The theatrical baroque architecture in and around the Piazza Navona is surely one of the area's main attractions. It is outdone, however, by the theatrical rush of water splashing from the fountains and the variety of street performers happy to receive donations from tourists who might otherwise be spending money on more formal performances. In addition, for those who have finished watching everything going on, there is the wide diversity of vendors offering to sell almost anything that somebody in the piazza might desire.

Piazza Navona, Rome (2012). The cafés and restaurants around this famous square have made it into an even more popular tourist destination. (Alexander Garvin)

For many decades the ground floor of many of the buildings has been occupied by restaurants and cafés, where, for less than the price of a theater ticket, spectators can sit in the shade of umbrellas and enjoy the show in this remarkable square. Whenever I am in Rome, I never miss the opportunity to watch what is going on from one of the tables at Tre Scalini, a restaurant established in 1882, which serves its version of tartufo, a very special lump of dark chocolate enrobed in chocolate ice cream covered with an even darker layer of chocolate.

Animating a Multifunctional Public Realm

Chicagoans had little difficulty adapting Washington Park to accommodate whatever they wanted to do there. Their activities are what transformed it into a great locale. Sometimes, as was the situation at the end of the twentieth century when Market Square and PPG Place in Pittsburgh were initially opened to public use, people will avoid a place because it lacks facilities that are easily available elsewhere. Once those activities were made available there, they became the attraction, transforming the people who used it into actors and spectators in a theater of place.

Market Square and PPG Place, Pittsburgh—In the plan of Pittsburgh's 1784 grid, Market Square was established as an important civic destination. Over the next two centuries Market Square's 1.5-acre (0.6-ha) site had been occupied by buildings containing a courthouse, a city hall, a succession of market buildings, and stores.[8] However, in 1961 the last of these buildings was demolished and replaced with four barren, grass-covered rectangles left over from the vehicular traffic that had earlier cut through the square on Forbes Avenue and Market Street. At that time, this new green space was anything but a desirable addition to the public realm.

The modern reclamation of Market Square as an actively used part of the public realm began when the city eliminated through traffic from the square and redesigned, refurnished, and reprogrammed it for popular activities that take place at different times of the week and seasons of the year. Ironically, the first step in reclaiming the area from motor vehicles occurred in 1984, when another public square opened half a block south of Market Square. This new privately owned and managed square was designed as the centerpiece of the seven-building headquarters of the Pittsburgh Plate Glass Co. (PPG). In retrospect, it appears to be a brilliant urban design strategy conceived by PPG's architect, Philip Johnson. At the time, however, it seemed to be primarily a political ploy to obtain city approval for the project.

Piazza San Marco, Venice
(2006). (Alexander Garvin)

When Johnson presented the project to the public officials whose approval was necessary to begin construction, he promised that when PPG was done, Pittsburgh would be the beneficiary of PPG Place, a spectacular, colonnaded public square that would rival Piazza San Marco in Venice.[9] Everybody was so thrilled with the comparison to Venice that the project was approved even though Piazza San Marco is six times the size of PPG Place and its colonnade shelters stores, restaurants, museums, and hotels serving hundreds of thousands of tourists every year rather than merely providing access to a few office buildings occupied by white-collar workers. When the pedestrian hardscape at the center of PPG Place opened with a squat obelisk in its center, it attracted few people who were not on their way to work in the buildings or to do business there. In fact, PPG Place was nothing like Piazza San Marco.

PPG Place, Pittsburgh (1987). Without places set aside for people to use, this square became a barren passageway. (Alexander Garvin)

PPG Place, Pittsburgh (2014). A water feature, tables, chairs, umbrellas, and planters transformed this once-barren open space into a popular part of Pittsburgh's public realm. (Alexander Garvin)

Later, however, in an attempt to attract people to PPG Place, the city scattered tables and chairs around the square and enclosed the obelisk in a water feature. Although it still was a far cry from the Piazza San Marco, the square became a delightful destination for children and adults alike. The movable furniture provided a place for people to eat lunch or have a conversation. During the summer children are encouraged to splash in the spurting fountain. During the winter, when the water is mechanically frozen, they return to ice skate.

Market Square, Pittsburgh (2014). Visitors enjoy Market Square's summertime offerings. (Alexander Garvin)

Market Square, Pittsburgh (2013). At Christmastime, the square hosts small retailers offering gifts and goodies that attract people from the entire metropolitan area. (Alexander Garvin)

When the city realized that Market Square was not performing as promised, it took the next and much more significant steps to reclaim the square for residents and visitors. In 1997 it established the Pittsburgh Downtown Partnership, a downtown business improvement district (BID). A BID is a funding mechanism that uses money from an annual surcharge on its members' real estate tax payments to pay for services and capital spending that city governments had reduced or terminated.[10] Nine years later, the city, together with the Pittsburgh Downtown Partnership, commissioned *A Vision and Action Plan* from the Project for Public Spaces, a New York City–based nonprofit planning, design, and educational organization. The plan's recommendation was strikingly simple: *put the "market" back in Market Square*.[11] Accommodating a full market, however, required making enough room in the square. Consequently, city officials banned traffic from travelling through the square and replaced the four grass rectangles with a single large gathering place. A few vehicles still make their way cautiously around the square and some find room to park along the sidewalks in front of restaurants, bars, and retail stores that line the four sides of Market Square. At the same time, the sidewalks in front of the buildings enclosing the square were extended to accommodate outdoor dining, and lighting was improved throughout the square.

Equally important, the Downtown Partnership began programming events that would attract people to Market Square.[12] Each Thursday a farmers market attracts 7,000–10,000 office workers, residents, and visitors to the square. There are afternoon concerts on Mondays and Wednesdays. On Tuesday mornings it sponsors "KidsPlay," which consists of different educational programs every week, as well as the Carnegie Library of Pittsburgh's mobile branch "Reading Room." During the Christmas season, a special holiday market provides booths for merchants to display a variety of gifts and artisanal crafts. Like other BIDs, the Downtown Partnership manages the square and provides day-to-day maintenance, in part by supplementing municipal sanitation and security services. Pittsburgh's Market Square and PPG Place thus eventually came to provide a successful multifunctional public space.

Opposite page:
Central Park, Manhattan (2007).
(Alexander Garvin)

A Place for Everything and Everything in Its Place

One Sunday in May 2014 as I strolled through the Central Park, I marveled at how everybody in the park was able to "do their thing" without interfering with those others strolling, playing baseball, lying in the sun, reading a book, having a picnic, sitting on a bench, rowing a boat, sleeping on the grass, playing tennis, listening to a concert, riding a bicycle, watching birds, feeding the ducks, flying a kite, skateboarding—any of the other activities going on simultaneously.

I knew the answer because I had spent more time at the park and knew it better than perhaps any other part of the public realm in any city. I had discussed it in every one of my books and written about it in great detail in *Public Parks: The Key for Livable Communities*. Furthermore, as a lifelong New Yorker, my earliest trips to Central Park began before I was born. I had played there as a toddler, and now, as a septuagenarian, I thought I truly understood why this wonderland attracted 40 million visits annually.[13] As I shall explain, its inspired design and excellent management ensure that visitors can pursue all their interests, whatever they may be, simultaneously.

The 843 acres (341 ha) of Manhattan that Central Park occupies are large enough to accommodate almost anything. But because its designers chose to divide all that space into a myriad of smaller, interconnected places, everybody can fit into the park without interfering with any of the thousands of others who are there, regardless of their different reasons for being there.

Central Park, New York City—In 1858, Olmsted and Vaux conceived of the plan of Central Park for a design competition. At that time Olmsted was a 36-year-old resident of Staten Island who had unsuccessfully pursued careers as a farmer and a publisher and Vaux was a 34-year-old English-trained architect, who had moved to New York to begin his professional practice. The two men had never worked together or designed a public park. Still more astonishing, at that time there were no completed public parks specifically developed for recreational purposes in America, so they could not even go to see what their American forbears had done in such places. Indeed, the only expertise they brought to the competition was the knowledge of the site that Olmsted had gained as superintendent of the property, a position that he had assumed just three months before the two men decided to enter the competition. Nevertheless, their design was the winner among thirty-three submissions to the competition. And their plan would ultimately determine the fate of this enormous rectangular site in the middle of Manhattan Island.[14]

Olmsted and Vaux's design called for regrading the land, establishing lakes and ponds, and introducing an entirely new circulation system. Though visitors often think of the park as a reflection of Manhattan's original natural state, the designers actually prescribed a tremendous amount of work to transform the space: the occasional but nonetheless prominent rock outcrops are the only remains of the original landscape. An average of 4,000 workers a year using "pickaxes, hammers, shovels, and 166 tons of gunpowder" cut through more than 30,000 cubic yards of rock, and "excavated, moved, or brought into the Park nearly 2.5 million cubic yards of stone and earth," 35,000 barrels of cement, 65,000 cubic yards of gravel, 19,000 cubic yards of sand, 40,000 cubic yards of manure, and 270,000 trees and shrubs.[15] The park that emerged consisted of hundreds of carefully considered, landscaped destinations that have been in continuous use for more than 150 years.

Central Park (2011). Rock outcrops and boulders are all that remain of the park's original landscape. (Alexander Garvin)

On a typical Sunday in 1872, ten years after the park officially opened, 70,000 of the city's 940,000 residents, most of whom lived at the lower end of Manhattan, walked "at least three miles to reach the lower end of the park," while many others travelled in horse-drawn omnibuses.[16] On a nice day in May 2014, more than 200,000 people came to Central Park.[17] Central Park had become the center of a high-density city with a resident population nine times as large as when it was constructed, but despite the city's dramatic growth and the changing demands of its far larger population, most activities that took place in the park that day were similar to those that took place over a century and a half ago.

Central Park, Manhattan (2014). The park comfortably accommodates hundreds of thousands of visitors each day—far, far more than when it initially opened. (Alexander Garvin)

In my lifetime I have seen people continue climbing the rock outcrops, lying in the grass, strolling in the shade, sitting on benches, rowing in the lake, and so much more—activities that park-goers enjoyed as much in 1862 as they do in 2016. Still others do things that were unheard of when I was a little boy: playing with hula hoops, skateboarding, practicing yoga, and tossing Frisbees. Though its planners did not envision these modern diversions, I am sure that Central Park's adaptability will enable it to handle the recreational activities invented in the twenty-second century with similar ease.

There are four reasons why so many people continue to actively use Central Park. First, its landscaped destinations are attractive and easy to use for the simple recreational activities for which people go to any park. Second, those recreational destinations—the paths, fields, and paved spaces that adorn the park—are not single-purpose facilities: they are designed to be large enough to accommodate many uses simultaneously, thereby providing a place for everybody to enjoy the park and preventing conflict. Third, the destinations are easily accessible via the three-part circulation system, which separates pedestrian and vehicular circulation using a system of roadways:

> · four crosstown east-west arteries sunken into the ground and landscaped so that regional traffic can traverse the park without being noticed by the people in the park or interfering with their activities,
> · an independent, limited-access, circumferential artery, originally designed for carriages, that until recently allowed motor vehicles and still allows bikers to drive through the park without intersecting with the crosstown arteries,
> · plentiful, convenient pedestrian paths that connect recreational destinations and which, because of the numerous pedestrian bridges and underpasses, park-goers can reach without encountering vehicular traffic.

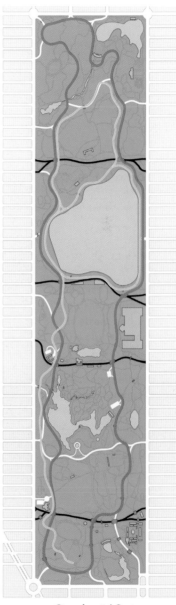

— Circumferential Carriageway
— Crosstown Transverse
— Bridle Path
Buildings
Water

Previous page–right: The circulation system in Manhattan's Central Park includes separate pathways for through traffic, vehicles circulating within the park, and pedestrians, and provides underpasses and overpasses to prevent collisions. (Joshua Price, Alexander Garvin) Previous page-left: Sheep Meadow, Central Park (2014). Park-goers relax in one of Central Park's many landscape destinations. (Alexander Garvin)

Below: Passeig de Gracia, Barcelona, Spain (2013). The street includes separate areas to store motorcycles, bicycles, vehicles that stop to unload, and long-term underground parking. (Alexander Garvin)

Finally, the great variety of landscape destinations, which Olmsted and Vaux designed in response to the different topographical conditions within the site, provide a huge number of spaces for visitor activities. Central Park places sports fields, meadows, lakes, shady woods, and playgrounds all within walking distance, among other attractions. In sum, the Olmsted and Vaux design maximized the choices that could be selected by anybody going to Central Park and made these choices attractive, easy to use, accessible, spacious enough to accommodate the masses, and diverse enough to entertain them.

Like Central Park, the Passeig de Gracia, Barcelona's premier shopping street, is specifically designed to provide places for all the activities that take place there, yet the problem of providing something for everybody using even a relatively wide street, like the Passeig de Gracia, is very different from accomplishing this task in Central Park, where there is ample space for the hundreds of thousands of people who use it. Like Central Park, however, the Passeig de Gracia requires a design where there is a place for all the activities that would otherwise conflict with one another.

Passeig de Gracia, **Barcelona**—Mention Barcelona and most people think of the pushy, unruly crowds of that city's most famous street, La Rambla. As it turns out, however, there are often just as many people roaming the equally busy but far more elegant and civilized Passeig de Gracia. Passeig de Gracia, however, works surprisingly well to inspire harmonious street behavior and is far more pleasant a place to visit. One reason for its success is that Passeig de Gracia is 200 feet (61 m) wide from property line to property line,[18] whereas La Rambla can become alarmingly crowded with people at its narrowest point of 72 feet (22 m).[19] Passeig de Gracia also provides a great deal of room for all social and commercial activities to operate freely, thereby increasing the ease with which people mingle on the street without intruding on one another's business or privacy. That is more difficult in smaller components of the public realm where there is not enough room to set aside a place for every activity at every time of the day. People who use narrower streets, like many in Copenhagen (see chapter 8), whether pushing a pram, driving a delivery van, riding a bicycle, eating lunch in an outdoor café, or just walking somewhere, have to adjust their activities to provide room for everybody.

Passeig de Gracia, Barcelona, Spain (2013). The street's layout reduces potential areas of conflict by providing specific places for popular activities. (Alexander Garvin)

City officials in Barcelona went out of their way to accommodate the people and activities on Passeig de Gracia. For example, starting at the building line, they constructed a 36-foot-wide (11-m) sidewalk bordered with comfortable benches. At the edge of the sidewalk, there is a tree-lined area designated for parked motorcycles and bicycles, a service road, a lane for diagonally parked taxis, delivery vehicles and cars, and another for vehicular and pedestrian access to underground parking. The city also added a narrow sidewalk, a bus lane, and five lanes of motor traffic. This neatly organized setup is mirrored on the opposite side of the street where spacious sidewalks allow hundreds of people to move about freely without getting in one another's way. Finally, and within the limits of the law, people on Passeig de Gracia have designated areas in which they can do all the things they have come there to do, thereby encouraging lively street life.

The ease of doing so many things on the Passeig de Gracia attracts lots of people. Their presence is one added attraction for people out for a stroll. The many fine stores are another attraction, as are some of its famous buildings, like Antoni Gaudi's Casa Milà, known locally as the Pedrera. Streets such as Passeig de Gracia are the reason so many residents and tourists spend hours wandering in Barcelona's public realm.

Reclaiming Bits of the Public Realm for Public Use

Mary Magdalen Square, Krakow, Poland (2007). Seven boys trying to outperform one another on skateboards in a small square. (Alexander Garvin)

Though it is relatively easy to provide something for everybody on a large property in undeveloped territory, such as the site selected for Central Park, doing so is more difficult in densely packed cities. Creative additions to the public realm, however, do not necessarily require the ample dimensions of Central Park or even of a major street, like the Passeig de Gracia.

Indeed, there are ample opportunities for small-scale transformations of underused bits of the public realm in unexpected places. Sometimes they are informal interventions by city residents that require no money at all. In other places, they are initiatives of private property owners and businesses seeking to improve nearby underutilized space. Often these improvements to the public realm are the product of citizen activism. They also often inspire public officials who are particularly inventive in finding tiny bits of property that can be transformed into actively used components of the public realm.

During the twentieth century, mass-produced recreational equipment made possible the widespread construction of local playgrounds to which children went to have fun. By the end of the twentieth century, however, toddlers, teens, and adults no longer needed to go to a place specifically set aside for recreation. They could go anywhere in the public realm and bring inexpensive equipment with them. As a result we see hula hoops, skateboards, Frisbees, and other popular items in whatever part of the public realm we wish to occupy. For example, while visiting Krakow, Poland, I saw teenage boys transform an unused corner of a small square into a skateboard competition site.

Rockwell Imagination Playground, Toronto (2014). Small children put together lightweight polyethylene foam equipment, brought to the site by supervisors who assist them in building their own personally imagined world. (Alexander Garvin)

Architect-designer David Rockwell and his firm have devised a particularly inventive way to enable active recreation and play to take place almost anywhere within the public realm. Rockwell's standard Imagination Playground, as it is known, consists of 105 pieces of brightly colored polyethylene foam that together weigh about 250 pounds (113 kg). The pieces can be stored in one box, two carts, or five bags. Small children connect, stack, or arrange the lightweight pieces into a playland that is the creative product of their own fantasies. As always with small children, their own imaginations are far more engaging and exciting than the fixed ideas provided for them by adults in conventional facilities.

All they need for an Imagination Playground is a site no bigger than 225 square feet (0.002 ha), an area that is smaller than most studio apartments. Empty publicly owned sites of that dimension are prevalent throughout every city in the world. Besides an unused section of street, square, or park, the only other requirement is a worker who keeps the play area safe and ensures that small children can pursue their dreams without interference from teenagers.

Keisersgracht, Amsterdam (2006). Café patrons chat and relax on a small patch of sidewalk near the Pulitzer Café, which has been transformed into a small, corner section of the public realm outfitted with tables, chairs, and small planters. (Alexander Garvin)

Retailers, especially those who operate bars and restaurants, frequently increase revenue and attract customers by expropriating the sidewalks in front of their establishments, in the process expanding the range of offerings within the public realm. Businesses in Amsterdam are particularly clever about finding and using leftover corners. For instance, shopkeepers place tables and chairs along a narrow edge of the Keisergracht Canal and other portions of unused territory, transforming them into places for people to sit and chat, or have a cup of coffee or a glass of beer.

Sporenburg, Amsterdam (2013). Children enjoy playing on a small corner of the public realm that was once an underutilized section of roadway. (Alexander Garvin)

Public officials in Amsterdam are often as inventive as local retailers. In the Sporenburg section of the city, for example, they transformed the stub end of a street into a playground, transforming a useless portion of roadway into a recreational facility for children. Amsterdam is just one of many cities making the public realm more welcoming and usable. Chicago has established a program called Make Way for People, which converts portions of street, parking spots, plazas, and alleys into community assets.[20]

The process works in reverse as well. Once a city government does something that people like in one neighborhood they demand the same for theirs. That happened in New York City as soon as Janette Sadik-Khan, the transportation commissioner (2007–2013), began a major program of reclaiming portions of street for cyclists and pedestrians. The process began in a few places by painting lines around the areas where motor vehicles were prohibited, measuring the impact, making any needed adjustments, and then making permanent changes to the pavements.

One of the earliest places this was tried was a section of Broadway in Manhattan. In 2008, a triangle next to Madison Square (see illustration on page 149) was reclaimed for use as a plaza with tables and chairs. As Sadik-Khan explained, the pedestrian projects on Broadway were intended to put "the square back in Madison Square."[21] Citizen activists from all over New York City started demanding the same thing for their neighborhoods. The program was so popular that in 2013 the Horticultural Society of New York established the Neighborhood Plaza Partnership to help neighborhoods reclaim and transform streets into public plazas. It became so popular that by 2015 there were forty-nine completed neighborhood plazas and another twenty-two in planning, design, or development.[22]

Corona Plaza, Queens, New York (2013). With the help of the city's Department of Transportation, this leftover triangle of open space was appropriated by merchants for a green market, by children as a play area, and by adults as a gathering place. (Alexander Garvin)

Corona Plaza is a typical example of the effectiveness of citizen activism aimed at improving the public realm. The site had been a triangular parking lot established at the intersection of several streets and the elevated #7 subway line running between Manhattan and Queens. Because so many people from the ethnically diverse surrounding neighborhoods came and went to the subway stop, stores along the street leading there were filled with customers. After seeing the success of other neighborhood plazas, residents and retailers came together to transform the parking lot into a plaza. They obtained support from the Queens Museum, the Queens Economic Development Corporation, City Council Member Julissa Ferreras, and Queens Community Board #4, as well as a donation of $800,000 from Chase Bank.[23] When the Department of Transportation opened Corona Plaza in 2013, it was an instant success. The weekly green market attracts families, some adults sit at tables and chairs that they can move around into convenient groupings for conversation, and others purchase fresh produce, while their children play games surrounded by trees and flowers.

Plenty of People

Corona Plaza is a particularly successful addition to the public realm because there are plenty of things for people to do there. But this phenomenon begs a question: how does a city get enough people there in the first place? In her seminal work, *The Death and Life of Great American Cities*, Jane Jacobs maintained that peopling a city requires high population densities and a diverse combination of building uses and ages. She believed that this urban fabric would ensure the presence of enough people to sustain a vibrant public realm.[24] The next chapter is devoted to explaining how a great public realm attracts those people and keeps them coming year in and year out.

Third Street Promenade,
Santa Monica, California
(2011). (Alexander Garvin)

Attracting and Retaining Market Demand

I did not need to travel anywhere to know that a great public realm attracts and retains market demand. If it is particularly satisfying it will attract people from locations both nearby and far away. These people are potential customers for businesses that might open in the vicinity, and these businesses, in turn, are potential tenants for the privately owned properties surrounding the public realm. When there are enough customers, some property owners will erect buildings. Others will sell to developers who will supply the market by building for it. The process is the same when enough people want to live in the area: If property owners don't build residences for them, developers will purchase their property and build. Either way urbanization starts when property owners initiate development.

Private development will continue as investments continue to be made in the public realm and in infrastructure such as water, sewer, utility and transportation systems, making it cost-effective for businesses and residences to locate in proximity to these investments. Property that is as yet undeveloped will become sites for new businesses and additional residences. Their success will, in turn, attract even more people, who come to shop, be entertained, do business, gather with friends, and for a multitude of other reasons. The additional customers will result in property owners replacing underperforming assets with larger scale buildings.

The more people who use the public realm and spend time there, the more likely they are to spend money there as well, and the more revenue business owners will earn. As the street's popularity increases, a greater number of people will desire to live, work, and shop there, in the process providing still more reasons for real estate development. Equally important, the increasing market demand will keep surrounding neighborhoods alive, preventing the decline that might otherwise accompany aging buildings.

Richard Florida, in *The Rise of the Creative Class*, argued that cities attract people when they are the location of choice for a creative class of people who "constantly revise and enhance every product, process, and activity imaginable, and fit them in new ways."[1] Although I agree that these residents play an important role in making cities great, great cities are the product of all their residents, not just a few of them, however talented. But I do believe that Florida is correct in arguing that great cities require "a supporting environment—a broad array of social, cultural, and economic stimuli . . . work environments, lifestyles, associations, and neighborhoods."[2] I would further argue that this requires ongoing interaction among generations of people enjoying the city's public realm and reshaping it to meet changing market demand.

This chapter describes an interdependent relationship between market demand and the public realm in which the government is *not* a passive bystander, but an enabler of or barrier to economic growth. After all, government agencies own, manage, and maintain the vast majority of parks, squares, and streets. As time passes government may need to expand the public realm to accommodate growing market demand and/or reposition the public realm to retain existing market demand or attract additional customers. Thus, in the 1960s, when city governments worried about losing customers to suburban shopping centers, Santa Monica, California, and other cities made investments in the existing public realm to retain local business, employment, and taxes. Sometimes they succeeded and sometimes they did not.

Third Street Promenade, Santa Monica (1930s). During the 1930s, the street was a conventional roadway with diagonal parking space for automobiles. (Santa Monica Historical Society)

Over time, the public realm of Third Street in Santa Monica has undergone a number of transformations, each one evolving in response to market demands. The initial transformation of Third Street began at the beginning of the twentieth century when city officials made room for private automobiles that had become popular. Then, in a reversal in 1965, the city eliminated cars from three blocks between Broadway and Wilshire Boulevard, transforming the territory between flanking buildings into a pedestrian-friendly concourse that resembled the central open-air, linear malls of outdoor shopping centers then popular in Southern California. This new Third Street Pedestrian Mall was flanked by 2,600 city-built parking spaces in six new garages, which could accommodate customers who would otherwise have driven to those outdoor shopping centers.[3]

Third Street Pedestrian Mall, Santa Monica (1979). Pedestrianizing Third Street made it an attractive destination for local shoppers. (Alexander Garvin)

Although customers flocked to the Third Street Pedestrian Mall, civic leaders soon began to worry that they would be drawn away by competition from newer air-conditioned, skylit shopping malls that were opening throughout Southern California. So, seven years later in 1972, the Santa Monica Redevelopment Agency began planning a redevelopment site at the south end of the pedestrian mall, just off the Santa Monica Freeway. The agency believed that an up-to-date, air-conditioned shopping mall on this site would retain and even increase the number of retail customers coming to Santa Monica. A partnership between two of the nation's most successful shopping center developers, the Rouse and Hahn Companies, agreed. It sought and won the right to develop the project.

In 1980, when this development, christened Santa Monica Place, opened, it was a huge success. This state-of-the-art, three-level, 120-store, air-conditioned shopping mall with a parking structure that could accommodate more than 2,000 cars quickly became the fifteenth-highest-grossing mall in the country. It also immediately began drawing away customers from the three-block pedestrian mall. Faced with a loss of customers, disappointed Third Street businesses and store owners began to disinvest, switching their merchandise to low-priced items, moving away, or going out of business.

And so in the mid-1980s, around the time that New York City formed its first business improvement district (BID), the Bryant Park Corporation, Santa Monica invested in remodeling the public realm, rebranding its pedestrian mall as the Third Street Promenade, and turning over management to a specially created BID, similar to the Bryant Park Corporation (discussed further at the end of this chapter). This was long before Denver and Pittsburgh created the BIDs discussed previously.[4] The management, additional services, and programming provided by the BID made the new promenade such a success that by the turn of the twenty-first century, many shoppers no longer went to Santa Monica Place; they stayed on the Third Street Promenade.

Third Street Promenade, Santa Monica (2011). Three decades later, after extensive remodeling, Third Street had again become a popular shopping destination. (Alexander Garvin)

However, Macerich, a large Santa Monica–based owner of shopping centers, identified the slow leaking away of Santa Monica Place customers as an opportunity. It purchased the mall with the express purpose of repositioning it as an upscale retail destination (with Nordstrom, Bloomingdale's, and Vuitton) and extending the booming promenade into Santa Monica Place. It eliminated the skylight and air-conditioning, tore out the wall and doors that separated the (formerly interior) mall from the outdoor promenade, and reconfigured the mall's entire ground place so that it appeared to be a continuation of the Third Street Promenade. The redesigned and reconfigured public realm, which reopened in 2010, became part of a four-block public realm that remains (along with the beach) one of the most popular destinations in Santa Monica and the west side of Los Angeles.

Third Street Promenade, Santa Monica (2015). The even more popular Third Street Promenade now extends into what was once an air-conditioned shopping mall and now offers customers the opportunity to shop at Nordstrom, Bloomingdale's, and Vuitton. (Alexander Garvin)

The story of Third Street illustrates the intimate relationship between government (the owner, creator, and manager) of the public realm and property owners and businesses that depend on it for their customers. By studying that story, one quickly learns that government can make mistakes in dealing with the public realm, as Santa Monica's government did when they opened Santa Monica Place. After all, the government's main concerns and skills are in providing public services, regulating public activities, and raising the money to pay for them, not estimating market activity or operating businesses.

Using the Public Realm to Trigger Private Development

Governments tend to be more successful when they make their public realm investments in largely undeveloped territory, thereby avoiding opposition from the people and businesses affected. When government agencies want to initiate development in this territory, they often do so by first establishing the main component of the public realm, which is most likely to attract a market that will spill over into surrounding territory and trigger private investment there. Market development was, in fact, the rationale behind the creation of the Place des Vosges in Paris. Sometimes, as in the case of London's Regent's Park and countless American privately developed communities, such as Irvine, California; Sugarland, Texas; and Reston, Virginia, the public realm is created by a property owner.

Place des Vosges, Paris (2014). (Alexander Garvin)

Place des Vosges, Paris—At the start of the seventeenth century, when the Place des Vosges was established, the public realm of Paris consisted of a tangled web of alleys, lanes, and twisty streets that were rarely wide enough to accommodate more than a single horse-drawn delivery cart. There were sumptuous gardens and impressive forecourts to major edifices—all privately owned—but relatively little open space, other than narrow streets, open to the public at large.

King Henri IV believed that the best way to attract business to undeveloped sections of the city was by creating attractive public spaces not available in the older sections of Paris. Consequently, in 1604, the king announced the creation of a new public square, then called the "Place Royale," which became known as the Place des Vosges in 1800. He offered to six of the city's wealthiest citizens land on the north side of the new square, titles of nobility, and tax-free status. In exchange they had to build workshops, provide worker housing, and manufacture silk.[5] Property on its other three sides was transferred by the state to people who agreed to erect residential buildings with deep arcaded galleries that provided access to shops at ground level.

Place des Vosges (c. 1600). In its original incarnation this square had no planting whatsoever. (from *The Paris of Henri IV*, by Hillary Ballon, MIT Press, Cambridge, 1991)

It took three years for the attempt to jump-start a silk industry to fail, but the Place des Vosges did not fail in every respect: because Paris had a growing population that provided the necessary customer base, developers erected residential buildings instead. The public realm that emerged was 468 feet (143 m) square.[6] At first there was nothing but sand in the Place des Vosges, then residents erected a fence to restrict circulating carriages from taking a shortcut through the square. In 1639 an equestrian statue of Louis XIII was placed in the middle of the square. The statue was melted down during the French Revolution and replaced during the Bourbon Restoration (1814–1830) with a copy, along with decorative fountains in the four corners of the square.

Just as Henri IV had intended, the Place des Vosges enhanced the city's appearance, offered a glamorous setting for public ceremonies, and provided Paris for the first time with a large, public open space that could be used for a great variety of recreational purposes.[7] The Place des Vosges became a model for Place Dauphine (1607), Place des Victories (1692), and Place Vendôme (1699), each of which initiated private development in surrounding neighborhoods because of intense demand for additional housing throughout Paris. The new public squares provided the immediate vicinity with a competitive advantage over more densely developed parts of the city. More important, the Places des Vosges encouraged development in the surrounding neighborhood, which became known as the Marais. After nearly three centuries, however, the Place des Vosges succumbed to changes in market demand and had to be reconceived to better serve its customers.

The Revival of the Place des Vosges—The area of Paris commonly known as the Marais, which grew up around the Place des Vosges, had been in decline since the end of the nineteenth century. After World War II, however, by which time the neighborhood had become a predominantly working-class district, a series of investments in the public realm triggered the area's revival.

Place des Vosges, Paris (2014). In the late twentieth century, this square became popular with a very different population from those who used it a century earlier. (Alexander Garvin)

In 1964 Minister of Culture André Malraux persuaded the French government to declare the Marais the first historic district in Paris. Twelve years later the city invested in major restoration of the square: it enclosed the statue of Louis XIII with spectacular flowering chestnut trees, replanted the clipped linden trees that had once dominated the square's periphery, and installed benches for adults

Below: Map of Regent's Park and St. James Park, London. Sir John Nash devised Regent Street as a way of connecting Regent's Park with parkland to the south. (Ryan Salvatore, Alexander Garvin)

Below right: Regent's Park with Hanover Terrace in the background, London (2014). (Alexander Garvin)

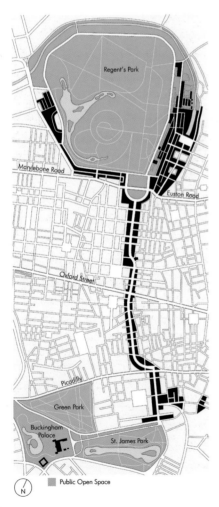

and placed play equipment for children around the square.[8] The city and national governments also restored some of the neighborhood's mansions and converted them into museums.

Pioneering households identified bargains among the area's government-designated landmarks and soon purchased and transformed them into comfortable residences. Merchants as well as café and restaurant operators perceived the new residents as potential customers, so they responded to the market demand by opening businesses in the arcades of the Places des Vosges. Eventually, more and more Parisians wanted to live in the historic structures on or near the square, especially once fine meals, great wines, and fashionable articles of clothing and furniture became easily available from the retail outlets in the arcade and along neighboring streets. Indeed, the square itself became a favorite hangout for parents to meet one another and for children to frolic under the trees. A similar evolution occurred in London over the first half of the nineteenth century on crown property that became Regent's Park.

Regent's Park, London—The prince regent (later King George IV) owned 500 acres (202-ha) (now Regent's Park) just north of the center of London. The land had been leased until 1811 to farmers who used it for grazing cattle and growing hay.[9] The prince regent decided to increase crown revenues by transforming the land at the heart of the property into a large park.

At the prince regent's request, in 1810 architect–developer Sir John Nash prepared a comprehensive plan for the 395 acres (160 ha) that are now Regent's Park, the territory around it, and a new street (Regent Street) connecting it with the largely developed district to the south. Later Nash also prepared a plan for St. James Park and property at the southern terminus of Regent Street.[10]

Cumberland Terrace and Regent's Park, London (2014). In between the service road of each terrace (apartment complex) and the park, there is a gated recreational area that is used in common by terrace residents. From the windows of the Cumberland Terrace, however, because of the clever placement of the common garden Regent's Park appears to be the private garden of a lavish country estate. (Alexander Garvin)

Nash himself developed about thirty properties on leased land facing the park, including long blocks of row houses called terraces. These terraces face gated private parks that run the length of each property. Though each terrace has the appearance of a grand palace, the occupants live only in apartments with windows that open onto what seems, at least from the vantage point of the interior, to be the occupant's own vast estate garden, when it is actually Regent's Park.

Other developers continued building on crown land and nearby properties in other hands. Thus, by 1851, when the Crown Lands Act transferred management of Regent's Park and London's other Royal Parks to the national government, much of the land in this section of the city had been fully developed.

Louis Napoleon, president of France (1848–1852), who crowned himself Emperor Napoleon III (1852–1870), was quite familiar with London's Royal Parks from his years living in exile there. In fact, he had lived in a Nash terrace facing St. James Park. The emperor adopted the development strategy that had been, so successful for Regent's Park, donating to the city of Paris the vast royal 2,090-acre (846-ha) property known as the Bois de Boulogne that occupied a location on the western outskirts of Paris, similar to the property on the northern edge of London that had been transformed into Regent's Park. Napoleon III wanted to transform it into a park that would, in a similar manner, trigger private development,[11] but to do so he needed a major attraction to induce people to move to the outskirts of Paris. Just as importantly, he needed adequate roadways to get them there.

Avenue Foch, Paris (1872). Etching by Jean-Charles Alphand, chief engineer and landscape architect of the Services des Promenades et Plantations, which was responsible for the creation of Avenue Foch. (from *Les Promenades de Paris*, by Charles-Adolphe Alphand, Connaissance et Memoires, Paris, 2002)

Avenue Foch, Paris—Emperor Napoleon III in 1852 ordered the creation of a new artery leading from the Arch of Triumph westward to the new public park that would be created from the Bois de Boulogne. He commissioned the architect Jacques-Ignace Hittorff to design the new Avenue de l'Impératrice, intending to make it as impressive as possible because it was to be named in honor of his wife, Eugenie.

In 1853 the emperor then took a step that would deeply and forever affect the destiny of his beloved city: he appointed Baron Georges-Eugène Haussmann (1809–1891) prefect of the Seine (essentially CEO of the entire Paris region), instructing him to make Avenue de l'Impératrice one of his foremost priorities. On seeing Hittorff's initial design for a forty-meter-wide (131-ft) treeless avenue, he exclaimed, "The Emperor does not want that . . . Triple it! [Make it] 120 meters [in width]—add to your plan two [flanking] lawns . . . of 32 meters . . . which will allow me to plant groups of trees."[12] Haussmann's glorious new 1,200-meter-long (3,937-ft), 120-meter-wide (394-ft) landscaped boulevard opened a year later.[13]

As part of an ambitious development program, Haussmann and his colleagues set out to make the blocks that lined the new boulevard (along with the entire sixteenth arrondissement through which it was to pass) one of the most expensive and exclusive residential sections in the city.[14] The easy access the proposed avenue provided to the new Bois de Boulogne park and to the rest of Paris made real estate in this area highly desirable, as did the charming and convenient neighborhood park islands opposite all the residences. As more and more properties along this new roadway were transformed into expensive living quarters, the thoroughfare itself went through several name changes before it was finally dubbed Avenue Foch in 1929. It remains the neighborhood's most impressive address and still is lined with mansions, townhouses, and apartment buildings occupied by wealthy Parisians.

Avenue Foch, Paris (2006). The green space on both sides of this central roadway and the adjacent Bois de Boulogne park make it one of the city's most attractive areas in which to live and visit. (Alexander Garvin)

Avenue Foch, Paris (2006). The lavish park islands lining the avenue have become popular recreational resources for nearby residents. (Alexander Garvin)

Enlarging the Public Realm to Accommodate a Growing Market

Where there is ongoing and substantial demand for new residential or commercial development, massive investment in a great public realm, such as the combination of the Avenue Foch and the Bois de Boulogne, will attract development to an undeveloped section of the city. The reasons are obvious: government can easily acquire open land and make investments there, just as the private sector can easily acquire undeveloped territory around the new public realm and invest in buildings that will supply the ready market. Adding to the public realm of an already built-up city is far more difficult, however, and often requires considerable demolition and hardship. For example, large sections of medieval Paris had to be cleared during the nineteenth century to make room for its streets and squares. In the early 1900s, Chicago had a similar problem of growing market demand, and responded by building a bridge linking North and South Michigan Avenue, making nearby territory more attractive for development (discussed below) but without causing nearly as much hardship.

An Administrative Center for the Modern City of Paris—Paris, which had a mid-nineteenth-century population in excess of one million people, needed a large public market.[15] In Paris, the creation of the city's central market, known as Les Halles, had begun before Haussmann became prefect of the Seine.[16] The construction of Les Halles required taking private property, displacing its occupants, and demolishing existing buildings. However, the laws of France required Haussmann and the government of Napoleon III to employ relatively complex means to acquire the necessary property for additions to Paris's public realm. Before beginning demolition, they had to prepare and publish a redevelopment plan and obtain approval from the minister of the interior, the appropriate national ministries, the Council of State, the National Assembly, the Paris Municipal Council, and the councils of the individual arrondissements (districts) that would be affected by the construction. Then a commission had to evaluate the proposed indemnification of the property owner and the court had to approve the expropriation and the condemnation payment.[17] Thus, create Les Halles, property owners were paid what the courts decided was a fair price for their land.

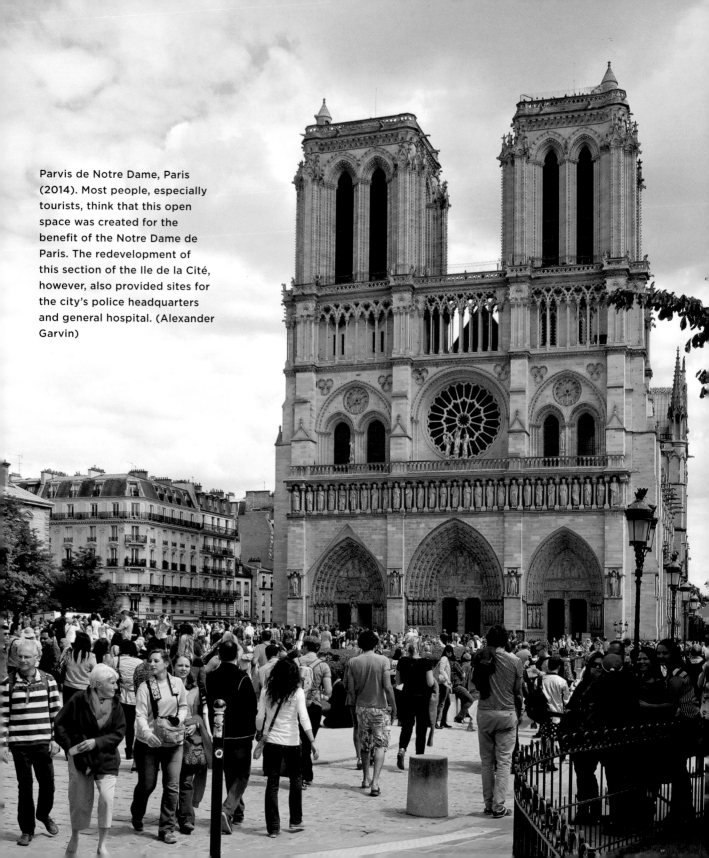

Parvis de Notre Dame, Paris (2014). Most people, especially tourists, think that this open space was created for the benefit of the Notre Dame de Paris. The redevelopment of this section of the Ile de la Cité, however, also provided sites for the city's police headquarters and general hospital. (Alexander Garvin)

Haussmann did not clear away the dilapidated houses dating from the Middle Ages that encrusted much of central Paris merely to create a central market or enlarge the open space in front of Notre Dame cathedral. Rather, he wanted to concentrate administrative, judicial, medical, and university activity at the very center of the city so that Paris would become "the world's leading city" and "a capital worthy of France."[8] To provide the center of the city with prominent, easily accessible destinations, Haussmann and his team pierced broad avenues through the medieval city and assembled large sites for the institutions that would occupy the impressive structures that they erected there.

To achieve this goal on the Ile de la Cité he erected magnificent buildings for the Ministry of Justice, the general hospital, and police headquarters; created a new public realm of streets and squares; and connected everything to the rest of the city with new or improved bridges across the Seine River. This new public realm consisted of

- one broad new north-south street, Rue d'Arcole, connected by new bridges to the left and right banks of the Seine River;
- two widened north-south arteries: Rue de la Cité and Boulevard du Palais;
- three new squares: (i) Place du Parvis (an open space used by people going to Notre Dame, police headquarters, and the city's main hospital, the Hôtel-Dieu), (ii) Rue de Lutece, which is in effect a public square for users of the Ministry of Justice, and (iii) Place Louis Lépine, which is essentially a flower market.

When this complex of streets, squares, and public buildings was finished, it was soon filled with lawyers, doctors, public administrators, and business leaders. They provided the market that was essential to the transformation of the center of Paris, a role they could perform because it was a short walk across one of the bridges to the rest of the city.

Opposite page: Haussmann supervised retrofitting of the center of Paris to accommodate modern facilities for the central administration of the city of Paris, its police headquarters, its central produce market, the national Ministry of Justice, and the Sorbonne (a complex of national universities). (Owen Howlett, Alexander Garvin)

Model of Ile de la Cité circa 1800. As this model from the Museum Carnavalet demonstrates, delivering goods and services within the maze of narrow streets of old Paris was a nightmare. (Alexander Garvin)

The government of Paris also wanted to displace the residents from the Ile de la Cité. In that way, it would eradicate what Haussmann called the "ignoble district" that had become a "refuge or meeting place for . . . criminals . . . rejects of the Parisian population . . . ex-convicts, swindlers, thieves, and murderers."[19] He achieved just that, through a fair, deliberative process that compensated the residents of Ile de la Cité for their property.

Just as in France, local governments in the United States cannot take private property without due process of law or fair compensation for property owners. The difference is that during the mid-nineteenth century the government of Paris was able to take a comprehensive approach to the creation of its public realm (without producing a comprehensive plan) and implement what it had in mind. Chicago, in part inspired by Paris, was one of the first American cities to take a similar comprehensive approach. The *Plan of Chicago,* published in 1909, is arguably the first and the most influential such plan ever produced in America. Among its most effective proposals was the extension of Michigan Avenue north of the Chicago River, which had as powerful an impact on the north side of the city as the Avenue Foch did on the west side of Paris.

Rush Street Bridge, Chicago (1900). The bridge provided only one lane of north-south traffic in each direction crossing the Chicago River. (Chicago History Museum)

North Michigan Avenue, Chicago—A half century after Avenue Foch was conceived, Chicago planned to extend a similar but less ambitious artery into partially developed territory north of the Chicago River and beyond. The city had already considered numerous proposals for connecting the two sides of the Chicago River. One of the most utilitarian called for either a bridge or tunnel that would extend Michigan Avenue across the Chicago River and into partially developed land north of the river.

In 1909 architects Daniel Burnham and Edward Bennett published their proposal for a new bridge in *The Plan of Chicago;* it would be one of many proposals in the plan that the city ultimately implemented.[20] Burnham and Bennett's scheme called for more than just the creation of a single wide street. Unlike Paris, Chicago already had plenty of wide streets, the larger ones extending 80 feet (24 m) from property line to property line, the smaller ones measuring 66 feet (20 m) wide. Unlike Paris, however, Chicago's streets were evenly spaced every three or four hundred feet throughout the entire city.

The most important of these streets, a section of Michigan Avenue that lined Grant Park, was 130 feet (39.6 m) wide, broader even than some of the boulevards of Paris. As Michigan Avenue continued northward, however, the roadway narrowed to 66 feet (20 m), causing major traffic jams all the way to the Chicago River, where vehicles were forced to make a sharp turn and then climb a steep grade to reach the Rush Street Bridge. Even after enduring this trek, motorists found that the bridge carried only one lane of traffic in each direction, and it soon gained the reputation as being "one of the most crowded bridges in the world."[21]

To alleviate the traffic nightmare, Burnham and Bennett suggested widening Michigan Avenue and extending it to a new bridge they proposed across the Chicago River. They also proposed widening Pine Street at the other end of the bridge to 130 feet (40 m), renaming it North Michigan Avenue, and extending this new artery northward from the river to the outskirts of the city.

Although there was ample support for the new street, the plan encountered opposition from property owners who were concerned that they would not be treated fairly. Thus, it took four years from the publication of the plan for condemnation to be approved by the city council and three more years of litigation to settle on compensation for the property owners.

Burnham and Bennett's bridge opened in 1920 and within ten years the modest buildings lining Pine Street had been replaced by the landmark Wrigley Building, the Chicago Tribune Tower, and several other major structures. Empty lots several blocks east and west of the new street likewise became sites for important new office buildings. By the end of the twentieth century Burnham and Bennett's improvements had helped turn North Michigan Avenue into the most important shopping street in the entire American Midwest. And the neighboring low-density residential area extending east to Lake Michigan became the high-rise residential district known as the Gold Coast, which today plays host to some of the city's most luxurious buildings.

Opposite page: Proposal for North Michigan Avenue (1909). Burnham imagined extending Michigan Avenue in the Loop across a new bridge over the Chicago River that would continue northward as a widened North Michigan Avenue. (Chicago History Museum)

North Michigan Avenue, Chicago (2012). Today North Michigan Avenue has become the main shopping street for Chicago and the entire Midwest. (Alexander Garvin)

This intense private-market reaction to investment in the bridge and street extension occurred because the improvements allowed the surrounding area to respond to massive and rapidly growing market demand. In 1910, just after the project was proposed, Chicago had a population of nearly 1.7 million people. The year the bridge opened, however, this population had grown by half a million people to almost 2.2 million, and it reached 2.7 million by 1930. The new bridge and avenue provided a public realm armature around which developers found attractive locations for new buildings where many of those additional million people could live, work, and shop.

Responding to Diminishing Market Demand by Repositioning the Public Realm

When an area loses its customer base, it may be from any number of conditions not limited to the size, scale, or design of the public realm. In the case of the Place des Vosges, for instance, the changing demands of the population that moved to the area forced the city and local businesses to adapt. The physical character of the public realm may also be an issue. For example, on Kärntner Straße, a major street in Vienna, the problem was the inability to physically accommodate existing and potential demand. Making Kärntner Straße more accessible to customers through mass transit, eliminating vehicular traffic, making more room for pedestrians, and reconceiving the design and operation of the street itself could help the street satisfy that demand. Inadequate government services also can be the problem. The repositioning of the public realm, which took place in Manhattan's Bryant Park during the 1980s, for instance, was achieved by reconceiving the way the park functioned and dramatically improving safety and the park experience.

Kärntner Straße, Vienna (1900). (Imagno)

Kärntner Straße, Vienna—Unlike streets in Chicago, Vienna's ancient streets were simply not designed to handle the twentieth-century invasion of trucks, buses, and automobiles. The public realm had to be adjusted to handle the traffic. Vienna also desperately needed efficient public transportation that would allow more people to visit and patronize its commercial districts. A combination of both would keep important businesses downtown, increase the number of customers patronizing its stores, preserve much-admired historical buildings, and clean up what was fast turning into a crowded, chaotic environment where cars and pedestrians intermingled in a snarled, noisy mess. Particularly hard hit were Kärntner Straße and Grabenstrasse, Kärntner Straße's four-block-long perpendicular extension. By the 1950s both streets were losing customers as a result of excessive noise, traffic congestion, air pollution, and the absence of ample sidewalk space to accommodate shoppers. Some businesses on these streets relocated. Others simply closed their doors.

To combat this downward slide, Vienna's leaders decided on a three-part prescription: (i) make Kärntner Straße accessible to many more people via public transportation, (ii) alter the physical structure of the street to make it safer, cleaner, more convenient, and more attractive, and (iii) provide the additional management that would allow more activities to go on as necessary.

In 1968 the city council, which had long discussed augmenting its seventy-year-old metropolitan rail system (Stadtbahn) with an underground subway system, voted to create an 18.6-mile (30-km) underground network called the U-Bahn. One of its most important stations, Stephansplatz, was located under the intersection of Kärntner Straße and Graben, and was completed in 1978, making both these streets easily accessible to hundreds of thousands of subway customers who no longer needed to suffer the travails of road traffic to get there. By 2013 the U-Bahn extended 49 miles (78.8 km) and served more than 1.3 million passengers daily, all of whom were potential Kärntner Straße customers.[22]

Kärntner Straße, Vienna (2013).
Once vehicular traffic was
removed from Kärntner Straße,
there was enough room to
increase the street's customer
base. (Alexander Garvin)

Of course, something still needed to be done to improve conditions for shoppers and tourists once they arrived at these streets. Consequently, Vienna sought recommendations from the Viennese-born American architect and city planner Victor Gruen. His 1971 report, prepared in consultation with the city's planning department, recommended banning all vehicular traffic from the entire central business district contained within the Ringstrasse.[23] Gruen had proposed something similar for downtown Fort Worth, Texas, in 1956 and failed to convince the city of the importance of pedestrianizing the entire business district.[24] Rather than begin implementing Gruen's comprehensive demotorization plan, however, the city decided on an experiment: they would close Kärntner Straße to vehicular traffic for three months beginning in November 1971, but only on weekdays between 10:30 a.m. and 7:30 p.m. The experiment proved that Gruen's plan could be successful: the volume of customers on Kärntner Straße quickly increased during the traffic ban.

Over the next two and a half years the city continued its improvement program, eliminating curbs on Kärntner Straße and Grabenstrasse, regrading and repaving both streets, and transforming the entire area into one continuous pedestrian zone. It added trees, seating areas, tables, benches, cafés, new lighting, planters, and street furniture. As a result, Kärntner Straße became a popular pedestrian destination once again, and when the Stephansplatz subway station opened in 1978 it was on its way to regaining its former status as one of Europe's most elegant shopping streets.

Kärntner Straße, Vienna (2013). Providing subway access to the commercial center of Vienna allowed Kärntner Straße to serve even more customers. (Alexander Garvin)

Indeed, the program did not stop with physical improvements. Over the next three decades the city made sure that merchandise delivery, street cleaning, and street maintenance were completed before 10:30 a.m. so that any disagreeable noise or activity would be out of the way before the tourists arrived. By 11:00 a.m. the trucks were gone, along with any hint of exhaust and congestion. Moreover, because of its proximity to the city opera house and many of the city's finest hotels and restaurants, nearby customers and those now able to get there by public transportation poured into the area well into the night, keeping Kärntner Straße and Graben alive and hopping long after many of Europe's premiere shopping streets had closed for business. Today these streets remain among the most successful shopping sites in all of Europe.

In Bryant Park in New York City, the importance of good urban management is more starkly evident. There was no easy way to increase the number of people who could access the park; it was already well connected by transit and large, nearby populations of workers. This nine-acre (3.6-ha) area, however, had become such a dangerous and unpleasant place that most people who worked in the area or were visiting avoided it. The situation was so bad that during the 1980s the city agreed to transfer management of the park to a specially created institution that made minor but very effective adjustments to its design and made major changes to its administration. These managerial and design changes were enough to turn the park into one of Midtown Manhattan's major attractions.

Bryant Park, New York City—Bryant Park, along with the New York Public Library at Fifth Avenue and Forty-Second Street in New York City, occupies a site that replaced the Croton Distributing Reservoir in 1899. During the early part of the twentieth century, New Yorkers avoided spending time in the shadow of the noisy elevated subway that ran along its western edge on Sixth Avenue. In 1905 the *New York Times* reported that the park had "papers strewn over the grass, loafers fast asleep and sprawled out over the benches." In 1921 every night four hundred to six hundred men hung out at the park playing poker and drinking, leaving it in the morning looking "like a junkman's cellar after a flood."[25] Conditions improved dramatically during the 1930s when the elevated subway was replaced by an underground subway and the park itself was completely renovated, but unfortunately the renovation also sowed the seeds of its later decline.

To better support the trees and other plantings that accompanied the reconstruction, the level of the park had been raised by adding four feet of earth (taken at no cost from nearby excavations for the Sixth Avenue subway) to the street-level

Bryant Park, Manhattan (2008). (Alexander Garvin)

grade. In addition, over the next four decades the bushes lining Bryant Park's street edges were allowed to grow large enough that neither pedestrians walking along the street nor, perhaps more importantly, policemen driving in patrol cars or walking their beats on the sidewalk could see into the park.[26]

Parks, like streets and squares, do not take care of themselves. They deteriorate when local governments do not employ the necessary personnel or spend enough money to maintain them. As I explained in chapter 4, that was the situation in New York City during the 1970s when the city's capital budget allocation for parks, calculated in constant dollars, was less than one-fifth of what it had been only two decades earlier and parks department staff had been reduced by a similar amount.[27]

Given this decline in funding for care and supervision, it was no wonder that Bryant Park was described at the time by Laurie Olin, the landscape architect who was responsible for its redesign, as "trees overgrown—ground beaten bare—trash overflowing the waste cans, stuffed into the long-abandoned light boxes—lights broken off and missing; pavement not repaired—hedges allowed to grow up to hide the ugly lights, themselves neglected and ugly."[28] In addition, given the increasing amount of crime in the city at that time, one should not be surprised that in those days many people avoided most city parks, including Bryant Park.

By the 1980s more than nine hundred arrests per year were made in the park. In response, neighboring real estate and business interests decided to intervene and engaged Daniel Biederman, then a recent graduate of Princeton University and Harvard Business School, and William H. Whyte, a social scientist who had been studying people's behavior on streets, sidewalks, and in squares and parks for many years, to help them deal with the situation. Whyte explained that the park had become a hangout for "dope dealers and muggers" and was underused because it was "cut off from the streets by walls, fences and shrubbery." Therefore, people could not see in or see out, and the park had thereby become a territory that attracted undesirables.[29] He recommended actions that would attract many more people to the park: removing the fences, cutting back the shrubbery, and adding points of entry from surrounding streets.

Surrounding businesses and property owners enclosing the park, including the New York Public Library, created the Bryant Park Corporation, an independent, nonprofit institution to implement Whyte's proposals, and appointed Biederman to administer the new institution. The Bryant Park Corporation was the city's first BID, funded with a surcharge on city real estate taxes paid by the properties surrounding the park. At its inception, the corporation sought modest charitable contributions and a continuation of the annual city budget expenditure, which had been $210,000. In fiscal year 2013, however, the budget of the Bryant Park Corporation had grown to $7.9 million, including $1.1 million from the real estate tax surcharge, $2.5 million in rents, $1.5 million in sponsorships, and $2.8 million from user fees and other sources. It spent the full $7.9 million annually, primarily for sanitation, security, public events, and capital projects. Most importantly, the corporation has a staff of eighty-five people caring for this intensely used park space.

Bryant Park, Manhattan (2014). (Alexander Garvin)

Opposite page: Bryant Park, Manhattan (2010). During the winter months the central lawn is covered over with an ice skating rink. (Alexander Garvin)

When the Bryant Park Corporation renovated the park again between 1991 and 1995, low-growing plants replaced overgrown bushes so that police and passersby could again see what was going on in the park and would no longer be afraid to go there. These latter-twentieth-century changes to the physical design, as important as they were, however, did not play as important a part in the park's rehabilitation as the introduction of new facilities that attracted thousands of people to Bryant Park, the programming of the many events that now take place in the park every day, or the establishment of a management team that makes sure that the park is safe, clean, and attractive.

In 2015 visitors to the park could go to a restaurant; outdoor café; "Southwest Porch" bar and grill; kiosks selling coffee, sandwiches, ice cream, and other frozen treats; an outdoor library; tables for ping pong, chess, and backgammon; a petanque court; and a carousel. The rest of the park includes a 1.1-acre (0.4-ha) open lawn for lying in the sun (transformed into a skating rink during the winter), moveable chairs that can be arranged into conversational groups, tables with umbrellas, and shady tree-lined walks. When the weather is appropriate the park schedules outdoor movies, ice skating, dance performances, concerts, yoga, tai chi, lectures, fencing, birding tours, juggling—in short, something for everybody. It is no wonder that after work on nice days there are around three thousand people in Bryant Park. The quantity of people in the park makes it extremely difficult to identify the vagrants (who were prominent in 1980) or the twenty-four-hour security guard roaming the park. In all of 2013 the only crimes reported in the park were seventeen incidents of larceny (down from nine hundred arrests when Biederman came to the park).

The improvements to the public realm made at Bryant Park—design, additional facilities, programmed events, maintenance, and management—generated additional demand for the retail stores and office buildings surrounding the park. Area office rents, for example, more than doubled between 1990 and 2002, outstripping such nearby areas as Grand Central Terminal (where the increase was less than 60 percent) and Rockefeller Center (where the increase was less than 45 percent). That increase was enough to trigger the development of an additional 2.8 million square feet of office space.[30]

Continuing Investment

Paris, London, Chicago, Vienna, New York, and the other great cities discussed in this chapter all made public realm investments that appealed to an ever greater market—a market that spread out through those cities' public realm network. They demonstrate that whether streets, squares, and parks are extended into new territory, inserted into the existing fabric of a busy city, or repositioned to meet contemporary demands, simply creating a container for public activities is not enough. To be successful, that public realm must have enough appeal and provide sufficient opportunity to attract people *and* keep them there. And once this is accomplished, greater concentrations of people benefit these spaces, surrounding businesses, and the city as a whole. Thus, the present and future prosperity of a great city can be ensured only by continually adjusting the public realm framework to satisfy contemporary and future market demand.

Boulevard Saint-Germain, Paris (2004).
(Alexander Garvin)

Admiralty, St. Petersburg, Russia
(2014). (Alexander Garvin)

Providing a Framework
for Successful Urbanization

I n 2014, I traveled to St. Petersburg to have yet another look at Palace Square (Dvortsovaya Ploshchad). I had been there in 1959, when people in Nikita Khrushchev's Russia called the city Leningrad; in 1996, when people in Boris Yeltsin's Russia had renamed it St. Petersburg, and in 2004, when it was Vladimir Putin's beloved jewel of a city. As I had done each time before, I climbed to the top of St. Isaac's Cathedral to photograph the city from above. There, looking at the spire of the Admiralty, I understood how and why a great public realm provides a physical framework for urbanization.

From high above St. Petersburg, where one can see crowds passing through city streets, the importance of physical framework became clear. In a great city, once people arrive at their destination, they must be able to orient themselves and then to get to the other places they wish to visit, stop along the way to deal with whatever incidental errands may arise, and move around easily throughout the public realm. It is the readability of this framework that attracts people and makes it easy for them to find their way to the places they wish to go.

Peachtree Street Corridor, Atlanta (2004). The development of Atlanta evolved in a linear fashion along the ridge line of Peachtree Street. (Alexander Garvin)

Alternative Frameworks

Kevin Lynch, in *The Image of the City*, proposed five elements to organize the image of a city: paths, edges, districts, nodes, and landmarks.[1] These are certainly helpful in perceiving any public realm framework. To provide a framework for private development, however, those components must be combined into very simple geometric patterns that take the form of axial vistas, a radio-concentric pattern of circulation, or a rectilinear grid. It is these geometric patterns that provide the public realm framework for development. But whatever the geometric form, the public realm will be successful in shaping further urbanization only if it is well maintained and well managed.

The public realm's physical framework is never accidental. It may grow along well-traveled paths or adjust to the topography, as do the streets of Atlanta, Georgia, and the Croatian city of Dubrovnik. It may consist of a set of destinations cleverly connected by axial roadways, as is the case in Rome, Italy, or St. Petersburg, Russia. It may take the form of easily recognizable geometric shapes such as concentric circles with radial arteries that connect the circles, as in Paris, Vienna, and Moscow. It may appear as a rectilinear grid, like the streets of New York, Chicago, and countless other American cities.

It is not destinations, however, that determine the framework. Rather, the easy-to-understand, abstract, geometric pattern of cities determines the flow of people, goods, and vehicles and, thus, spending patterns and private development. Clarity of form is sometimes difficult to identify, but its presence is immediately perceptible. The rectilinear grid of Manhattan, for example, is instantly recognizable, as are the diagonal boulevards leading to the Admiralty tower in St. Petersburg and the circle of the Ringstrasse in Vienna. As the previous chapter explains, however, whatever form the public realm assumes, for the city to remain great, its residents and the city will have to make continuing adjustments to meet present and future market demand.

If that framework is not properly managed and maintained, it loses its ability to shape the character of the city and may even retard its development. As this chapter will illustrate the proportion of the public realm devoted to vehicular traffic and its regulation can have a deleterious effect on street life, which is what happened with New Arbat and Tverskaya Street in Moscow. As this chapter goes on to explain, on Thirty-Fourth Street in Manhattan, the reduction of spending for public services resulted in an increase in crime and a decrease in retail activity, which was reversed by the establishment of a business improvement district that more than replaced city spending on public services and restored the street's role as one of New York's retail and entertainment destinations.

Atlanta—The absence of any perceptible pattern for Atlanta's street system has led observers to joke that it is the product of a "planned attempt to confuse everyone, especially visitors."[2] That public realm framework is anything but confusing, however, when seen from the air. Flying overhead in a helicopter one can see that all the city's high-rise buildings are grouped on either side of Peachtree Street, the ridgeline running through the city along what is the highest ground in the area. On the ground the confusion is compounded by seventy other streets that "incorporate the name Peachtree."[3] Nevertheless, the block and lot patterns that emerge on either side of the Peachtree Street corridor all adjust to high ground of the Peachtree ridge. As a result Atlanta's residents orient themselves in relation to a linear corridor, rather than a numbered street grid like that of New York or Chicago.

Atlanta's other dominant landscape elements consist of abandoned railroad rights-of-way; interstate highway I-285, which encircles the city; and the limited-access, radial arteries leading from I-285 to Peachtree Street. Unfortunately, they are not accessible to anybody who is not in a train or a motor vehicle. Moreover, they are single-function arteries that provide nothing for anybody else. Thus, they cannot be considered genuine components of the public realm.

One more component of Atlanta's public realm is emerging as I write this chapter: the Atlanta BeltLine (freight railroad tracks that used to encircle the city but are now being transformed into a combination trail, park, and gathering place), which is already changing the character of life in this exploding metropolis (see chapter 10).

Dubrovnik, Croatia—The organizing element of Atlanta's public realm (the linear ridge of its main street, Peachtree Street, which runs through the city and suburbs for miles) is the obverse of Dubrovnik's roughly 1,000-foot-long (305-m) linear depression of Stradun (also called Placa), its main street. Stradun, the depression that bisects this medieval walled city on the coast of Dalmatia, was created at the close of the eleventh century by filling in the marshy channel that separated the island settlement south of what is now Stradun from settlements on the hills north of Stradun. In 1667, an earthquake destroyed this landfill and it had to be reconstructed.

Nowadays, Stradun runs from Dubrovnik's harbor wall on the east to the western wall. The limestone houses that were built after the earthquake are essentially the same in height, width, façade treatment, and interior layout.[4] Stores and artisan workshops occupy the ground floors, while residences occupy the second and third floors. Like Peachtree Street, it is the main shopping street in Dubrovnik and a gathering place for residents and tourists. In addition, the narrow streets perpendicular to Stradun are laid out almost like ribs at regular intervals. Those on the north side have steep steps leading up the inland hillside, while those on the south have a more gradual slope, but are stepped as they get further south.

Stradun, Dubrovnik Croatia (2015). The development of Dubrovnik evolved in a linear fashion on either side of this street created at the low point of the city. (Alexander Garvin)

Unlike Atlanta, everybody, even visitors to Dubrovnik, can understand the importance of its public realm: It is impossible to get lost in the city. Wherever one is in the city, the clock tower at the eastern end of Stradun and the church tower at the western end are visible. The rest of the public realm consists of the narrow streets leading directly to Stradun or a few east-west streets that connect them. Rome, Paris, Moscow, and the other international centers discussed in this chapter are multiple times the size of Dubrovnik, but benefit from the same clarity of form.

Rome—The street layout of Rome offers a particularly interesting axial design formula to orient residents and visitors alike. Rather than a single corridor, such as Peachtree Street or Stradun, most of this city's great avenues began as arteries leading to major basilicas, including St. Peter's. In 1585 when Sixtus V (1521–1590) was made pope, one of his priorities was to mark these religious destinations in a clear way for the thousands of pilgrims who poured into the city every year. To do so he erected four ancient Egyptian obelisks at critical points, creating landmark vistas that instantly identified specific destinations and gave them a certain cachet.[5] Today, as any visitor to Rome will testify, these obelisks make it easy to find one's way around the Eternal City, serving both to orient one's directional sense and to please the eye.

Worthy of mention as well is the Via Sistina, a street also built by (and named after) Sixtus V. This central city corridor runs from Trinità dei Monti up and down various hills, then straight on to the obelisk at the back of the Basilica di Santa Maria Maggiore. In Sixtus's time this church was one of the four main pilgrimage churches in the city, and he believed it deserved an appropriately imposing and beautiful marker. The placement of obelisks to highlight vistas and identify important destinations, however, continued long after Sixtus's papacy. The obelisk in front of Trinità dei Monti, for example, was added during the Napoleonic era.

The axial vistas terminating at obelisks in Rome are also the reason why certain streets became so special over time. The Via dei Condotti, for instance, probably the most fashionable shopping street in Rome, is today filled with tourists who are there not only to shop but to make their way to and from the obelisk in front of Trinità dei Monti above the Piazza di Spagna, where the Spanish Steps are located. The remarkable view offered there of the famous steps and of the picturesque obelisk, along with the street's many chic stores, makes the Via dei Condotti an alluring, heavily trafficked, and successful thoroughfare. St. Petersburg's prime shopping street emerges from a similar axial vista, but directed at the gleaming gold spire of the Admiralty, rather than an obelisk.

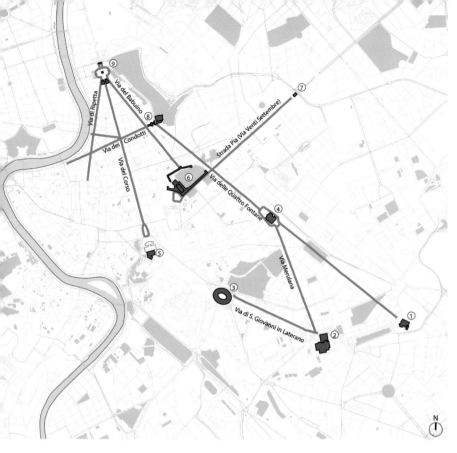

Pope Sixtus V's obelisks and the corridors extending from them make it easy to identify specific destinations and move around central Rome. (Owen Howlett, Alexander Garvin)

1 Basilica di Santa Croce in Gerusalemme	6 Palazzo del Quirinale
2 Basilica di San Giovanni in Laterano	7 Porta Pia
3 The Colosseum	8 Piazza di Spagna
4 Basilica di Santa Maria Maggiore	9 Piazza del Popolo
5 Basilica di Santa Maria in Aracoeli	

St. Petersburg, Russia—A particularly effective example of axial urbanization began in 1703 when Czar Peter the Great ordered the construction of a new city along the Neva River, a city that was to replace Moscow as the capital of Russia and create what Peter famously dubbed "Russia's window on the West," with access via the Gulf of Finland to other important ports of Europe.[6]

For its setting the czar selected a marsh dotted with more than one hundred islands, an utterly flat territory without a hill or outcropping to spoil the view. The metropolis that resulted, St. Petersburg, was the work of a huge, low-wage labor force, as well as of Peter himself, a skilled carpenter and mechanic who helped lay the city's brick and mortar. Its design was the product of a single powerful organizing principle: a series of vistas leading to the gilded spire of the Admiralty, headquarters of the Imperial Russian Navy and the institution that would open Peter's desired window on the West.

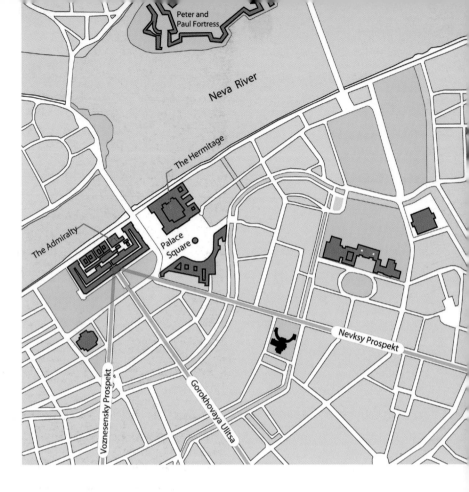

The main arteries of St. Petersburg, Russia radiate out from the Admiralty tower. (Owen Howlett, Alexander Garvin)

St. Petersburg's city center quickly grew southward from the Admiralty along three broad avenues: Nevsky Prospekt, Gorokhovaya Ulitsa, and Voznesensky Prospekt.[7] In a flat city such as this one, the spire of the Admiralty became the central landmark, providing residents with a reliable means of orientation from practically any street, plus an appealing view. Over time one of its three main avenues, Nevsky Prospekt, lined with delightful stores and important institutions that attracted virtually everybody, became St. Petersburg's most important artery. As the celebrated Russian writer Nikolai Gogol wrote in 1835, when the city had reached a population of 452,000: "This is the one place where people put in an appearance without being forced to, without being driven there by the needs and commercial interests that swallow up all Petersburg."[8] It has remained this way ever since.

Nevsky Prospekt, St. Petersburg
(2014). (Alexander Garvin)

Map of Paris boulevards. The design structure of Paris is a combination of a "Grand Croisée" (the crossing of the city's main east-west boulevard and its main north-south boulevard) and three concentric boulevard rings created on the site of demolished former city walls. (Joshua Price, Alexander Garvin)

The Paris Street Network—Paris was already one of the world's preeminent cities with a population that was more than double that of St. Petersburg when Napoleon III and Haussmann began their work. The city had a few radial avenues like those of St. Petersburg and the beginnings of two circumferential boulevards.

The evolution of a discernable radio-concentric pattern to Paris began in the 1660s, when King Louis XIV began erecting a ring of technically advanced fortifications around France's frontiers. The Sun King believed that he was rendering his territories impregnable with these up-to-date defenses,[9] and consequently he decided that the wall of Charles V that had encircled Paris since the fourteenth century was outmoded. In 1676 he ordered its demolition.[10]

Map of the wall of Charles V (fourteenth century) demolished to make way for the Grands Boulevards. (Cortez Crosby, Owen Howlett, Alexander Garvin)

By creating the Boulevard Saint-Germain, Haussmann connected the Grands Boulevards with the Left Bank and created the first of the city's radio-concentric boulevard rings. (Cortez Crosby, Owen Howlett, Alexander Garvin)

1 Place de la Concorde	6 Boulevard Poissonniere	11 Boulevard des Filles du Calvaire	16 Musee du Louvre
2 Boulevard de la Madeleine	7 Boulevard de Bonne-Nouvelle	12 Boulevard des Beaumarchais	17 Les Halles
3 Boulevard des Capucines	8 Boulevard St. Denis	13 Place de la Bastille	18 Place des Vosges
4 Boulevard des Italiens	9 Boulevard St. Martin	14 Boulevard Henri IV	19 Ile de la Cite
5 Boulevard Montmartre	10 Boulevard de Temple	15 Boulevard Saint-Germain	20 Palais Royale

At one time, we are told, long stretches of grass grew along the top of Charles V's old wall, rendering it an attractive place for people to congregate and enjoy recreationally. Voltaire remarked that the wall served as a kind of green corridor where people often gathered to play the popular game of "boules." When the wall was finally replaced by tree-lined streets, the word *boulevard* came into existence:[11] Voltaire suggested that the word *boulevert* referred to these elevated green (*vert*) ball (*boule*) fields. Others ascribe the origin of the word to a corruption of the Dutch word *bolwerc—bulwark* in English.[12]

The boulevard that replaced the wall of Charles V took its form from a double row of stately elms that Louis had planted along its edges. Over time this route became a broad concourse devoted as much to leisure activities as to transportation.[13] Nothing like this sequence of wide, tree-lined arteries had ever been seen in densely packed and populated Paris, or for that matter in any other European city. Each individual section of this and other new Parisian avenues took on the character of its surrounding district and was given a distinctive name. At nearly 115 feet (35 meters) in width, these tree-lined corridors, which thrust through 3 miles (4.9 km) of the crowded city, soon became known as the "*Grands Boulevards*" (the great boulevards).[14]

In 1784, when the population of Paris had reached 650,000 people, the city had been enclosed by a 15-mile-long (24-km) structure known as the Farmers-General Wall, built to control the carriage and foot traffic coming into the city and to collect taxes on imported goods passing through the wall's main gate.[15] This great stone structure became rapidly outmoded as the city's population passed one million people. Accordingly, in 1844 the Farmers-General Wall was torn down and replaced with the new 21-mile-long (34-km) Thiers Wall, built about one mile beyond the rapidly developing outskirts of the city.

Even with a few axial avenues and the emerging circumferential boulevards, getting goods and services into and around the city was a real challenge. Thus, at the emperor's behest, Haussmann implemented several pre-existing plans for axial arteries and added important others.[16] These wide boulevards were cut through old city neighborhoods, connecting them with the gates of the city, with its railroad stations and bridges, and with other major destinations, eventually extending these roadways throughout the city.[17]

Haussmann believed the Grands Boulevards that replaced the wall of Charles V and the arteries that replaced the Farmers-General Wall provided an opportunity to tie together all of central Paris. Among his initial projects was the creation of the 98-foot-wide (30-m) Boulevard Saint-Germain. It became the primary artery of the city's Left Bank, integrating the Latin Quarter with the Grands Boulevards. This new road completed a loop that began at the Place de la Bastille on the Right Bank, continued along the new Boulevard Henri IV, crossed the Seine River on the Pont de Sully (Bridge), the Île St. Louis, and onto the Boulevard Saint-Germain, passed through the Left Bank to the Pont de la Concorde (bridge across the river) and Place de la Concorde on the Right Bank again, around the Grand Boulevards and back to the Place de la Bastille.

In addition to axial arteries and concentric rings of boulevards, Haussmann added the "Grand Croisée," or great crossing that tied them all together. It was a broad east-west artery that went from the west end of the city to the east end (starting at the Avenue de la Grand Armée, encircling the Arch of Triumph, continuing as the Champs-Élysées, crossing the Place de la Concorde where it jogs north becoming the Rue de Rivoli and then the crooked Rue Saint-Antoine, until it encircles Place de la Bastille. From that square it extends east along the Rue du Faubourg Saint-Antoine until it reaches the Place de la Nation). This east-west artery crosses another going north-south. It begins in the south as the Boulevard du Général Leclerc, turns into the Avenue Denfert-Rochereau, and then curves to connect to the Boulevard Saint-Michel. The route jogs slightly at the Seine River to cross bridges connecting the two ends of the Boulevard du Palais on the Île de la Cité with the Boulevard de Sebastopol,

Champs-Élysées, Paris (2010). The first leg of the east-west Grand Croisée (the Avenue de la Grande Armée, the Champs-Élysées, and the Rue de Rivoli) was created by Napoleon at the start of the nineteenth century. (Alexander Garvin)

which leads to the Gare de l'Est railroad station. It then jogs back to connect to the Rue du Faubourg Saint-Martin, which leads to the north end of Paris.

Neither the axial avenues nor the circumferential boulevards of Paris are continuous straight lines of the sort promoted by Beaux-Arts design principles. Rather, they are the incremental product of several centuries during which their creators (including Haussmann) had to adapt to the realities of property ownership, political power, and pre-existing landmarks. It is the imperfect geometry of the Grand Croisée and the circumferential boulevards that keeps many people from perceiving the city's radio-concentric plan—the very same imperfect geometry that provides pedestrians with continually shifting vistas, a wide variety of

The wall (in red) enclosing the city of Vienna was demolished by order of Emperor Franz Josef I in 1857, at which time the grassy open area surrounding the wall became sites for public buildings and their accompanying public squares as well as substantial private development. (Cortez Crosby, Owen Howlett, Alexander Garvin)

building forms, and a unified but constantly shifting cityscape that make Paris one of the most beautiful cities in the world. The physical framework of Paris is complex but nevertheless provides a logical armature for residents to find their way around, and for businesses to thrive.

Property owners reacted to each new boulevard in the same way as their predecessors had. They erected buildings, opened retail stores, installed places of entertainment, and created residential neighborhoods. Indeed, the same thing happened in the twentieth century when the Thiers Wall was replaced with the Boulevard Périphérique ring-road highway, a structure that spurred additions to the already substantial amount of new suburban housing.

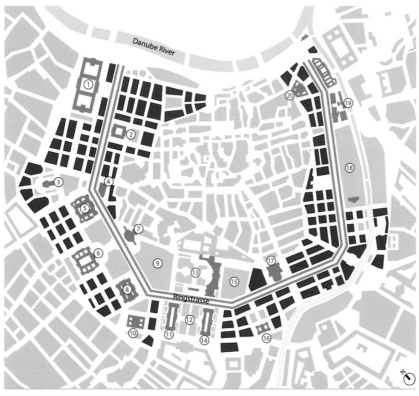

The Ringstrasse, which replaced the walls of Vienna, provided the public realm framework for the city's major institutions. (Cortez Crosby, Owen Howlett, Alexander Garvin)

Rossauer Barracks	6 Town Hall & Town Hall Park	11 Museum of Natural History	16 Academy of Fine Arts
Vienna Stock Exchange	7 Austrian National Theatre	12 Maria-Theresien-Platz	17 Vienna State Opera
Votive Church	8 Parliament	13 Neue Burg & Burgtor	18 Stadtpark & Kursalon
Palais Ephrussi	9 Volksgarten	14 Kunsthistorisches Museum	19 Museum of Applied Arts
University of Vienna	10 Palace of Justice	15 Burggarten	20 Austrian Postal Savings Bank

**Kärntner Ring Straße, Vienna
(2013). (Alexander Garvin)**

Ringstrasse, Vienna—The various governments of France paid little attention to the placement and location of most buildings along the avenues they created, believing that this was a private-sector responsibility. However, when Emperor Franz Josef I ordered the encircling walls of Vienna to be replaced by a circular tree-lined boulevard in 1857, transforming this ring-shaped corridor into the city's main avenue, he paid considerable attention to the placement of surrounding buildings.

Franz Josef ordered that the Parliament building, the city university, an opera house, the Burg Theater, City Hall, a stock exchange, major museums, and an array of other important public destinations be erected along the ring, thus creating a true urban center. Private real estate developers soon followed the money, tapping into new markets by building residential dwellings in between the ring's official public buildings.[18] As a result, virtually everything of any importance in downtown Vienna was, and still is, within walking distance of the Ringstrasse. No wonder it is so easy to find one's way around the center of this delightful city. No wonder people like being on the Ringstrasse.

Radio-Concentric, Moscow—Just as with growth in Paris and Vienna, the growth of Moscow included replacing city walls with new boulevards, but these boulevards differ significantly in character from the Ringstrasse and Haussmann's avenues. The walls of the Kremlin are still standing, but the three walls that were erected thereafter have all been replaced by vehicular arteries and augmented with an additional outer highway ring. The multifunctional boulevard rings of Paris and Vienna were designed to include people on horseback and in horse-drawn vehicles and to be packed with pedestrians. The same was true in Moscow, but in the twentieth and twenty-first centuries Moscow's ring roads were reconfigured to move as many vehicles as possible.

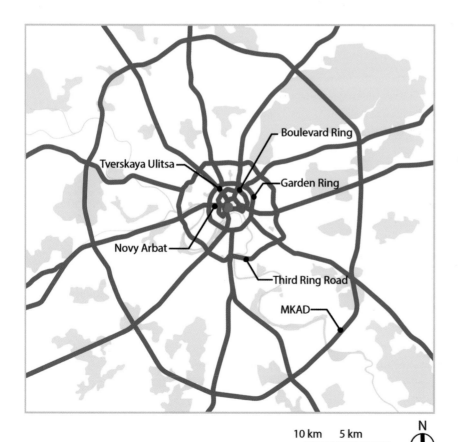

Map of Moscow's ring roads. As in Paris and Vienna, the walls enclosing Moscow were demolished for the city's initial concentric ring of boulevards. (Owen Howlett, Alexander Garvin)

Engineering technocrats dominated Moscow's planning during the twentieth and twenty-first centuries. Their objectives were set forth in the 1935 *General
Plan of the Reconstruction of the City of Moscow*. To accommodate an ever-greater
number of vehicles they proposed adding a fourth ring road built 3 miles (5 km)
beyond the Kremlin, widening some of the radial arterials penetrating all the
way to the center of the city, and adding a radial avenue, now known as the Novy
Arbat (or New Arbat), which would be even broader than the Champs-Élysées.

What remained of the first wall outside the Kremlin, an earthen rampart
that enclosed the city's "trading quarter," had been cleared during the 1930s to
reduce traffic congestion.[19] The second, or Boulevard Ring, and the third, or
Garden Ring, replaced sixteenth- and seventeenth-century ramparts, emerging
as boulevards in stages largely during the first part of the nineteenth century.
Successive government initiatives "updated" the landscaped boulevards by substantially increasing the area devoted to vehicular traffic.

The 22-mile-long (35-km) Garden Ring was completed after World War II. A
fourth ring, the 68-mile-long (109-km) MKAD Highway, which was widened to
ten lanes with grade-separated intersections with radial arteries, was completed
at the turn of the twenty-first century.

Besides ring highways, the 1935 general plan also called for the construction
of broad radial avenues.[20] These new roadways took the form of eight- to ten-
lane, fast-moving arteries intersected at 1,500–2,000 foot (457–610 m) intervals
by pedestrian underpasses. To prevent collisions with oncoming vehicles, pedestrian crossings were forbidden except at marked locations sometimes situated as
much as half a mile apart. The 1935 plan also called for major vehicular underpasses where the Garden Ring crossed the broad radial arteries, many of which
were erected during ensuing decades.

The most dramatic of Moscow's new roadways proposed in the 1935 plan was
the New Arbat, an artery constructed between 1962 and 1968 and known as Kali-
nin Prospekt until 1994. This giant-sized construction cut mercilessly through
the old Arbat neighborhood, sweeping away everything in its path, which "the
political ideologists of reconstruction considered as an unfortunate provincial
anachronism which needed to be promptly rectified."[21]

When the new tree-lined avenue opened to the public in the late 1960s it was
intended to demonstrate Moscow's glorious Communist future. Everything about
it was enormous; even the sidewalks were broader than those on the Champs-
Élysées. The trees were removed at the end of the twentieth century to make more

New Arbat (Street), Moscow.
(2014). (Alexander Garvin)

room for motor vehicles.[22] By the second decade of the twenty-first century, the street's appeal had begun to wane. The noise and exhaust fumes from the traffic were increasingly unpleasant, and opportunities for pedestrians to cross the huge highway were too few and far between.

At the turn of the twenty-first century, related problems began occurring on the other broad avenues in downtown Moscow that had been widened pursuant to the 1935 general plan.[23] Traffic engineers introduced regulations to many of these arteries forbidding parking, standing, stopping, or unloading along pedestrian sidewalks. In response to these restrictive laws, potential downtown customers chose to take the subway or drive to other, more convenient shopping complexes near their increasingly suburban residences. As a result, stores along the broad arterials suffered from a gradual departure of their customer base and some closed.

Tverskaya Ulitsa (Street),
Moscow (2014). Parking and
unloading along this street is
prohibited, creating what is in
effect a limited-access highway.
(Alexander Garvin)

Tverskaya Ulitsa, known as Gorky Street between 1935 and 1990, provides a vivid illustration of the problem. It had been one of the city's most popular retail centers and continued to be even after the late 1930s, when it was widened from 52 to 131 feet (16 to 40 m) and lined with trees. As was the case with the New Arbat, the trees were removed to make more room for motor vehicles. But once traffic regulations forbade stopping to unload or pick up passengers and allowed cars and trucks to speed uninterrupted for as much as a half mile (0.8 km) between pedestrian underpasses, customers began patronizing shops on other streets, especially pedestrianized streets, such as Kuznetsky Most, Nikolskaya Ulitsa, and the Old Arbat.

Although the radio-concentric geometry of Moscow, like that of Paris or Vienna, is the product of replacing city walls with boulevards, by thrusting fast-moving vehicular corridors into the city, Moscow's leadership transformed an asset into a liability. Moreover, its ill-conceived management during the past quarter-century has degraded what remained of a once-great public realm.

Moscow's radio-concentric geometry superficially resembles the limited-access highway rings of many American cities. In Moscow, however, planners attempted to beat the traffic monster by erecting high-rise apartment complexes on the edge of the city—the exact opposite of the low-density residential subdivisions that were then being built in suburban areas in the United States. Highway loops may provide a framework for the development of tall buildings and high-density districts. By themselves, however, they are not enough to sustain a livable environment, increase personal well-being, or nurture a civil society.

Map of Houston's Highways. The rings of highways around Houston were financed through the Interstate Highway System. (Owen Howlett, Alexander Garvin)

Houston's Highway Rings—Nevertheless, it is possible to combine high-rise buildings with highways in a manner that results in a great business district. As the extensive discussion in chapter 10 of the Uptown District of Houston demonstrates, the dehumanizing impact of interstate highways can be overcome by intelligent, continuing investments in the public realm, such as are being made to Post Oak Boulevard, a 135-foot-wide (41-m) landscaped avenue that runs parallel to the I-610 highway. Those investments have already attracted a substantial residential population to the high-rise condominiums that are as prominent as the district's office towers and retail stores. As a result, the Uptown District, five miles from downtown Houston (the eighth largest business district in the United States), by 2015 had become the country's sixteenth largest business district.

Precisely organized frameworks need not preclude a great public realm. The rectilinear street grids of most American cities, for instance, are even more prominent than radio-concentric plans that dominate cityscapes of Paris, Vienna, and Moscow. Even in Los Angeles, Atlanta, or Houston, where highways are more prominent than in Moscow, it is the rectilinear street grid that provides the framework for their privately developed skylines. Nowhere is the central role of the grid more evident than in New York, the city with the world's most recognizable and privately built skyline.

Opposite page: York Avenue, Manhattan (2012). (Alexander Garvin)

Map of the Manhattan street grid. (Owen Howlett, Alexander Garvin)

1	Union Square	6	Bryant Park
2	Madison Square	7	Grand Central Station
3	Penn Station	8	Times Square
4	Herald and Greeley Squares	9	Columbus Circle
5	The United Nations	10	Central Park

Broadway and Park Ave. (atypical streets)	
Major Cross Streets at x feet wide	
Avenues at x feet wide	
Typical Cross Streets at x feet wide	

The Manhattan Grid—It is no accident that the streets of Manhattan have been called The Greatest Grid.[24] From almost the moment they arrive in the city, people learn their way around this ingeniously designed urban framework. Significantly, while residents and visitors alike believe they are walking due east or due west when they make their way across Manhattan (just as they might do in any city based on the national grid established by the U.S. Congress in the Land Ordinance of 1785)[25] this is not quite the case; Manhattan's grid conforms not to the compass, but to the island. In fact, Manhattan's grid has nothing to do with the 1785 ordinance. Rather, it was designed by a professional surveyor, John Randall Jr., and approved by the New York state legislature in 1811. Randall placed the grid parallel and perpendicular to the island's river edges—the East River to the east and the Hudson River to the west—rather than aligning it to a true north-south axis.[26] Consequently, New York City's grid is twenty-nine degrees off standard compass orientation. The result of this misalignment, however, is that residents and visitors can easily orient themselves within the city and to the two rivers that enclose it.

Another common misconception about New York is that its streets and blocks are all the same size. In fact, the Manhattan grid is not a regular checkerboard at all but contains long blocks and short blocks alike. For example, while the north-south edges of New York City blocks are all 200 feet (61 m) long, its east-west edges vary from less than 100 feet (30 m) to more than 900 feet (274 m) in length. Street widths differ as well, from 60 to 150 feet (18 to 46 m). Nor is the city grid entirely flat, as it appears to many visitors on first impression. In fact, it rolls up and down hills and valleys following the natural topography of the island. Though many of its knolls and prominences, especially those in lower Manhattan, were leveled during the nineteenth century, many others were left intact and remain so to this day. Indeed, there are areas of the Upper East Side in Manhattan where walking up hill is tantamount to a workout on a treadmill.

The Manhattan grid, furthermore, is not geometrically precise or without interruption. A perfectly laid out grid can be as overpoweringly monotonous as an ideal Beaux-Arts street plan composed of properly axial roadways, and New York, like Paris, is anything but monotonous. Randall's 1811 grid avoided this pitfall by making use of Broadway, an already well-used and somewhat winding artery that runs from the bottom of Manhattan to the city of Albany 135 miles (217 km) due north. A redundant north-south corridor, Broadway crosses and forms intersections with six adjacent streets that run parallel to it. These intersections include Columbus Circle, and Union, Madison, Herald, Times, and Verdi Squares.

Broadway at 23rd Street, Manhattan (2013). Where Broadway cuts across the Manhattan grid, it creates open space that is not needed for vehicular traffic and is being reclaimed for pedestrian use. (Alexander Garvin)

Manhattan's grid, moreover, frequently contains small aberrations in the form of parks, almost all of them added after 1811, and by sites of major significance also built after this time. Such sites include the United Nations, Grand Central Terminal, Pennsylvania Station, the U.S. Post Office, the main branch of the New York Public Library, Columbia University, City College, and several major hospitals. The resulting vistas that cut through heavily built-up parts of the city add yet another factor that makes New York so navigable.

Finally, besides creating livability, walkability, clear orientation, and aesthetically pleasing vistas, the genius of New York's grid is that it guides and supports so much of the city's private real estate development. For example, the city's zoning resolution mirrors the grid by allowing taller buildings and greater density on wider streets, and by requiring lower building heights and less bulk on narrower streets.[27] Because many more people use the wider avenues, developers built in this way long before the government adopted its first official zoning policy in 1916.[28] Similarly, New York's zoning mirrors its grid by restricting commercial development on narrower residential streets.

Thus, although on first impression a street grid may seem a mechanical and boring way to organize a city, the techniques in New York City's grid show how coherent design, insightful planning, and appropriate innovation can make an ordinary rectilinear grid extraordinary. But whether that grid is or is not extraordinary, it is directly responsible for what property owners build.

With a few exceptions, virtually all the numbered streets and avenues on the island of Manhattan have the same configuration and dimensions. The city's major east-west arteries run two ways, measure 100 feet (30 m) wide, and permit parking along their sidewalks. The narrower east-west streets are 60 feet (18 m) wide, permit traffic only in one direction, and have places for parking along the curb. Yet New York's residents, it turns out, use or avoid these streets for reasons other than their physical design. They patronize certain streets because they are convenient or because they offer specific attractions; stay away from others to bypass traffic or because they are repelled by their chaos, noise, and litter; and avoid still others due to fears, real or imaginary, of the dangers lurking there.

The supply of 60-foot-wide (18-m) east-west streets in mid-Manhattan, however, is interspersed with five major aberrations: 100-foot-wide (30-m) commercial arteries that run east to west at Fourteenth, Twenty-Third, Thirty-Fourth, Forty-Second, and Fifty-Seventh Streets. The design of all five streets and the land uses along them are essentially similar.

In the early part of the twentieth century retail activity naturally gravitated to these wide east-west avenues where there was plenty of room for truck deliveries and ample sidewalks to accommodate consumers. The subways soon followed suit by opening stations on those streets, and the zoning resolution certified those locations in 1916 and again in 1961, permitting very high density commercial use.

By the mid-twentieth century each of these east-west arteries had evolved in a different way. The most famous of them, Forty-Second Street, had become an integral part of New York's entertainment industry on its west side. Grand Central Terminal, on its east side, served the bulk of the Midtown office district. Elsewhere, the Thirty-Fourth Street area was by then home to the Empire State Building (at that time the world's tallest skyscraper), while nearby it hosted other landmark buildings such as Pennsylvania Station, the U.S. Post Office, and

Macy's, Gimbels, and B. Altman department stores, plus major hotels that serviced the adjacent Garment District. When the original Penn Station was demolished in 1965, it was rebuilt with Madison Square Garden, retail stores, and two large office buildings above it.

In the 1970s, the market that had been attracted to Thirty-Fourth Street, Forty-Second Street, and these other major arteries began to look elsewhere because Midtown Manhattan, like much of New York City, began a period of decline—a decline that "the greatest grid" could not prevent. No street layout can prevent litter, graffiti, pickpocketing, or mugging. That requires determined and enlightened maintenance, supervision, planning, and management. Ultimately, businesses and property owners supplied the management that dramatically reversed the sad decline of the commercial streets of Midtown Manhattan, eventually brining new life to what had become a deteriorating public realm. In Times Square (see chapter 8) and on Thirty-Fourth Street they brought a second wind to the powerful economic engine that generated jobs and taxes for the city. The story of Thirty-Fourth Street explains that attracting a market and creating a great public realm are not enough. Responsible players must always be there to manage and maintain a great city's framework of urbanization.

Maintaining the Public Realm Framework

As a result of a fiscal crisis during the 1970s the State of New York created an Emergency Financial Control Board to supervise city finances. In fiscal year 1976, its first full year of operation, the control board forced the city government to eliminate 38,152 municipal employees (13 percent of the total number),[29] beginning New York's emergence from what was referred to as its "fiscal crisis."

As a result of these cuts, New York's streets, squares, and parks began to deteriorate (see chapters 5 and 7). The number of people assigned to collect litter, empty garbage, clean the streets, and provide police protection was severely curtailed, along with the frequency of service. These service reductions caused the Thirty-Fourth Street area to become increasingly litter-strewn, graffiti-covered, run-down, and crime-ridden. Meanwhile, the city's previous level of municipal services remained unrestored even after its fiscal health began to improve. Many of Thirty-Fourth Street's better stores had closed or moved elsewhere. They were replaced by low-end discount stores, bargain hotels, and fast-food outlets. Eventually, property owners and businesses in the area decided to reverse the area's decline.

West 23rd Street, Manhattan (1992). The more government services were cut back along major commercial streets, the more congestion and confusion increased. (Alexander Garvin)

Thirty-Fourth Street, Manhattan—In 1993, the slow deterioration of Thirty-Fourth Street finally led the owners of the Empire State Building, Macy's, Madison Square Garden, and many other local businesses to decide that the best way to reverse the street's decline was to replace services that had once been provided by city government and to pay for them out of their own pockets. To get the job done, businesses and property owners banded together, establishing a nonprofit entity, the Thirty-Fourth Street Partnership, a business improvement district (BID) like the ones described in previous chapters. Thereafter, the city government entered into agreements that transferred some day-to-day service delivery from city

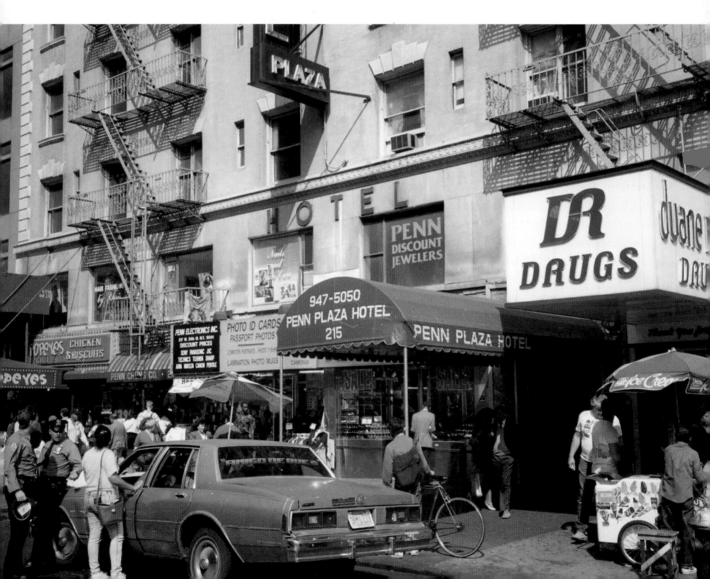

departments to the new business-operated agency. In addition to service delivery, the BID took responsibility for physical improvements on the thirty-one blocks along Thirty-Fourth Street and in neighboring Herald and Greeley Squares.[30]

Rather than concentrate on capital investments, as had been done on West Bloor Street in Toronto, the Thirty-Fourth Street Partnership based its approach on two of New York City's pioneering BIDs: Bryant Park Corporation (see chapter 5) and Grand Central Partnership, both initially conceived and managed by Daniel Biederman, who also became the Thirty-Fourth Street Partnership's president.

Governed by a fifty-four-member board of directors representing property owners and office and retail tenants, plus four ex-officio public officials, the partnership's 2013 operating budget of $11 million came from a payment by property owners of $0.29 per square foot of floor area collected by the city and transferred directly to the partnership. The rest came from concession rents, payments in lieu of taxes, advertising fees, program sponsorships, and other revenues. In return, the partnership agreed to provide all monies necessary to pay for its own activities, thereby allowing the New York City government to shed the responsibility and cost. It was a classic example of government of, by, and for the people it affected.[31]

West 23rd Street, Manhattan (2013). Once the Thirty-Fourth Street Partnership assumed responsibility for the area's streets and sidewalks, safety and cleanliness increased dramatically and developers began replacing obsolete, deteriorating buildings. (Alexander Garvin)

154

Street sweeping provided by the BID on 34th Street, Manhattan (2013). (Alexander Garvin)

Tourist information provided by the BID on 34th Street, Manhattan (2013). (Alexander Garvin)

Although the Thirty-Fourth Street Partnership did, in fact, replace services that had been reduced or withdrawn by the city government, it did not replace all government activity in the district. Today the transportation and police departments still manage vehicular traffic. The partnership collects and bags garbage, but the Department of Sanitation then carts it away. Water supply, sewers, noise and air pollution, and hazardous waste are still the responsibility of the Department of Environmental Protection. This specific allocation of responsibilities has evolved over two decades. By 2013 city services had been augmented by sixty-two partnership sanitation workers and twenty-seven partnership uniformed security officers. Today three staff members are responsible for improving the appearance of the area's 589 private-sector retail outlets, as well as designing and maintaining street furniture, planters, and signage. In addition, the partnership, in cooperation with district property owners, manages a sidewalk repair program responsible for the maintenance of over 11 miles (17.7 km) of concrete sidewalk. This combination of city and partnership services ensures that the area will remain safe, clean, convenient, and attractive.[32]

Macy's 34th St., Manhattan (2013). (Alexander Garvin)

Thirty-Fourth Street certainly will never rival the finest sections of the Champs-Élysées, the Via dei Condotti, or Unter den Linden, the most fashionable streets in Paris, Rome, and Berlin respectively, because in New York that role is played by sections of Madison and Fifth Avenues. Consequently, shopping on Thirty-Fourth Street is not as glamorous as on these legendary European streets. Nevertheless, Thirty-Fourth Street remains one of the busiest streets in the world, handling 430,000 passengers arriving daily from Pennsylvania Station alone. Depending on the season, Macy's attracts between 35,000 and 70,000 customers every day, and remains the largest department store in the world. And one block away the observation deck of the Empire State Building is a destination for 3.5 million visitors annually, while Madison Square Garden draws another 4 million every year to big-time sporting events. Tens of thousands more people use this street routinely for general shopping and for eating.

The litter, graffiti, and crime that characterized Thirty-Fourth Street before the establishment of the BID have today been replaced by a clean and safe business environment, the product of detailed attention to daily management of the district's capital plant and public services. This combination of physical improvement, public services, mutual cooperation, and careful management is what keeps the public realm attractive to its enormous market.

Determining the Location of Market Activity

Whether the public realm is dominated by a central spine, like Peachtree Street in Atlanta or Stradun in Dubrovnik; axial corridors, like those of Rome; radio-concentric arteries, like the ones in Paris or Moscow; or the ubiquitous American rectilinear grid, it determines how and where cities grow and change. It is the power of this geometry that provides customers with the orientation they need to circulate easily and quickly within the city and endows property owners with the ability to predict where their customers will be spending their time (and money).

When the people are unable to circulate freely, as happened on Kärntner Straße in Vienna, or are unwilling to do so because of unfavorable conditions, as happened on Thirty-Fourth Street in Manhattan, they will go elsewhere. Those cases require common action to alter the public realm in a fashion that will change market perception sufficiently for enough customers to return there.

Via dei Condotti, Rome (2012).
(Alexander Garvin)

Eastern Parkway, Brooklyn
(2012). (Alexander Garvin)

Sustaining a Habitable Environment

Eastern Parkway in Brooklyn is among the greatest designs produced by Olmsted and Vaux. From the time that I first encountered it I have been amazed at the wide variety of people and activities that take place there. Its success is the result of the designers' objective of *sustaining a habitable environment*, though they certainly would not have used this modern jargon.

They understood that Eastern Parkway would become a heavily used corridor challenged by changing patterns of use, an increasing population, fickle government administrations, and fluctuating financial conditions. It was not designed only for the horse-drawn vehicles that sped down its central artery in 1870, when it was opened to the public, or for the motor vehicles that replaced them. Rather, Olmsted and Vaux designed it to ensure that during every season of the year—and for generations yet to come—people who lived and worked around it would be able to breathe fresh air without being overwhelmed by noise and filth from the central artery. Equally important, when walking down the street they would be cooled by the shade of six rows of street trees, whose bare branches during the winter allowed warming sunlight to filter down.

What Does It Take to Sustain a Habitable Environment?

Three concepts help to illustrate the meaning of a habitable environment: livability, remediation, and resilience.

The amount of time anybody spends in the public realm depends entirely on its livability. If we go outside but are not dressed for cold weather, we will come in out of the cold; just as when it gets too hot, we find cooler places to spend our time. Similarly, when the noise is deafening, we go to quieter places, and when we are in the midst of polluted air, we find places where the air is fresher. Thus, it is useful to measure cities and the public realm in terms of *livability*.

Our cities are full of places that are already contaminated—privately owned and publically owned properties, as well as huge amounts of the public realm. Because we are directly responsible for the size, character, and condition of public property, *remediation* of the public realm whenever necessary sustains a habitable environment and is surely one of the requirements of a successful public realm.

Another measure of a successful public realm lies in its ability to handle routine activity and also accommodate intense waves of added use, as well as changes to its climate, economy, or population. Consequently, there is an increasing interest in *resilience*.

Any popular and successful part of the public realm will attract people who are often unaware that their actions may degrade or even eventually destroy the public realm that they came to enjoy. Moreover, they may even be "indignant at obvious constraints upon what [they regard] as harmless conduct." Thus, as Olmsted would have explained, the public realm must be designed and managed to sustain heavy use by the people it serves.

Eastern Parkway, Brooklyn—Like the Avenue Foch, Eastern Parkway is lined with park islands and service roads flanking a central roadway, only narrower than that Parisian street. The park islands were designed both to protect pedestrians on its sidewalks and to provide a green public corridor allowing a visitor's "park experience" to begin long before he or she reached the destination—the large and impeccably laid out Prospect Park in the center of Brooklyn.

When Eastern Parkway opened in 1870 motor vehicles had not yet been invented. Consequently, protecting residents from exhaust fumes and particulate matter was an unnecessary function, though reducing the noise of carriages, horses, and delivery carts, and keeping unnecessary traffic from local streets certainly was. By channeling this traffic into the central artery of the parkway

Eastern Parkway, Brooklyn (2006). Eastern Parkway diverts regional traffic away from neighborhood streets. (Alexander Garvin)

where it could move rapidly over long distances until it turned off to its destination, the parkway reduced traffic congestion on neighborhood streets, diverted noise and congestion from residential neighborhoods, and protected visitors with the trees and greenery that lined it.

Eastern Parkway, Brooklyn (2009). Eastern Parkway was intended to start the park experience for nearby residents before they actually entered Prospect Park. (Alexander Garvin)

Eastern Parkway, Brooklyn (2012). The trees that line Eastern Parkway provide cooling shade during the summer and the warmth of sunlight during the winter once the leaves have fallen. (Alexander Garvin)

Similarly, Eastern Parkway opened at a time when draining rainfall runoff was not yet a problem and when overburdened sewage treatment plants were not a concern. When these issues became serious worries for New Yorkers, however, it turned out that the park islands built along the parkway were well suited to the task of soaking up rainwater and stopping pollution from flowing into the city's waterways. One has to wonder whether the parkway's creators were prescient in this regard or simply amazingly perceptive in their approach to designing a road.

Using the Public Realm to Create a Habitable Environment

There is an unfortunate tendency among specialists to separate actions that improve livability, increase resilience, and remediate polluted territory. In fact, improving the public realm is an integrated whole—a single strategy that can address all of these concerns. This is the approach used by Olmsted during the creation of Boston's Emerald Necklace and by Robert Moses during the establishment

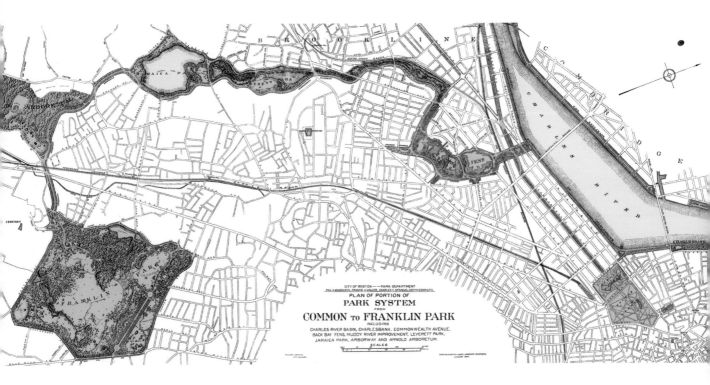

PLAN OF PORTION OF
PARK SYSTEM
FROM
COMMON TO FRANKLIN PARK
INCLUDING
CHARLES RIVER BASIN, CHARLESBANK, COMMONWEALTH AVENUE,
BACK BAY FENS, MUDDY RIVER IMPROVEMENT, LEVERETT PARK,
JAMAICA PARK, ARBORWAY AND ARNOLD ARBORETUM.

of Long Island's parks, beaches, and parkways. It leads not only to a successful public realm, but also to greater resiliency and a more habitable environment for all.

Boston's Emerald Necklace—Work on Boston's Emerald Necklace system of
parks began in 1876 when the Boston Board of Park Commissioners purchased
106 acres (43 ha) for a new park in the Back Bay, an area that, in the assessment of
the city engineer, combined "more disadvantages for a park" than any other place
in the state of Massachusetts.[2] The board purchased this territory because it was
much less expensive than properties that were already in use, because it lay in the
path of development, and because they wanted to eliminate what they correctly
perceived to be a hazardous nuisance.

The commission ultimately rejected the winning design among the twenty
that were submitted to a competition.[3] Instead, it asked Olmsted to be its "advisory landscape architect" for three years. What emerged by the late 1880s was a
plan for a 7-mile-long (11-km) park system that extended over 3,357 acres (1,358
ha) between the cities of Boston and Brookline, starting at the Boston Common
and ending in Franklin Park.[4]

Map of Frederick Law
Olmsted's "Emerald Necklace"
park system for Boston.
(Frederick Law Olmsted
National Historic Site, courtesy
of National Park Service)

Fens, Boston (2014). The Emerald Necklace provided a framework for real estate development in Boston and Brookline. (Alexander Garvin)

The initial site included the Muddy River and the Stony Brook, two waterways that flowed into the Fens and then, during ebb tide, into the Charles River. During high tide, brackish water from the Charles backed up, overflowing riverbanks and on some occasions covering as much as 300 acres (121 ha), a phenomenon made worse because for many years neighboring communities in Boston and Brookline disposed of their sewage in the river. Like the residents of those communities, Olmsted knew that this dumping rendered the water so filthy "that even clams and eels cannot live in it, and that no one will go within half a mile of it in summertime, unless of necessity, so great is the stench arising therefrom."[5] Indeed, Olmsted publicly stated that the superintendent of sewers was "better prepared" to deal with the challenges of the Back Bay than he was.[6]

Olmsted's solution was to deepen and redirect some portions of the waterways to create an invisible basin that could store large amounts of additional water "when an unusually high tide would for a few hours prevent outflow."[7] This approach is what we understand today as increasing territorial resilience. This is no doubt an expression that Olmsted would *not* have used, but a principle to which he was devoted. Terminating the stench, even then, was referred to as remediation. But although resilience and remediation were both objectives of the Back Bay improvements, Olmsted's overarching goal was the creation of a great park.

As a result of Olmsted's advice, Boston created Jamaica Park (120 acres [49 ha]) around the existing Jamaica Pond (70 acres [28 ha]), Arnold Arboretum (265 acres [107 ha]), and Franklin Park (527 acres [213 ha]) and the Fens and Muddy River

sections of the Emerald Necklace and connected them by tree-lined boulevards, which the Olmsted firm called parkways.[8] The combination of larger parks, creek corridors, and parkways provides a home for a variety of flora and fauna that would not otherwise have survived within a densely packed city such as Boston. In addition, Olmsted selected and developed appropriate portions of the system that were desirable for specific recreational activities. Thus, as in his work on Manhattan's Central Park (see chapter 4), there was a place for everything and everything had its place, which is why wildlife and people thrive in the Emerald Necklace, side by side. The Emerald Necklace thus accomplished multiple goals of a great public realm, increasing livability and resilience while remediating much of Boston.

Muddy River, Boston (2014). This park may have started as a remediation project, but since completion it has provided a remarkable recreational resource for the people of the entire Boston metropolitan area. (Alexander Garvin)

Dredging the Back Bay Fens (1882). (City of Boston, Doc. No. 20-1883)

Long Island's Network of Parks, Beaches, and Parkways—Boston's Emerald Necklace is tiny compared with the 175 miles (282 km) of parkway, 24 miles (39 km) of public beach, and fifteen major parks that Robert Moses created between 1924 and 1963 while he served as president of the Long Island State Park Commission.[9] As with Boston, Long Island's park network began with a small, environmentally challenged property: a 200-acre (81-ha) "mosquito-infested tidal swamp full of stagnant pools flanked by shifting dunes," which was already publically owned when Moses began his work in 1924.[10] Today, these 200 initial acres form the core of Jones Beach State Park, 6.5 miles (10.5 km) of Atlantic Ocean frontage that is part of a 2,400-acre (971-ha) maritime environment supplemented by another 18 miles (29 km) of state-operated public beaches on Long Island.[11]

Jones Beach, Long Island, New York (2010). (Alexander Garvin)

Transforming this desolate barrier island into a popular public park required pumping 45 million cubic yards (34 million m³) of sand from South Oyster Bay to raise the average island elevation from 2 to 14 feet (0.6 m to 4.3 m) above sea level for a distance of 17 miles (27.3 km). The commission planted hundreds of acres of beach grass to hold the sand in place. More amazingly, it built a boardwalk and two bathhouses with more than 10,000 lockers; a golf club; a huge swimming pool; a band shell, restaurant facilities, and dozens of picnic tables; paddle ball, tennis, and shuffleboard courts; and a marina and vast parking fields for visitors.[12]

From the beginning many people thought the project was foolhardy. The 1920 U.S. Census reported that there were only 237,000 people living on Long Island, of which 126,000 were in Nassau County, where the beach was located. The Regional Plan Association, for example, argued that the money allocated for Jones Beach would be better spent creating residential subdivisions now and creating parks later.[13] The more serious objection was that few people on Long Island owned cars and fewer still would be able to use the park because the only way to get there in 1924 was by car along inadequate local roads.[14] Within a few years, however, most people on Long Island would own cars and be able to travel on the system of parkways that the state park commission had been established to build.

By 2014, when Long Island had a population of more than 2.7 million people who owned more than 2 million cars, acquiring thousands of acres of parkland, opening tens of miles of oceanfront beaches for public use, and creating a system of parkways to make them accessible by automobile seems an obvious public policy.[15] This is not, however, what happened to many of the country's other valuable beaches. The shoreline of Malibu in California, for example, is similarly accessible by the Pacific Coast Highway, but public access is blocked by miles of expensive bungalows. Similarly, the shoreline of Palm Beach, Florida, is also accessible by car. The only people who can use it, however, are local residents who walk to the beach, because parking meters permit only a twenty-minute stay.

One can ask about the fairness of not providing access to public beaches for Long Island residents who do not possess automobiles. Although that may be a reason to object to the absence of public transportation to these beaches, it is not a reason for not providing the millions of Long Islanders who do own automobiles with the opportunity to use public beaches. New York City, on the other hand, decided to provide everybody with access to magnificent beaches.

When Long Island parks and parkways were being created there was only one mile of public beach in New York City—on Coney Island in Brooklyn. There were people who believed that New York City residents, especially those who could not afford cars, should have been given the opportunity to go to Long Island beaches, even if they were more than twenty-five miles (40 km) away. Robert Moses solved this problem between 1934 and 1960 while he was New York City's parks commissioner. He added 17 miles (27 km) of public beach to Brooklyn, Queens, Staten Island, and the Bronx—all of it easy to get to by bus or subway.

Northern State Parkway, Long Island, New York (2010). The greenery absorbs the noise and pollution from automobiles and drains the heavy rainfall during hurricanes. (Alexander Garvin)

When Jones Beach opened in 1929, Long Island residents immediately understood that they owned what essentially was an enormous country club for people who could not afford membership in typical but far smaller Long Island country clubs. Most car owners and their friends and neighbors could, however, afford to pay the fifty-cent toll and park their car in one of the huge parking fields next to the beach. Indeed, in 1930, the park's first full year of operation, 950,000 cars paid the toll to get to Jones Beach.[16]

The parkways that the Long Island State Park Commission created restricted traffic to private automobiles. Residents who used them to drive to Jones Beach had an experience unlike that on any other roads that were then available. The Meadowbrook State Parkway, for example, was the nation's first limited-access, landscaped roadway to separate traffic along its entire length "either by a center barrier or by splitting the parkway into separate roadways."[17] Furthermore, the broad landscaped corridors on each side of the pavement were so thickly planted that they gave drivers the impression they actually were in a linear park.

Southern State Parkway (2011). The broad landscaped areas separating the parkway from neighboring residents are a major environmental asset within the vast sea of suburban subdivisions into which they helped to transform Long Island. (Alexander Garvin)

Like the concrete ribbons that were extended across the United States during the second half of the twentieth century, Long Island's parkways opened huge territories for development as sprawling residential subdivisions. Unlike those highways, however, the generously landscaped parkways that were created in Connecticut, Maryland, New Jersey, and New York became major environmental assets within a vast sea of suburban houses. On Long Island, in particular, the combination of trees, grass, and bushes became linear parks that were wide enough to prevent nearby property owners from seeing cars or hearing the traffic, and the generous dimensions of the corridors allowed wildlife to move from one park habitat to another. The parkland on either side of the roadways was substantial enough to filter vehicular exhaust and drain away storm water, which during the fall hurricane season on Long Island could be quite substantial. Thus, these parkways played an important role in increasing resilience of what would otherwise have been an endless collection of vulnerable, single-family-home subdivisions, similar to most suburban housing built in the rest of the United States after World War II. As Moses eagerly explained, federally subsidized highways were the work of engineers whose "idea of landscaping [was] something to make the angels weep."[18]

In addition, the commission achieved one other environmental objective: preserving the quantity and quality of water supplied to residents of Brooklyn. In 1925 it arranged to manage over 2,000 acres (809 ha) of Long Island streams, lakes, and open space that had been originally acquired by the City of Brooklyn for water supply purposes, before its consolidation into the great City of New York in 1898.[19] In exchange for maintaining, fencing, policing, and taking care of the property, the commission was allowed to open this territory to the public for benign recreational purposes. The park system that emerged helped to ensure that Long Island could provide safe, clean drinking water and survive torrential rainfalls, hurricanes, and hordes of automobiles, while providing superb recreational facilities for a mushrooming population—all at a price that it could afford. Moses is perhaps best known for vociferously advocating for a controversial system of highways for New York City, and he is erroneously often thought to have built this system, which disrupted the lives of many local residents. But his legacy on Long Island is one of preserving, increasing resiliency, and fostering the habitability of the environment for everybody in the region, whether they owned a car or not. The same is true of the parkways for which he was responsible as NYC park commissioner.[20]

Reconfiguring the Public Realm to Improve Habitability

Acquiring open land to help sustain a habitable environment is relatively easy, whether by creating something akin to Boston's Emerald Necklace or the Long Island park and parkway system. It is much more difficult, however, to accomplish this acquisition in an already built-up city, especially if one wishes to avoid massive hardship and relocation such as happened in creating the avenues and boulevards of Paris, as described in chapter 5.

Portland, Oregon, however, provides a story of success in this area. In recent years, it has successfully repurposed one-acre sites that had previously been in both private and public hands to add to the public realm. New York City similarly repurposed public property by transforming tiny bits and pieces of street, averaging only 0.07 acres (0.03 ha) each, into thousands of Greenstreets sites (see below) scattered throughout the city. Both Portland and New York understand that the only way to sustain a habitable environment is to keep adding to the public realm and increasing its ability to improve air quality, reduce noise, and maintain a benign climate on an ongoing basis.

The Public Squares of Portland, Oregon—For more than four decades Portland has steadily acquired whole privately owned city blocks and turned them into public squares. Because the blocks are only 200 feet square (18.6 m²), acquisition does not require huge amounts of territory, money, time, or serious dislocation, but the impact on the public realm is great. Pioneer Courthouse Square (1984), for instance, provides a hardscape similar to many old European squares, though it is a late-twentieth-century design. In addition, the Ira Keller Fountain (1970) and Jamison Square (2002) combine hardscape with trees, grass, and other greenery. O'Bryant Square (1971), the Lan Su Chinese Garden (2000), and Tanner Springs Park (2006), like the squares of Savannah, are primarily natural landscapes that (unlike Savannah) incorporate flora that ranges from traditional Chinese garden plants to grasses and plants that are indigenous to the American Northwest. Whether these 200-foot-square blocks are squares or parks is open to interpretation, but regardless of terminology they remain actively used components of Portland's public realm.

Ira Keller Fountain, Portland (2007). (Alexander Garvin)

The Ira Keller Fountain has a long and complex history. It originally emerged from a nine-year struggle over the shape and contents of a federal urban renewal project, beginning in 1952 when the city proposed to clear the 54-acre (22-ha) "slum" that was occupied by more than 2,300 residents and 200 businesses.[21] In its first configuration, the project included only a new civic auditorium and supporting services, but four years later the plan was rejected in favor of a mixed-use district that retained the city's grid plan. This new version eventually included the auditorium, additional office buildings, apartment houses, a shopping complex, and small parks. Directly across the street from the civic auditorium is one of the project's most striking features, a 200-foot-square (18.6-m^2) public open space that contains the Ira Keller Fountain designed by landscape architect Angela Danadjieva of Lawrence Halprin & Associates.

The square lies at the center of a sloping site surrounded by busy streets on all four sides. Thus, it must deal with daily periods of heavy traffic and the heavy rainfall common in the northwestern United States. The foliage of the trees enclosing the square, however, filters out the noise, pollution, and particulate matter from vehicular traffic. The ground around the trees also soaks up storm water, so the square is not just a place for adults to enjoy and children to have fun, but also an integral part of the natural systems that sustain a habitable environment.

For more than four decades the Ira Keller Fountain delighted young people who cavorted in the water and older folks who kept watch over their children or strolled by and sat on benches under the tree-lined areas enclosing the square. Recently, however, there have been problems keeping the fountain in good repair and maintaining water pressure during periods of drought. As long as the fountain is kept running, this public square will continue to be one of the most successful components of Portland's rich public realm.

In another example, Pioneer Courthouse Square was a single-block downtown development project rather than a tiny part of a 54-acre (22-ha) federal urban renewal project. To maximize market attraction and, therefore, generate as much private investment as possible, Portland selected the single most accessible downtown block for a new public square. The site, which it purchased in 1979, was a parking garage on a typical, two-hundred-foot-square Portland block that also was the main downtown stop on the city's TriMet light-rail commuter system. Recognizing the mismatch between the block's potential and its use, the city sponsored an international design competition that attracted 162 submissions for the new public square. The winning design, drawn up by a team of local artists and architects led by Willard Martin, included red brick paving, a cas-

Pioneer Courthouse Square, Portland (2007). (Alexander Garvin)

cading fountain, classical columns, a TriMet ticket office, a visitor information center, a semicircle of steps that serves as an informal amphitheater, a Starbucks coffee shop, and outlets for small retailers.[22]

Since it opened in 1984, Pioneer Courthouse Square has been a major attraction, and its customers made the surrounding blocks attractive for further development. In the years since its opening, Nordstrom built a new store facing the square and Saks Fifth Avenue followed shortly thereafter with a store of its own. Later, the Rouse Company acquired the nearby Olds & King department store and converted it into The Galleria, a 75-foot-high (23-m) atrium surrounded by a variety of restaurants, cafés, and retail stores. Later still, Tom Moyer, a local developer, built a twenty-seven-story tower containing a ten-plex movie theater on the block next to Nordstrom, while the block next to Saks was rebuilt as Pioneer Place, a multistory, air-conditioned atrium with shops, restaurants, and tourist-oriented retail outlets. Recently, Apple has opened a store on the square and new buildings and stores have opened within a few blocks.

Not only has Pioneer Courthouse Square generated substantial private real estate development and shaped the urbanization of downtown Portland,

Jamison Square, Portland (2007). (Alexander Garvin)

it also encourages Portland residents to use public transportation alternatives to private automobiles. Because the square lies at the intersection of TriMet's four light-rail lines, commuters using any of the lines can easily transfer at the square to get to a destination that would otherwise only be easy to get to in their car. The resulting decline in air pollution and noise from the increased use of Portland's light-rail system contributes to providing Portland with a more habitable environment.

Elsewhere in Portland, Jamison Square is the product of the remediation of 34 acres (14 ha) in the city's popular Pearl District that had been the property of the Burlington Northern Railroad. The Portland Development Commission, which took charge of the project in 1987, removed 30,000 cubic yards (22,937 m³) of contaminated soil and,[23] two years later, held a design competition to determine the best reuse of the site. The winner, Peter Walker and Partners Landscape Architecture, conceived of two new 200-foot-square (18.6-m²) additions to the public realm surrounded by Portland's typical 200-foot-square residential blocks.

The first of them, Jamison Square, designed by Walker and Homer Williams and Partners Landscape Architecture, opened in 2002. Like the Ira Keller Fountain, it includes a water cascade. But, because the site is flat, water flows over steps that are just high enough to have become a favorite of toddlers. Their parents either participate in their splashing or relax on the tree-shaded grass lining the square. As with Pioneer Courthouse Square, families who do not live in the surrounding area can visit using TriMet light-rail lines that flank the square. Thus, Jamison Square is a rare case in which the environmental planning techniques used in previous projects were combined in an attempt to create something that would have an even greater role in sustaining a habitable environment.

The slow but steady addition of these 200-foot-square open spaces has helped to make downtown Portland more agreeable, eliminated small amounts of contaminated territory, and helped the city to withstand sudden shifts in the weather. It provides a model for other communities with limited resources that are seeking a more habitable environment.

New York City's Greenstreets Program—For the last two decades New York City has been transforming paved traffic triangles that were not essential to vehicular flow into parklets through the Greenstreets Program. The program began in 1996 as a joint effort of New York City's Department of Transportation and its Department of Parks and Recreation and has become a major success. By the end of 2013, 2,569 sites had been added throughout the city, covering 169 acres (68 ha) with new, lush, and sometimes garden-quality plantings.[24]

Greening abandoned and little-used public spaces eliminates sections of roadway and other unsightly surfaces, replacing them with living trees, bushes, grass, foliage, and flowers. These stretches of greenery automatically serve to beautify neighborhoods, calm traffic, delight pedestrians, and improve air quality. With public greening, sections of formerly dark, impervious, paved roadway surfaces that absorb solar energy and radiate heat in the middle of summer are turned into ecological assets. Rather than acting as magnets for heat and debris as blacktop did, areas of flowers, shrubs, and trees now cool the temperature, supply berries and other flora for a range of small creatures, and provide links for birds and other wildlife on their way to public parks and larger open spaces. In addition, the greenery brings shade during the summer months, dampens street noise, lowers ambient temperatures by as much as two to four degrees, filters particulates from the air, and absorbs gaseous pollutants emitted by passing vehicles.[25] Some Greenstreets plantings are extensive enough to encompass sidewalks and sitting areas, in effect transforming streets into small public parks.

Transportation Alternatives That Improve Habitability

Several alternative transportation strategies can increase habitability. The most direct way is to increase the amount of space in the existing public realm for activities that do not take place in cars, while reducing the territory devoted to traffic congestion. Many cities, including Paris, San Francisco, and Boston, have done this by investing in underground garages as a way to reduce traffic seeking curbside parking places. A second way is by making cycling to places more attractive than going by car. The third way is to reduce the number of vehicles entering the city. London, in particular, has reduced congestion by charging

Brooklyn (2010). The Greenstreets Program replaces abandoned and little-used sections of roadway with greenery, thereby beautifying neighborhoods, calming traffic, absorbing noise, and improving air quality. (Alexander Garvin)

Parking under Place St. Michel, Paris (2014). (Alexander Garvin)

motor vehicles for the use of downtown streets (discussed later in chapter). Perhaps the most dramatic way is the one adopted by Zurich, Switzerland (discussed later in chapter), which invested in a widespread streetcar system and installed a computer system that gave primacy to streetcars and trams over private vehicles.

When drivers arrive at their destinations, it is often difficult to find a parking place. Consequently, the cars cruise around, unnecessarily spewing carbon monoxide and particulate matter into the air. The more attractive the destination, the more automobiles it attracts, the longer it takes to find a parking space, and the greater the extent of air pollution. One popular way to reduce vehicular congestion and the air pollution it causes is to excavate streets, squares, and parks, constructing public garages beneath the public realm, thereby reducing

Union Square, San Francisco (2006). (Alexander Garvin)

traffic flow, exhaust fumes, and particulate matter in street water runoff, while also increasing the space available for pedestrians.

Union Square, San Francisco—Union Square in San Francisco was established in 1847 when the city's initial 1845 street grid was extended southward.[26] Though its name originated with rallies for the Union cause during the Civil War, for nearly a half century this 2.6-acre (1-ha) rectangle was more a park than a gathering place for rallies. The area around it, however, became the busiest retail shopping district in San Francisco. With this expansion in retailing came changes in the way the square was used, and in 1903–1904 it was remodeled to include prominent, paved sitting areas and a new central column commemorating the nation's victory at Manila Bay in the Philippines during the Spanish-American War.[27]

At that time, California's love affair with the automobile was just starting, but soon automobiles would inundate the San Francisco region; indeed, even the Great Depression could not stem the flood. Consequently, in 1941 Union Square was again remodeled, this time to accommodate a 985-car underground garage. The garage was a success, and with it retail activity in the area steadily increased.

Later, as the decades passed and the area's popularity continued to grow, the square on top of the garage no longer adequately served the district's clientele; it had become overcrowded. The new problem was how to make more room for people. Consequently, in 1997, the city sponsored a competition to redesign Union Square and three years later the square reopened with a design that retained the monument and palm trees, but added terraced steps where people could sit and watch the world go by; corner entrance plazas; large paved areas that are used for outdoor art exhibitions, concerts, and spontaneous demonstrations; and a popular outdoor café. Beginning with 1941, each of the reconstructions of the square increased its livability while simultaneously improving ambient air quality.

Post Office Square, Boston (2015). (Alexander Garvin)

Post Office Square, Boston—In 1954 Boston erected a four-story, 950-car downtown garage in the hopes that it would decongest city streets and shorten the time private automobiles spewed pollution into the air. Unfortunately, the garage could not accommodate enough of the cars seeking parking places. Moreover, the area was densely built up and provided virtually no place for relief from the congestion, so thirty-eight years later Boston took the idea that had been pioneered in San Francisco one step further.

The city replaced the old garage with a 1,400-car underground parking facility, covered by Post Office Square—a landscaped park with a café, walkways, and sitting areas. Thus, in addition to removing motor vehicles from the public realm and reducing their emissions, Post Office Square provided people with a more livable environment in which they could sit on a bench, lie on the grass, have a cup of coffee, or go for a stroll.

Oxford Street, London (2013). Charging private automobiles for entering London during the busiest hours of the week, certainly reduced the amount of traffic and improved the quality of life throughout downtown London. Nevertheless, the privately owned vehicles that do pay to enter the downtown business district, along with taxis, buses, and publicly owned vehicles, are still responsible for considerable traffic congestion. (Alexander Garvin)

Congestion Pricing in London—London has been at the forefront of the opposite strategy: reducing vehicular traffic itself as a way to remediate polluted streets. Its particular method is an economics-based system of traffic pricing that has helped to reduce street congestion and air pollution. First put into place in 2003 when the city established an 8-square-mile (21-km²) congestion charge zone (CCZ) encompassing the city's central business and entertainment districts,[28] the system charges most motor vehicles that enter this CCZ between £9 and £12 during the hours of 7:00 a.m. to 6:00 p.m. on any weekday. All-electric, plug-in hybrid, and other vehicles that emit reduced amounts of carbon into the air receive a discount.

In 2000, three years before the CCZ was established, 1.1 million people entered central London during the peak morning hours. This group included 137,000 people entering the city in private automobiles, 88,000 in buses, mini-buses, and coaches, 12,000 by bicycle, and 871,000 by rail, subway, or some other mode. Although the number of commuters had been steadily decreasing for more than a decade, downtown vehicular congestion and air pollution had become a serious threat to both the economy and the environment.

In 2003 the CCZ set out to reverse the decline in the number of people entering London and increase the number taking mass transit or cycling. By 2011 the number of people entering the CCZ had decreased by 10 percent. The fact that 70,000 fewer came by private automobile (a 49 percent decrease), while 66,000 more came by bus, 21,000 by bicycle, and 939,000 by rail, subway, or other modes, was even better news.[29] As a result, congestion thinned, bus service improved, travel time for drivers fell, truck deliveries occurred in a more efficient way, the number of traffic accidents declined, and air pollution substantially fell.

Although some people criticize London's traffic remediation system as being draconian, many more applaud its success, arguing that *whatever works* to reduce traffic is best. While the reduction in private automobile traffic in London has improved livability and enhanced circulation, congestion remains a problem. Zurich, on the other hand, has found a way to address all three of these issues.

Sechseläutenplatz, Zurich (2015). Frequent streetcar and tram service going everywhere in the city, together with computer-operated sensors regulating traffic flow on city streets and giving priority to public vehicles, have made Zurich a uniquely pedestrian-friendly city where less than 26 percent of residents travel regularly by private automobile, motorcycle, or motorbike. (Alexander Garvin)

Congestion Targets in Zurich—The people of Zurich wanted the most livable city possible. That meant removing the vehicular traffic that interfered with becoming overwhelmingly pedestrian-friendly, overwhelmingly transit-friendly, and super convenient. Rather than reduce the number of vehicles downtown by charging for peak-period access to the city, as London did, Zurich limited the total number of motor vehicles that may be in the city at any one time, as well as the total number of legal parking places. This sounds impossible to achieve in a city of 34 square miles (88 km²) occupied by 380,000 people within a metropolitan population of 1.9 million.[30] Nevertheless, the Swiss have found a way to make it work.

The city installed a network of more than four thousand sensors that monitor traffic throughout the city. The sensors are connected to computers that change traffic signals in response to the number of cars, motorcycles, motor bikes, and bicycles, trucks, buses, streetcars, and trolleys passing by—giving priority to streetcars and trolleys. When the sensors determine that the number of cars in the city is approaching the decided-upon limit, the duration of green traffic signals on the main routes into town is reduced to slow the flow of cars into town until congestion is reduced to manageable levels.[31]

In addition, since 1996 the target for allowable parking has been set at the 1990 level. Any new parking spaces must be built (at high cost) underground and at least one existing parking space eliminated.[32] The successful result has been to remove space previously set aside for parked cars and increase territory available for daily life.

In 2010 only 26 percent of Zurich's residents travelled regularly by private automobile, motorcycles, or motorbikes. The rest used 300 streetcars on fifteen different routes, eighty trolleys on six different routes, 240 miles of S-Bahn trains, and numerous bus lines—or just walked or biked.[33] There are more than 300 million annual public transit trips in this relatively small city. Nobody waits more than three minutes for public transportation. As Samuel Schwartz explained in *Street Smart*, public transit in Zurich is "clean, comfortable, and remarkably easy-to-use, [resulting in] the world's best on-time performance with frequencies that are almost incredible."[34]

Walking around Zurich, one sees streetcars everywhere. Many of the streets in the old center of the city are pedestrian only. On a nice day, downtown Zurich is packed with people, strolling, shopping, sitting outside in one of its many cafés and restaurants, or getting on and off one of the ubiquitous streetcars. The public realm provides something for everybody, even children playing in one of the fountains. So one is likely to meet almost anybody in the city.

An Ever More Habitable Public Realm

Both the environment and the public realm are complex systems where various elements work together as an integral whole. Thus, to sustain a habitable environment one has to deal with both the environment and the public realm as complex, interconnected systems. You can build them up in large segments like Boston's Emerald Necklace, or by adding small pieces like New York City's Greenstreets, or even by adjusting the way the public realm is used, as Paris, San Francisco, and Boston did by opening underground garages, but to have a truly overwhelming impact, a city needs to address the content and the configuration of its entire public realm in a comprehensive manner. This sort of systemic intervention is responsible for the reconception and redevelopment of two major examples of the public realm—the Chicago lakeshore and the San Antonio River valley.

Lake Michigan, Chicago (1892). The shoreline of Lake Michigan in Chicago was used as a dump until reclamation began in the twentieth century. (Chicago History Museum)

The Chicago Lakeshore—Today, nobody wandering along the shore of Lake Michigan in Chicago could possibly imagine it as anything but one of the city's most extraordinary assets, yet during the 1850s the waterfront consisted of "wharves, piles of boards, rocks and garbage," railroad tracks, and freight yards.[35] During the next century and a half, however, the city, through excavation and dredging, transformed all but four miles of its 33-mile (53-km) lakeshore into 3,130 acres (1,267 ha) of parkland containing twenty-five public beaches and nine harbors, which accommodate five thousand boats.[36]

Lake Michigan, Chicago (2008). (Alexander Garvin)

This extraordinary transformation began in in 1869, when the Illinois legislature created three independent park commissions to develop what would become Lincoln, Grant, and Jackson Parks. Sixty-five years later the state legislature consolidated them into one single entity known as the Chicago Park District, an agency that currently cares for 11,000 acres (4,452 ha) of open space, including more than 570 parks, 31 beaches, and 50 nature areas.[37]

Although over the course of Chicago's history many people favored transforming the shore into a continuous park, visionary architect Daniel Burnham succeeded in promoting this transformation. His direct involvement with the lakeshore began in 1893, when he served as codesigner and director of works for the World's Columbian Exposition, an international fair akin in scale to the modern Olympic games, that would be hosted on land on the outskirts of Chicago. After the fair, Burnham produced an evolving series of proposals for a continuous lakefront park, which he advocated in presentations to Chicago's business and civic leadership. Finally in 1906, the city's Merchants Club and Commercial Club began working with Burnham and his partner, Edward Bennett, to produce the *Plan of Chicago* (see chapter 5).

The plan proposed a linear park extending from the South Side of Chicago all the way north to Wilmette. Burnham and Bennett believed that "wherever possible, the outer shore should be a beach" and include a "quiet stretch of green," sloping down to the water.[38] To obtain that result, they advocated using the one million cubic yards (764,555 m³) of garbage, ashes, and basement excavations that the city dumped into Lake Michigan annually as landfill. It was this grand vision for a park-lined waterfront inviting people to settle and work along the lake that led the city to adopt the plan in 1911 that Chicago has been implementing ever since, and which has provided not only green space for the city's residents, but also a habitat for local wildlife and a barrier to absorb flooding from Lake Michigan.

Reviving the San Antonio River—Water is both a resource and a necessity, but it can also cause great harm. One example occurred in 1913, when four people died because the San Antonio River overflowed its banks and flooded downtown San Antonio. The proposed engineering solutions in the wake of the flood included creating bypass channels, building walls to retain floodwater, and relegating parts of it to underground conduits. Later, a 1920 engineering recommendation called for widening the river (including the horseshoe bend that ran through the central business district) to a standard width of seventy feet (21 m) and lining it with steep masonry walls. When residents realized that this remediation plan would require cutting down cypress and other trees that they admired, as well as prohibiting shrubbery along the river's banks, however, they protested and the plan did not move forward.[39]

San Antonio Riverwalk Map. San Antonio solved its flooding problem by digging a bypass channel and installing locks at either end of the San Antonio River horseshoe. When there is a threat of flooding the locks are closed so that the floodwaters bypass downtown. (Joshua Price, Ryan Salvatore, Alexander Garvin)

SAN ANTONIO RIVERWALK

When another flood hit in 1921, fifty people perished and nearly half of the city's twenty-seven bridges were destroyed, underscoring the need for active remediation. The city responded by building an 80-foot-high (24-m) dam with a 1,000-acre (405-ha) retaining basin behind it, widening and straightening some of the creeks feeding the river, and excavating a bypass channel that could divert floodwaters away from the downtown "horseshoe" path of the river—all without addressing the horseshoe itself.[40]

In 1929, local architect Robert Hugman proposed transforming the horse-shoe portion of the river into a park that would combine the charm of the French Quarter in New Orleans with a fantasy vision of San Antonio's Spanish heritage. The idea was quite popular, but during the Great Depression there was little conventional financing available for a park project of this sort. Nonetheless, nine years after Hugman had published his proposal, downtown property owners within half a block of the river formed the San Antonio Improvement District to finance the project. Nearby properties had to pay a tax of 0.015 cents per $100 of assessed value.[41] The resulting income stream provided the debt service for a $75,000 bond issue, which, when combined with a $355,000 Works Progress Administration grant, paid for a twenty-one-block-long linear park that was completed in fall 1941.[42]

San Antonio Riverwalk (1941) after its transformation into a park. (Institute of Texan Cultures, University of Texas at San Antonio)

San Antonio Riverwalk (2012) has become the city's busiest tourist destination. (Alexander Garvin)

To create this new Paseo del Rio, or River Walk, the city temporarily drained the river bend; transplanted many existing trees and shrubs; added 11,700 new trees and shrubs, 1,500 banana trees, and 1,489 square yards (1,245 m²) of grass; built 17,000 feet (5,182 m) of walkways, 21 bridges, 31 stairways, a water pumping station, and a theater; and regraded the riverbed to a uniform depth of 3.5 feet (1.1 m), which was deemed deep enough for small river boats but shallow enough to prevent drowning.[43]

During and just after World War II very little changed along the River Walk. Soon, however, as the city made physical improvements, residents began using the promenade on their way to and from downtown destinations, and tourists began enjoying shopping in stores and dining in restaurants that opened along the park. The buildings, whose backs had been turned to the river, made it their front door.

Later, the River Walk grew to accommodate the HemisFair World's Fair of 1968, alongside an accompanying convention center and hotels. Public and private investment continued in stages and the number of people using the River Walk surged. By 2013, the River Walk had become the top tourist destination for the 26 million tourists who came to San Antonio every year, attracting more visitors than even the Alamo.[44] That is an amazing private-market reaction to a public investment in a small park whose purpose was environmental remediation. This reaction demonstrates that though many conceptualize environmental remediation as opposed to economic development, improving the public realm can unite the two.

During the decades in which the downtown portion of the San Antonio River evolved, however, economic conditions, cultural preferences, and populations kept changing. Thus, at the start of the twenty-first century, when San Antonio decided to create additional parkland along the river, it adopted a very different approach that reflected a historical context different from the one that Hugman and his contemporaries faced—one that relied less on commercial activity and more on the native landscape.

Mission Reach II, San Antonio (2012). The city is now reclaiming and remediating a waterway that had become a liability. (Alexander Garvin)

Between 2002 and 2013 the U.S. Army Corps of Engineers and the San Antonio River Authority worked with a coalition of private and public organizations to restore 7.5 miles (12 km) of the San Antonio River, including the downtown section that is home to the River Walk. Together they have spent $384.1 million on flood control, ecosystem restoration, and recreational improvements.[45] The park that is emerging, like New York's Central Park a century and a half earlier, has required massive amounts of excavation, regrading, and replanting. And as with Central Park, the new landscape will look very different from what was there before. It is ironic, however, that the rationale behind the twenty-first-century earthwork is restoration of a "native landscape"—precisely the opposite of what Olmsted and Vaux had in mind.

The San Antonio River reaches that are under development now will have riffles to aerate water as it runs over imported stones, "natural" pools, fish habitats, greenery planted to simulate the landscape that probably predated human presence, and thousands of new trees. Recreational facilities will be mixed in with the native landscapes and parking lots, where nearby residents will leave their cars to enter the park. The evolving landscape also includes hiking and biking trails, picnic tables, playground equipment for small children, sitting areas, basketball hoops, imaginatively designed landscape overlooks, comfort stations, educational signs describing the local flora and fauna and the history of the area, and even a golf course.

Operating the Pubic Realm

Even well-designed places can suffer from a lack of popularity without skillful management. When space is scarce, there may be so many people and activities in an area that there may not be room for everybody. Physical deterioration also accompanies heavy use. Once deterioration sets in, the number of people who want to be in a particular public area declines, followed by increasing social conflict. In such cases appropriate management can eliminate potential difficulties.

In the mid-twentieth century, the decline of the public realm in the United States coincided with a decline in the proportion of public spending devoted to police and sanitation services, street and park maintenance, and replacement of obsolete and broken street furniture and equipment. In New York City, perhaps the most extreme case, the decline in spending was the direct result of a fiscal crisis that took the city to the brink of bankruptcy in the mid-1970s. As a result, in 1978 the New York City Planning Commission explained that "during the last three years the city has spent . . . less than a fourth of what it had spent *annually* during the previous five years. As a result, potholes mar the streets; parks are ill-repaired; bridges face collapse; and an alarming number of city vehicles and other equipment are out of service."[46] In New York, a decline in spending had led to dramatic deterioration of the public realm.

In many cities the response to deteriorating conditions came from civic leaders who established business improvement districts (see chapter 4) or nonprofit conservancies that raised money privately to compensate for the decline in public spending. The decline and revival of New York's park system, Thirty-Fourth Street (see chapter 6), Times Square (see chapter 8), and Bryant Park (see chapter 5) illustrate the importance of providing management and maintenance services to maintain a welcoming public realm.

Park Management in New York City—People will use the public realm for the first time because they are curious, but they will return only if they are comfortable there, and they will be comfortable only when a park is clean, safe, and attractive. This fact is particularly important when it comes to public parks. New York City's parks, for instance, were in good condition while Robert Moses was commissioner of parks between 1934 and 1960, but deteriorated quickly after he left office and funding dried up. While he was commissioner, parks accounted for roughly 1.5 percent of the city's annual operating budget. During the 1960s and '70s, however, the city began reducing parks department staff and expenditures. The inevitable result was physical deterioration, decreased use, and increased antisocial activity.

The situation changed in 1979 when Mayor Edward Koch appointed Elizabeth Barlow Rogers to be the first Central Park administrator. The following year she helped to found the Central Park Conservancy, a private, nonprofit institution that raises citizen contributions to pay for three-quarters of the park's maintenance and operations.

Just as he had appointed an administrator for Central Park, in 1980, Mayor Koch appointed Tupper Thomas the first administrator of Prospect Park in Brooklyn, and followed this appointment with creation of the Prospect Park Alliance, a nonprofit conservancy like the one that had been established for Central Park. Smaller private contributions than were obtainable in Manhattan financed the alliance, but despite the more limited budget and, by extension, the longer time it took to execute the planned improvements, the alliance shares a similar structure with the Central Park Conservancy, using a combination of city and conservancy staff and with similar community participation in decision making.

Central Park, Manhattan (1980s). Years of deferred maintenance resulted in significant physical decay. The establishment of the Central Park Conservancy and the substantial sums of money it raised reversed years of deterioration. As a result, by 2015, the park was in better condition than at any point in its history. (Sarah Cedar Miller, Central Park Conservancy)

Indeed, the alliance has devoted even more energy to involving the community in diverse park activities and assisting with park management. Those activities include storytelling, nature walks, and fitness classes; operating Celebrate Brooklyn (New York's longest-running free, summer-long outdoor performing arts festival); and sponsoring numerous other events.

By offloading a portion of park management, maintenance, and capital improvements to these and a few other conservancies, the condition of these facilities greatly improved. The amazing fact was that although by the 1990s the city had reduced the number of funded park maintenance positions in its budget to one-sixth the number employed while Moses was in office, conditions everywhere had steadily improved. Part of the loss had been offset by the Workfare Program that allocated to the parks department 3,000 people who were formerly on public assistance.

In addition, the parks department began actively recruiting at major universities whose recent graduates did not commonly take entry-level government jobs. It started career-training programs and initiated rigorous staff performance reviews. Most importantly, it initiated a Parks Inspection Program based on site reports sent from handheld computers and digital photographs used during field inspections.[47] Thus, for the first time, the department was able to use real-time statistics in making management, maintenance, repair, and replacement decisions. These decisions were supplemented by regular meetings with neighborhood groups and community boards.[48]

The impact of improved management is easy to understand by examining Central Park. When the conservancy issued the park's first renovation and management plan in 1985, about 12 million people a year went to Central Park and the police reported nearly 1,000 felonies there annually. Despite a more than threefold increase in park attendance by 2013, the police reported fewer than 100 felonies.[49] Over those three decades, under the leadership of Elizabeth Barlow Rodgers and

Douglas Blonsky (Central Park administrator since 2004), the conservancy has completely restored the park and established a regular maintenance and management cycle using a full-time staff of 350 people and thousands of volunteers.

An Ever-Improving Public Realm

London, Paris, and Vienna were great cities in 1800, when Boston was a very small city and Chicago, Portland, and San Francisco didn't even exist. By 1900, however, these new cities had become great; they were still great in 2000; and they are likely to remain so throughout the twenty-first century because they keep adjusting to meet the challenges of sustaining a habitable public realm.

Sometimes, as in the case of Boston's Back Bay, the challenge has come from the refuse citizens were dumping into its waterways or, as in the case of London or San Francisco, from the onslaught of motor vehicles taking over too great a portion of the public realm. On other occasions the challenge to sustaining habitability has come from natural disasters, such as the flooding of the San Antonio River. As we have seen, some cities have met these challenges by decongesting the public realm, others by increasing its size to accommodate increasing demand from its citizens, or by combining different strategies that put them on the road to an ever-improving public realm. Whatever the approach, however, as this chapter demonstrates, the goals of maintaining a habitable public realm, economic development, and resiliency are not necessarily incompatible. Rather, using the public realm itself to sustain a habitable environment often accomplishes multiple goals.

Long Meadow, Prospect Park, Brooklyn (2006). The Prospect Park Alliance increased park attendance by sponsoring special events in the park. (Alexander Garvin)

Speakers' Corner,
Hyde Park,
London (2013).
(Alexander Garvin)

8

Nurturing and Supporting a Civil Society

O n my way to visit Regent's Park, London (see chapter 5), yet another time, I decided to pass through Hyde Park, where I immediately encountered a colorful parade of Hindus in traditional dress. A few minutes later I stopped to watch a procession of banner-carrying Muslims. Well, I thought, maybe my hometown, New York City, is not "the world's second home," after all. Later, as I approached Speakers' Corner, I saw small crowds gathered around individuals trying to make their case about topics they believed to be of great importance. Moreover, as I watched these spectacles, I noticed that, despite the crowds, I had seen almost no litter except in the park's trash baskets, nor had I seen any disorder among the many types of people who occupied the park. What a vivid example, I thought, of how disparate groups can live together in harmony!

The public realm does not take care of itself; people must take care of it. When litter covers a street, a square, a park, or any component of the public realm, somebody tossed it there. When trash bins overflow with rubbish, it is because they are not emptied frequently enough. When pavement shows cracking and crumbling, it is because those responsible for maintaining it are neglecting their job. We can be sure that these and similar conditions occur due to one problem in particular—the interaction between the public realm and the people in it. That is to say, the people who pass through the public realm, the business and property

Hyde Park, London (2013).
A Hindu parade passing
through the park.
(Alexander Garvin)

owners who use it, the government agencies that maintain it, and those who live and work in the area are not taking care of the public realm.

On the other hand, when the public realm is well conceived and managed, such situations are addressed, remediated, and sometimes even eliminated. This too is society at work, but this time for the best.

Even in cities that have their share of filthy streets, higher-end arteries are usually well maintained. Certainly it is difficult to imagine the Champs-Élysées in Paris, Regent Street in London, or the main street in any city being in a constant state of disrepair. The residents of these cities usually care enough about these main streets to prevent their sullying, while the people who visit them are usually on their best behavior. The result of such attention is that residents of these cities look on both themselves and their environment in an increasingly positive way. Everyone wins.

Government plays the most important role in managing and maintaining the Champs-Élysées and most other famous examples of the public realm. As we have seen, there are, however, numerous examples of modest but marvelous places that contribute to a great public realm. Mike Lydon and Anthony Garcia, in *Tactical Urbanism: Short-Term Action for Long-Term Change*, demonstrate the importance of small, incremental, easy-to-implement actions taken by citizen activists to alter and improve the existing public realm.[1] The stories in their book tell how residents successfully obtained pavement repairs, created bike paths, installed wayfinding signs, opened temporary sitting areas by placing tables and chairs in the public realm, transformed vacant city-owned property into parklets, and made countless small improvements to their neighborhoods. They demonstrate that the public realm is not a completed part of the city, but an ongoing interaction between the physical environment and its users. That interaction nurtures a civil society. But what does that interaction consist of and how does it take place?

Grand Central Terminal, Manhattan (2011). Miraculously, hundreds of people rush around the great hall of Grand Central only rarely bumping into one another or getting into an argument or fight. (Alexander Garvin)

Grand Central Terminal in New York City is a vivid example of a civil society in operation within a great public realm. Whenever I am in the great hall of Grand Central there are hundreds of people rushing around to make a train, to get to work, to get to a store. It certainly is not a model of orderliness, but, miraculously, people almost never bump into one another or get into an argument or fight. That ability to avoid entering into the physical space of others or interfering with their rights, it seems to me, is essential to a civil society. Being able to share a place with others, however, is insufficient. A parade of Hindus in traditional dress would interfere with everybody else in Grand Central. Adding a procession of flag-carrying Muslims would bring everything to a halt.

Indeed, everybody in a civil society must be on an equal footing, balance individual actions with collective aspirations, and live together peacefully. It is not enough, however, just to avoid doing anything that might harm others. People also need a place where they can express themselves, do things together with others, protest against what they consider inappropriate or destructive of a civil society, and advocate societal improvements to their fellow citizens. Hyde Park provides a place for all that.

Hyde Park, London (2013). The walk from Cumberland Gate to Knightsbridge is as popular today as it was in the nineteenth century. (Alexander Garvin)

The space I walked through had been informally used by Londoners even before Henry VIII acquired the territory in 1536 as a royal hunting preserve. People continued to go there by the grace of the Crown until it was officially opened to the public and management was transferred in 1851 to the Royal Parks Agency. Thereafter it became a haven for individual expressions of outrage, peaceful protests, and orderly demonstrations by every possible group of aggrieved citizens while at the same time providing recreational facilities which, in good weather, also accommodated tens of thousands of park-goers.

One of its most popular landscape destinations even before it was officially declared a public park was the walk from Cumberland Gate to Knightsbridge. Dandies went there for morning and evening strolls "to see and be seen."[2] And later, the lovely trees that shade that walk and the view across meadows have helped the walk to remain a favorite landscape destination for two centuries.

The recreational facilities added to the park also attract large numbers of people. The Crystal Palace is probably the most famous such facility ever erected in Hyde Park. Created for the World's Fair of 1851, the building drew hundreds of thousands of visitors from around the world. Three years after the fair it was

Winter Wonderland, Hyde Park, London (2013). (Alexander Garvin)

moved to a suburban location, where it remained until it burned down in 1936. Among the park's more popular contemporary facilities are the Lido Café, the boat rental booth on the Serpentine Lake, and the skating rink operated during the holiday season. Large numbers of people also come for the events that are scheduled throughout the year. Many of the most actively attended programs take place around Christmas and New Year's Day. Every year visitors come to a specially created Winter Wonderland to shop at the Christmas market, go to a show at Zippos Circus, or attend one of the Wonderland's other programmed events.

Because the landscape, facilities, and programmed events in Hyde Park attract so many people, visitors have had to learn to share the park with one another—that is one way in which this extraordinary public realm nurtures a civil society.

Hyde Park, London (2013). The "park stewards" manage the traffic in the park during particularly busy periods. (Alexander Garvin)

In addition, the tradition of demonstrations and orations in Hyde Park going back to the nineteenth century shows the importance of the role played by the public realm in nurturing improvements to an already existing civil society. At a time when crowds became unruly, the police frequently came to the park to restore order. In 1866, however, the police set aside a place where crowds were permitted to assemble for debate, discussion, and public speaking events.[3] Six years later, they formally established the Speakers' Corner as a place where anybody who wishes may speak on any subject to those who wish to listen, provided what they say is not obscene and does not incite a breach of the peace.[4] By formally providing a place for people to assemble and express themselves, Hyde Park ensures Londoners the opportunity to be part of a civil society, so formerly routine police enforcement became less necessary. Nevertheless, large crowds can still become unruly, so the Royal Parks Agency employs "park stewards" to keep large assemblages of people in the park from interfering with vehicular traffic, getting into trouble, or causing harm to other visitors.

Fredensgade Street, Copenhagen (2006). A cyclist using hand signals to indicate a turn. (Alexander Garvin)

The Nurturing Role of the Public Realm

What I had witnessed in Hyde Park was a public realm that was welcoming to a large, diverse population. Each group of park-goers felt comfortable and able to express themselves. More importantly, they understood that their very presence required them to respect the rights of the others who were there. That is the very essence of a civil society. This becomes increasingly difficult as the number of people begins to exceed the amount of space that can comfortably accommodate them. Intelligent management that nurtures civil behavior can increase the capacity of the public realm to handle increased utilization. That is the function of park steward in Hyde Park.

Taking this system of social regulation a step further, countries such as Denmark that are known for their civility avoid such clashes by instituting regulations *and* by encouraging group courtesy, in the process using both a legal and a moral incentive to keep things moving peacefully. Of course, one can ask the question of the chicken and the egg. If a young woman riding her bicycle in a protected bike lane on Fredensgade Street in Copenhagen uses hand signals to indicate a turn, does she do so because it is the law or because she wishes to be courteous to others on the street? The answer is most likely a bit of both.

Civil society has to be nurtured because it is the product of institutional memory and traditional government practices, regulations, and management techniques. As previously discussed, London's Hyde Park, which has become an auspicious setting for the public to express outrage or demonstrate support, is a vivid example of this effect. Places such as Hyde Park in every great city have been adapted for regular events and become traditional places for social gatherings following an initial public action (in this case, the creation of Speakers' Corner). Sometimes, however, simple rule changes are not enough to maintain the public realm. At times when there are *too many* people even for places that are well designed, for instance, conventional delivery of public services can bog down and sometime grind to a halt. In such cases, added regulation and management become necessary. As discussed at the end of this chapter, the complexity of demands placed on city streets, squares, and parks explains why so many American cities have created special business improvement districts and public-private conservancies to ensure a public realm that nurtures a civil society.[5]

Finally, in addition to nurturing civil society, the public realm often also provides a backdrop against which societies protest and evolve. As critic Michael Kimmelman explained, "The conflict over public space is always about control versus freedom, segregation versus diversity. What's at stake is more than a square. It's the soul of a nation."[6] Sometimes the public realm becomes the location for that struggle or for events of great historical importance, such as the protests that have taken place in Palace Square in St. Petersburg, Russia, and Red Square in Moscow, or more recently in Tiananmen Square in Beijing, Taksim Square in Istanbul, and Tahrir Square in Cairo.

The Streets of Copenhagen—Courteous behavior by pedestrians, bicycle riders, and drivers of private motor vehicles and public transit is widespread throughout Copenhagen. You even encounter civil behavior when passengers board and leave buses on heavily trafficked streets. The city's residents pursue their different objectives efficiently, politely, and without getting in each other's way. Clearly, Copenhagen's leadership wants its city's bicycles, delivery vans, buses, and private cars to use its streets for safe travel wherever and whenever they wish because this is a very civil thing to do, and fosters a climate that makes its citizens civil in return.

Tietgensgade Street, Copenhagen (2014). Courteous behavior results in room for cyclists, pedestrians, cars, buses, and the people using them. (Alexander Garvin)

Copenhagen began investing in its protected cycling lane network during the 1920s. From the beginning its intent was to reduce conflict, lower traffic volume, and enhance civil behavior. Because this vast network of lanes connects virtually every part of the city, bicycles were (and still are) in use throughout the day and night. This network, which in 2010 covered 246 miles (396 km), made it easy for people to get anywhere in the city.[7] That is why by 2005 more of Copenhagen's residents were using bicycles to commute to work than were using public transportation or private automobiles.[8] As a result, besides curtailing traffic and reducing driving woes, the city's population today is especially healthy and fit. According to government estimates, in 2010 the physical (and very aerobic) act of cycling reduced the cost of providing health care to its citizens by approximately $91 million per year.[9]

Strædet, Copenhagen (2014). The civil society on this street is so powerful that cyclists, café-goers, mothers with prams, delivery vehicles, tourists, private cars, and countless pedestrians mingle without curbs or traffic lights. (Alexander Garvin)

In addition to providing bicycle lanes, Copenhagen has restricted automobile use on many of the roadways within its city center. One of these roadways, Strædet, illustrates the fascinating *woonerf* approach that Copenhagen has taken to the pedestrianization of some streets. A *woonerf*, also known as a complete street, is designed so that a street's entire right-of-way can be simultaneously used by everybody, regardless of age, purpose, or ability, whether they are sitting, standing, walking, cycling, driving, picking people up, or making deliveries.[10] As a result, it is not entirely linear or direct.[11] Strædet, for example, allows automobile traffic, but has no curbs, and permits cafés and restaurants to spill out onto its roadway. Moreover, in some parts of the street road signs identify places where delivery vans and cars can park on a temporary basis, further regulating traffic flow. Motor vehicles and bicycles thus drive slowly as they make their way down this relatively narrow, crowded street, going around obstacles, and in the process they coexist with pedestrians, café-goers, restaurant customers, and tourists engrossed in window shopping. In this way, people using this street respect both its regulations and its design, which protect other peoples' privacy and space.

Few arteries anywhere in the world are as successful as Strædet in nurturing a civil society. The public realm, however, also must provide and even encourage self-expression, welcome social interaction, and even host celebrations and demonstrations. Although streets perform that role during parades and strikes, no public squares play this role more dramatically and sometimes tragically than in Russia.

Palace Square, St. Petersburg (2014). During the day people are dwarfed in this vast public square. (Alexander Garvin)

Palace Square (Dvortsovaya Ploshchad), St. Petersburg—Created over the course of a century beginning with completion of the tsar's Winter Palace in 1762 (now better known for the art contained inside what has become the State Hermitage Museum), Palace Square in St. Petersburg is a striking example of the role of public space in the evolution of civil society. In 1834, to celebrate Russia's victory over Napoleon, the government erected the 156-foot-high (47.5-m) red granite Alexander Column at the center of the square.[12] This gigantic 538,000-square-foot (49,982-m²) outdoor space is dominated not by the Winter Palace or the Alexander Column, but by the huge bow-shaped building that faces the Winter Palace.[13] That building, completed in 1829, houses Russia's military General Staff, Ministry of Finance, and Ministry of Foreign Affairs. It also includes an enormous double triumphal arch connecting the square with the city's main boulevard, Nevsky Prospekt.

In the nineteenth century people flocked to Palace Square for fairs, games, celebrations, and religious holidays such as Maslenitsa, the traditional Russian Orthodox holiday event held during the last week of Lent. Moreover, throughout its history Palace Square also has been a traditional place of protest, the most famous of which, Bloody Sunday, occurred on January 9, 1905, when members of the Assembly of Factory and Mill Workers and their sympathizers decided to appeal to the tsar for justice. Tens of thousands of peaceful demonstrators made their way through the city's wide boulevards to Palace Square, where two thousand soldiers, supported by artillery, fired on them, "leaving the square littered with torn bodies from which blood poured onto the new-fallen snow," and setting off what became known as the failed revolution of 1905.[14]

On November 7, 1920, the square was the setting for an amazing mass spectacle that presented eight thousand performers and five hundred musicians in a dramatic restaging of the Storming of the Winter Palace. This outdoor theatrical event, which portrayed one of many events that brought communism to Russia, was "more dramatic by far than the Bolshevik's seizure of power had ever been . . . [and] involved several times more people, than the events of October 1917."[15] In the dramatic finale, actors and spectators all sang the communist "Internationale," certifying the success of the revolution. Obviously, Palace Square had played a role in transforming a tsarist autocracy into what citizens hoped would be a more civil society. How ironic that a spectacle exaggerating that role was actually the harbinger of a very different outcome.

Over the next three quarters of a century under communist rule, however, Palace Square hosted fewer and fewer public events. Parades on World War II Victory Day and celebrations of May Day numbered among the few regular events.

The decrease in the number of public events that took place in Palace Square was accurate reflection of the waning of civil society in the Soviet Union. The declining importance of the square was reversed, however, in 1991, when people flocked there to maintain all-night vigils during the so-called second Russian Revolution, in which the Soviet Union and communist hegemony over Eastern Europe came to an end. Those vigils reflected hope for a revival of civil society in Russia.

By the beginning of the twenty-first century Palace Square was again a social gathering place for parades, musical performances, festivals, fairs, and other celebrations. There are now regular festivals in the square on New Year's Day, Independence Day (celebrating passage of the 1993 constitution), and City Day (celebrating St. Petersburg).

I went through the Palace Square in June 2014, on my way to the Hermitage Museum. At that time, daytime tourist visitors were little more than small spots within its vast space. I returned after 10 p.m., when there was still plenty of daylight this far north. There were costumed performers seeking contribu-

Palace Square, St. Petersburg (2014). During the "white nights" when it is light virtually 24 hours a day, small groups of residents take over the square for impromptu meetings and small concerts. (Alexander Garvin)

tions from passersby, a man and his two boys playing roller hockey, cyclists riding through the square, several sets of skateboarders, and a crowd of about eighty young adults engrossed in a performance from four musicians. What I thought improbable that morning had happened: city residents had again taken possession of Palace Square, though in this latest incarnation it had been incorporated into their daily routines, rather than being appropriated as a stage for political pageantry or revolutionary zeal. I went back to my hotel that night thinking that the people who had participated in the all-night vigils during 1991 had succeeded in fostering a civil society.

Red Square, Moscow—Few places have hosted events of such historical importance as Palace Square. However, many equally important public squares have hosted regular events and become traditional places for social gatherings. Tens of thousands of people, for example, congregate annually to participate in Easter, Christmas, and other special masses in St. Peter's Square in Rome, or to listen to speeches in Detroit's Cadillac Square on Labor Day. Few such events are as politically significant as the fireworks in Moscow's Red Square that have taken place on Russia Day since 1992, when the Russian Federation replaced the Soviet Union.

Although it is half the size of Palace Square, Red Square is an even more famous, huge space (248,000 square feet [23,000 m²]). It provides a dramatic

Red Square, Moscow (2014).
(Alexander Garvin)

setting for the Kremlin, Russia's most famous fortified complex of public buildings and churches that has been the seat of Russia's government except between 1712 and 1728 and between 1732 and 1918, when St. Petersburg was that nation's capital.[16]

Over the centuries, Red Square has been identified with an accretion of events, rituals, fairs, markets, religious services, executions, parades, celebrations, and demonstrations. In addition to the Kremlin, the square is the site of St. Basil's (the iconic church with the colorful concoction of onion domes that has become one of the most famous religious structures in Russia), Kazan Cathedral (built to commemorate the victory over the Poles in 1612), Lobnoe Mesto (a white stone dais erected in 1534), GUM (an enormous sky-lit department store that opened in 1893), and the Lenin Mausoleum (a large granite structure displaying the remains of the man who led the revolution of 1918).[17] Each of these structures hosts important activities, some unique occurrences and other regular, ritual events.

Historically, Red Square is where the dead bodies of traitors used to rest on public display. These included the first False Dmitry (one of three pretenders to the throne then occupied by Boris Godunov), the beheaded and quartered rebel Cossack leader Stenka Razin, and the streltsy (palace guards) who were executed on orders from Tsar Peter the Great.[18] It has hosted more recent, less bloody events as well, such as the World War II victory parade of June 1945, a 1987 demonstration by two thousand Crimean Tartars demanding a return to their homeland from which they had been deported during World War II, and a 2003 Paul McCartney concert. Perhaps the most famous of the rituals that took place in Red Square was the annual May Day parade. Until the dissolution of the Soviet Union in 1991, Communist Party leaders lined up on a reviewing stand on top of the Lenin Mausoleum. Every year "Kremlinologists" used to debate the relative power of Russia's political leaders based on their position on this stand.

Ensuring That the Public Realm Continues to Nurture a Civil Society

Truly large-scale public spaces, such as Palace Square, Red Square, and Times Square in Manhattan, help to nurture civil society because they have a high level of shared cultural significance and symbolic value, or because they manifest some kind of collective memory. But they also require regulation and management, which the various governments of Russia have always readily supplied—sometimes barbarically, sometimes tragically, but usually quite effectively.

In America, however, local governments often cut back on the public services and management that every well-functioning public realm requires, particularly during periods of financial strain. These cutbacks have inevitably produced a decline in the physical condition of the public realm followed by increasing civil disorder. Nowhere was this effect more evident than in New York City, where alarmed property owners and businesses surrounding Times Square devised and financed enormously successful remediation efforts in response to the poor condition of the public realm, the withdrawal of public services, and the accompanying increase in antisocial activity. That activity demonstrates that intelligent design of the public realm, such as Strædet, even in a frequently benign political environment, such as post-communist Russia, is not enough to nurture a civil society. It also requires effective management.

Times Square, Manhattan—Few public squares offer the variety of spectacle and excitement of Times Square. After all, the square competes with dozens of playhouses in New York's Theater District, which surrounds it. On New Year's Eve the crowd, often estimated at a half million people, reaches from below Forty-Second Street for nearly a mile, all the way to Central Park. In addition, the crowds that fill Times Square are not just well-heeled theater-goers. Visitors of every age, ethnicity, and income eat hot dogs and pizza beneath a dazzling display of neon signs and LED screens.

Two centuries ago, Times Square was essentially a 90,000-square-foot bow-tie-shaped traffic intersection, one-sixth the size of Palace Square in St. Petersburg.[19] The area was rarely visited by city residents, most of whom lived far south of the site. Between the Civil War and the turn of the twentieth century, at which time the intersection was known as Longacre Square, it had accommodated stables, carriage makers, and scattered businesses. During that time the entertainment industry, which had been concentrated around Union Square, began moving northward and initially clustered around the bars, brothels, music halls, and theaters in the Tenderloin, one mile to the south of the square.[20]

By the last decade of the nineteenth century, however, the entertainment industry was expanding to Forty-Second Street, which already was "ablaze with electric lights and thronged by crowds of middle- and upper-class theater, restaurant, and café patrons."[21] In 1895 Oscar Hammerstein's Olympia Theater began the march of downtown playhouses northward into the district. Nine years later, when the city's first underground subway opened with a stop at Forty-Sec-

Times Square (1902).
(Museum of the City of New York)

ond Street and the *New York Times* moved its headquarters to a new building diagonally across from the Olympia Theater, Longacre Square was renamed Times
Square. Other newspapers and magazines did not follow until many decades
later, but the entertainment industry continued its move to the area. By 1926 the
square was home to sixty-six Broadway theaters and dozens of vaudeville houses,
music halls, burlesque houses, and movie theaters.[22]

The Great Depression started one of the area's first downturns, which accel-
erated conversion of some theaters into movie houses. The golden era of musicals
and the post–World War II tourist revival, however, reversed the decline. This
was the first of many revivals for the area, symbolized by a brief resumption of
twice-daily vaudeville performances in 1951 during the first of entertainer Judy
Garland's comebacks at the Palace Theater.[23]

Times Square (2014). During the second decade of the twenty-first century motor vehicles were eliminated from redundant traffic arteries, which were transformed into pedestrianized precincts. (Alexander Garvin)

The next revival came in the late 1960s. Developers had been purchasing theaters with the aim of replacing them with more profitable ventures: large modern office buildings. The city responded by rezoning the entire theater district to allow construction of additional rentable office space by any developer who included a new theater in their building. That bonus resulted in construction of five new theaters, the first addition of theater venues since the Great Depression. [24]

In an attempt to increase its customer base, in 1968 the New York theatre industry created the Theatre Development Fund, a not-for-profit organization with a mission of identifying and supporting theatrical works of artistic merit and attracting diverse audiences to live theatre and dance events. Five years later it opened the TKTS Discount Booth in Father Duffy Square at the northern end of the Times Square bow tie. This new facility, which sold tickets at bargain prices to shows that were not sold out, certainly increased theater patronage, but it could not reverse national and regional economic trends.

As New York City confronted a broader fiscal crisis in the mid-1970s (see chapters 6 and 7), Forty-Second Street, the main east-west corridor of Times Square, grew increasingly seedy. Initially, subsidized construction of the Marriott Marquis Theater, along with the more important acquisition and redevelopment of both sides of Forty-Second Street between Broadway and Eighth Avenue, began to reverse the area's decline.[25] This redevelopment program included several components intended to reclaim the area: First, the Walt Disney Company restored and reopened the New Amsterdam Theater; then mainstream stores displaced low-end and sex-related retailing. One of the theaters that had long been a single-screen movie house was converted into a multiplex cinema, supplemented with a second multiplex. Later, four legitimate theaters reopened (one of which combined two old theaters), while the frontages of Seventh and Eighth Avenues became tall office buildings and a hotel.

Two underestimated public actions probably did the most to establish the current character of Times Square: (i) illuminated signage and complementary design requirements enacted in 1987–1988 and (ii) a business improvement district—the Times Square Alliance—established in 1992. Illuminated signs had contributed to the city's fame long before the first of Time Square's downturns and continued doing so for decades. In the 1980s, when the city was coming out of a major recession and developers were again beginning to assemble sites for new office buildings, the city government became concerned that this construction would lead to the elimination of the district's trademark neon-lit advertisements. Its response was to enact zoning that required any new building in the area to have a minimum of one illuminated sign with a surface area of at least 1,000 square feet (93 m²) for each 50 linear feet (15 m) of street frontage. A quarter century later there was so much light coming from these signs that it was impossible to hide antisocial activity. Consequently, the police department now reports that criminal incidents have been reduced by more than 75 percent, far more than in New York as a whole or the many other cities that have experienced a similar reduction in crime.[26]

Today the Times Square Alliance produces, manages, or hosts hundreds of outdoor events in and around the district. It also markets Times Square to the world through globally watched events like the ball-drop on New Year's Eve and a massive outdoor yoga event on the summer solstice, which in 2013 attracted 14,000 people.[27] These marketing activities have been remarkably effective in reversing negative perceptions of Times Square and Forty-Second Street and transforming it into a desired location for corporate headquarters, as well as enhancing it as a retail and entertainment center. The Alliance also played a significant role in the redesign of all the district's public areas, which has increased the square's ability to accommodate ever greater numbers of people.

In 1999, the Alliance, the Theatre Development Fund, the Van Alen Institute, and other local groups, sponsored a series of design studies and a competition for a new TKTS Discount Booth. The result was a red glass staircase with seats facing south and ticket sales windows facing north under the stair. The red stairs, however, did not provide enough seats for all the people in Times Square who wanted a place to watch the world go by. Consequently, the Alliance started putting out moveable chairs and tables. These physical improvements increased the territory available to pedestrians and added places for them to engage in the activities for which they came to Times Square.

Times Square (2014). The Times Square Alliance erected steps that provide space underneath for the sale of discounted theater tickets. Visiting tourists climb the steps and pause to watch the huge array of activities taking place in every corner of this famous place. (Alexander Garvin)

The Department of Transportation, under Commissioner Janette Sadik-Khan, working with the Times Square Alliance, found additional ways to expand the public realm and make it safer and more hospitable. One of the most successful of these banished vehicular traffic from Broadway between Forty-Second and Forty-Seventh Streets and rerouted traffic southward along Seventh Avenue. Because Broadway runs diagonally across the grid, removing traffic reduced the number of required traffic light signal changes from three to two, thereby actually speeding up traffic by 17 percent.[28] Consequently, this section of roadway that was once filled with motor vehicles is now actively used by many more pedestrians, all of whom are now less likely to be hit by passing cars. Between 2004 and 2009, the first five years during which the street was closed, the average number of traffic crashes with injuries fell 14 percent.[29]

Sometimes events scheduled in public squares (even ones as large as Times Square) attract too many people to avoid conflict. Additional management and even the reorganization of the public spaces themselves become necessary. The Times Square Alliance, for example, deploys seventy sanitation workers and fifty security officers who keep Times Square and the area around it safe, clean, and attractive. Many people who used to think of Times Square as dirty and dangerous now believe it is safe enough and clean enough to come there in even greater numbers than ever before. In 2012, 142,300 people were counted on Broadway between Forty-Sixth and Forty-Seventh Streets on a summer Saturday, between 8 a.m. and noon, up from 48,600 in 2002.[30] Perhaps because of this near tripling in the number of people in the area over ten years the number of reported criminal incidents in the area had declined 48 percent.[31]

By mid-2015 an estimated 480,000 people per day visited and passed through what has long been the busiest public square in the world.[32] High-end office buildings and popular national retailers have become as inseparable a part of Times Square as the tourists who come to gape at the flashing lights, the teenagers out for fun, and the theater-goers who want to see the latest show. "The open-air drug deals, streetwalkers, and other signs of serious disorder" were gone.[33] As in popular squares throughout the world, however, the huge number of tourists attracts costumed characters seeking money from passersby who want their pictures taken with them. As more and more people crowd into Times Square the possibility of disorderly behavior increases. So the police department has augmented Times Square Alliance personnel with a neighborhood policing unit.

The colorful history of Times Square illustrates that when uncivil behavior in the public realm escalates, there are three effective ways to nurture a civil soci-

Times Square (2014).
Everybody comes to Times
Square, even Mickey Mouse
and Spider Man. Some people
think these "street performers"
entertain tourists, others call
them aggressive panhandlers,
but many more want to have
their picture taken with them.
(Alexander Garvin)

ety, by (i) adjusting the configuration of the public realm, (ii) altering the regulations governing its use, and (iii) improving management. The effectiveness of these techniques is emblazoned in my mind every time I see the neon signs and LED screens that light up "the Crossroads of the World."

The Public Realm as a Setting for Self-Expression

Hyde Park, Palace Square, and Red Square provide plenty of space for self-expression. When enough people gather in these vast public spaces, they learn that to express themselves they must respect others who are there often for the same reasons. As we have seen, that process can go awry, as it did in mid-nineteenth-century Hyde Park, when nurturing a civil society led the government to establish Speakers' Corner, pass laws, and regulate public activity so as to guarantee self-expression.

The reaction to intense use of the public realm was very different in St. Petersburg in 1905 when the government of Russia felt threatened by the demonstrators who filled Palace Square and slaughtered them to prevent self-expression.

Maintaining a civil society is relatively easy in large spaces like Hyde Park. Some parts of the public realm, however, may not be ample enough to provide an adequate setting for self-expression. For example, some streets in Copenhagen do not have enough room for everybody who wants to be there. In such instances the role of the public realm in nurturing a civil society becomes particularly important. As we have seen, the government dealt with this problem in Strædet by eliminating regulations that assigned specific uses to each part of the street and also removing curbs and other physical obstacles to general use of the public realm. This encouraged the people who used the public realm to ration scarce public space and to respect the rights of others who were there at the same time.

Making physical changes and altering regulations may not be enough. When places in New York City, such as Times Square, became too crowded to fit the many people who wanted to be there, nurturing civil behavior required redefining the roles of different public agencies and supplementing them with additional institutions, such as the Times Square Alliance and the TKTS Discount Booth. Together, they reconfigured, managed, and programmed an improved public realm, making Times Square a safer, cleaner, and more prosperous place than it had been a half century before. People like me, who remember the filth, crime, and disorder of Times Square during the 1970s, believe their activities are a persuasive demonstration of the importance of a well-designed, well-regulated, well-managed, and well-programmed public realm to the nurturing of a civil society.

Cleveland Square,
London (2013).
(Alexander Garvin)

Using the Public Realm
to Shape Everyday Life

———————

By now it should be evident that the public realm must possess a range of different attributes to succeed. It must be a multifunctional constellation of streets, squares, and parks that is open to anybody. It must have something for everybody, attract and retain a market, provide a framework for urbanization, and sustain a habitable environment that nurtures a civil society for all citizens. As important as these six characteristics may be, however, what ultimately matters is the impact that the city's entire public realm network has on the everyday life.

In most places the public realm evolves in response to incremental actions by many people over a long period of time. Later, however, the changes to the public realm require action on everybody's behalf by some entity, even when operating in its self-interest. Thus, it is important to understand the entities that are empowered to do so and what actions they can take.

Whose Realm Is It?

The public realm, like all property, can be in individual, common, or public ownership. Too often, people fail to recognize this tripartite division. They instinctively know what is "mine" and what is "somebody else's." But they often assume that the rest is "public." Much of it isn't. In a condominium, for example, the open space that property owners share is owned in common. For that reason, I insist on making the distinction between *private open space* (a home-owner's back yard), *common open space* (the paths and roadways within a condominium), and *public open space* (city streets).

Many of us inaccurately refer to "our" residence, when it isn't. I refer to *my* home, for example, when I know full well that it is an apartment that I rent from the building's owner. Buildings in London and other parts of the British Commonwealth are often not owned by the occupants, who may, in fact, be inhabiting them pursuant to a ninety-nine-year or even longer-term lease. The same may be true of the area's streets, squares, parks, and every other component of what we have been referring to as the public realm. Nevertheless, the actions taken by the owners can affect far more than just the shape, character, and use of the public realm. They can also significantly alter the daily life of a city. In London, for instance, squares are the critical component; in Minneapolis it is parks; in Madrid it is management of city streets.

Determining the Daily Life of a City

Sixteen centuries after the Romans founded it, London had reached a population of just under eighty thousand people. At this point, property owners began to develop their land around privately owned squares and in doing so determined the character and pace of real estate development in London. More important, the approximately four hundred squares that eventually emerged determined the nature of family life around them, as well as the city's tourist, university, and commercial life.

In the United States, Minneapolis had also reached a population of about eighty thousand when it decided to invest in a system of public parks. Like the squares of London, that park system has continuously determined the character of its development for more than a century. Today, those parks still provide residents of the city with such remarkable recreational amenities that many families, who in similar midwestern American cities might have chosen to move to the suburbs, instead chose to remain in this prospering urban center.

Some cities update their approach to the public realm as a response to changing conditions. Madrid, for instance, already had a well-developed public realm created over five centuries that supported a population of nearly 2.9 million people in 2000, when it decided that it could no longer continue to thrive without completely altering its approach to organization and management of its public realm. In 2000, the city's streets were essentially the same as they had been a half century earlier. But by altering the management of its public realm, Madrid altered the pattern of activity on the street surface, and, in some instances, below the street surface as well.

The Squares of London—Beginning with Covent Garden in 1631, property owners in London adopted the urbanization strategy pioneered at Place des Vosges (see chapter 5) in 1604 and continued initiating development around new squares into the early twentieth century.[1] By that time, the London Squares Preservation Act of 1931 identified 461 squares and enclosures within the County of London.[2] Though these squares occupy a relatively small portion of London's land, no observer can doubt their effect on daily life in London.

In 1631 Francis Russell, the fourth Earl of Bedford, commissioned architect Inigo Jones (1573–1651) to prepare a design for land that the King of England had granted to the family ninety years earlier.[3] The result was Covent Garden, the first real square in London.[4] Like the Place des Vosges, buildings with ground-floor arcades encircled it and, like its French progenitor, the square was intended as an investment that would generate further private development on surrounding territory. The square's appearance, however, was rather different from the Place des Vosges. The London version was dominated by a prominent church on one side and, after 1671, by a daily vegetable market vividly portrayed at the start of George Bernard Shaw's *Pygmalion* and later in Lerner and Loewe's musical adaptation, *My Fair Lady*. Beginning at the end of the twentieth century, this vegetable market became a multipurpose market popular with tourists.

Though the two squares shared a similar design and purpose, the Parisian real estate development strategy embraced by Place des Vosges was altered to fit London property ownership patterns. Land in Paris, whether a possession of the Crown or private individuals, was owned in fee simple, and the owner held official title to the property. So when Henri IV wanted the Place des Vosges developed, he conveyed the property to other owners who agreed to comply with the terms of the conveyance (in this case: to build workshops, provide worker housing, and manufacture silk). Once the terms had been satisfied, the property was entirely owned by its developer.

Although much of London was also Crown-owned territory, large tracts were owned by families, who lived in splendid mansions that occupied their sizable properties. The Bedford estate, which owned the property that became Covent Garden, and other families who followed its example, wanted to live on their property while simultaneously earning income from it. Consequently, they subdivided the property into streets, blocks, lots, and open space, in the form

1 Ladbrook Square	6 Cadogan Square	11 Berkeley Square	16 Gordon Square
2 Cleveland Square	7 Belgrave Square	12 Hanover Square	17 Tavistock Square
3 Sussex Square	8 Bryanston Square	13 Fitzroy Square	18 Russell Square
4 Onslow Square	9 Montagu Square	14 Soho Square	19 Barnsbury Square
5 Egerton Square	10 Grosvenor Square	15 Leicester Square	

N

of fenced-in, landscaped squares, which the estate maintained for common use exclusively by present and future building occupants.

They leased the lots to speculative builders who acted as "developers." In some cases the builders also created the streets and squares on which their "leased" houses fronted. In all cases, they had to obtain financing for the project and contract with bricklayers, carpenters, and other tradesmen who did the actual work. Lessees made money on the buildings they erected by renting them out to occupants. At least in theory, these renters would pay enough rent to more than cover (i) rent to the familial estate that owned the property, (ii) debt service on the loan the developer had taken out to pay for the construction, (iii) the return the developer's investors expected on their equity, and (iv) compensation for the developer's work. This payment justified the real estate venture. In some cases the rent more than covered those costs and provided a handsome profit. In other instances, however, the lessee either absorbed the loss or declared bankruptcy.[5]

Typical leases provided a ninety-nine-year term. Thereafter, the property (land and buildings) returned to estate ownership. The estate could then re-lease the lot to somebody who paid a substantially higher price, reflecting the investment in the area as well as the value of the buildings that had been added to the property. It was not unusual, however, for the lessee to renegotiate the lease before it came due, because otherwise the lessee would lose the value of the building that had been erected on the site.

Under this arrangement, developers gave building occupants keys to the gates of the fenced-in squares. To protect and enhance the value of their property, the estates continued to invest in and maintain the streets and squares, exercised control over what the developers built, and supervised what happened to the property.

This is a drastically different legal arrangement from fee ownership that is typical in the United States. One of the benefits of leaseholds is that the principal landowners usually have enough money that they can afford to invest in their holdings in the surrounding area. Moreover, they have every reason to do so because, as owners of all of the land around the squares, they are the biggest beneficiaries of investment.

During four centuries in which the leasehold approach to London real estate development has been used, three types of squares emerged: those, such as Leicester and Russell Squares, for example, that were once estate properties and are now city public parks; those such as the squares in the Islington section of London that have been expropriated from their estate owners and now operate for

Covent Garden, London (2013). The first public square investment by a great estate interested in fostering development on its property. (Alexander Garvin)

Opposite page: The privately owned estates of London were responsible for the creation of over 400 squares (dark green), some of which are now publically owned and managed. Together with the public parks (light green) they are responsible for providing an open space framework for private development throughout London. (Owen Howlett, Alexander Garvin)

the benefit of the residents of the surrounding borough; and the overwhelming majority of the rest, which remain in the hands of the originating estate.

The majority of London's squares are available only to occupants of the buildings owned by the estate. Thus, building occupants have keys to a gated, often wondrous, common open space. The residents of Islington and other sections of London, where these once private facilities are open to the public, could not be happier about this bargain.

Grosvenor Square, London (2002). (Alexander Garvin)

Opposite page-top: Belgrave Square, London (2013). (Alexander Garvin)

Opposite page-bottom: Cadogan Square, London (2013). (Alexander Garvin)

Just as the Place des Vosges consisted of individual buildings that were similar in appearance, thereby creating a sense of place, London's lessee-developers often built blocks of individual structures that together took on the appearance of a single palatial building. Often, as in the case of Grosvenor Square, the work of different lessee-developers, bricklayers, carpenters, and architects reflected changes in fashion that had occurred over the longer development period that a 6-acre (2.4-ha) project required.[6] Because the estate determined what could be built, however, these buildings, constructed over long periods of time, share a similar scale and materials. In the case of other squares, like Belgrave and Cadogan Squares, which were developed over a short enough time and with common financial structures, developers, designers, and craftsmen, they maintained a consistent aesthetic, albeit often reflecting quite different architectural styles.

The unity of architectural character certainly provides a sense of place for the residents of the buildings enclosing London's squares and for the people passing by on the sidewalks or in an automobile. As important as aesthetics may be, however, what happens within the squares has affected the daily life of London much more.

No matter their architectural style, daily life within the squares is quite similar. When the residents of almost any of the squares of London pass through the gate, they enter a safe, secure world set aside for them—a world without the noise and confusion of the city beyond the fence. Whether they choose to stroll down a path or sit down to read a book, they have the comfort of trees, bushes, and flowers.

Bryanston Square, London (2014). Only the occupants of the surrounding buildings have keys to open the gates of this exclusive green hideaway. (Alexander Garvin)

On the June afternoon that I visited Bryanston (1810–1821) and Cleveland Squares (ca. 1855), I saw people going for a solitary stroll or taking the dog for a walk; soaking up the sun or taking refuge in the shade; picnicking with their family or hosting a garden party. All activities took place inside 1.5 acres (0.6 ha) of common open space.[7] Life in Bryanston and Cleveland Squares has remained similar over two centuries, even though London has changed greatly. Unlike these two examples, however, London's squares have not always been paragons of public order.

The increasing popularity of some of the other squares during the mid-eighteenth century, for instance, attracted unruly visitors. The presence of this disrespectful crowd, coupled with negligent investment and maintenance, threatened the relief these squares offered from less pleasant aspects of urban life. Robberies and crimes of violence in Hanover, Cavendish, Bloomsbury, Grosvenor, Berkeley, and other squares led to the installation of railings, improved street lighting, and patrols by guards.[8]

Bryanston Square, London (2014). The sumptuous plantings camouflage the noise and confusion of the surrounding city. (Alexander Garvin)

Leicester Square, for example, was described in the mid-nineteenth century by Charles Dickens as a "howling desert enclosed by iron railings."[9] Conditions were so bad that in 1865 the Metropolitan Board of Public Works, exercising the authority of the Public Gardens Protection Act that had been approved by Parliament two years earlier, tried to enclose the square in a 12-foot-high (3.7-m)

Cleveland Square, London (2013). Much of the social life of the occupants of the surrounding buildings takes place within the shelter of their landscaped common space. (Alexander Garvin)

wooden fence. The problems ended in 1874, when a wealthy entrepreneur purchased Leicester Square and donated it to the board of works, which paid for its redesign and reconstruction as a public facility.[10]

In some cases, however, even government "protection" did not safeguard many of the squares from further problems. The advent of World War II, for instance, led to the construction of trench shelters in many of the squares and to the removal of iron railings that could be melted down for the war effort. As the end of the war approached, many of the owners of private squares began reinstalling the railings. Their unfortunate rationale was the increase in crime that forced regular patrolling of the squares.

Soho Square (2013) is now a public park. (Alexander Garvin)

The squares that were opened to the public accommodated quite different activities from those that took place in private among a restricted group of users. These squares had to be made conveniently usable to the city as a whole, at different times of the day and in different seasons of the year. Accordingly, Leicester Square and other public squares began to provide more convenient sitting areas. Lawns changed from decorative outdoor carpets to places where people could lounge in the sun or find refuge from the heat.

Leicester Square (2014). In September hundreds of people enjoy strolling through the square, sitting on benches, and lying on the grass. (Alexander Garvin)

These public squares were altered to include additional recreational and social opportunities. Some, such as Russell Square, introduced cafés. Others, such as Soho Square, added ping-pong tables. Leicester Square has gone beyond common recreational opportunities to stage a winter carnival each December. During those weeks there is a Ferris wheel and kiosks that offer food, souvenirs, and a variety of games that attract people, especially young people, from all over London, enriching daily life for everybody in the city.

I do not know of any other city that has more neighborhood-scaled green spaces that are as evenly distributed or as actively used, except as I explain next, Minneapolis. Paris and New York have vast regional parks; but so does London. Consequently, access to nature is central to the life of communities throughout London. The squares, however, are not used merely for passive recreation. Some residents interested in gardening take care of the plantings; some organize picnics and other family events; but nearly everybody who has access to a neighborhood square puts it to active use.

The Minneapolis Park System—Like London's squares, the public parks of Minneapolis have a significant impact on the daily life of that city. The park system extends into every corner of the city. In 2015, the Minneapolis Park and Recreation Board reported that its 197 park properties covered nearly 6,743 acres (2,729 ha) of parkland and water,[11] approximately 19 percent of the territory of the entire city, an amount exceeded among large American cities only by Honolulu (33 percent), New Orleans (26 percent), Washington, D.C. (22 percent), and New York City (21 percent).[12] Within this vast open space, the Minneapolis system includes major regional parks; 17 lakes and ponds; 12 miles (19 km) of beach; 215 playgrounds; 181 tennis courts; numerous flower gardens, picnic areas, and nature sanctuaries; 49 full-service neighborhood recreation centers; 55 miles (88.5 km) of parkway; 51 miles (82 km) of paved trails; 43 miles (69 km) of off-street paths for walking, biking, and skating; 7 golf courses; and much, much more—all for only 383,000 residents.[13] The system is so accessible that The Trust for Public Land in its 2014 evaluation of parklands in fifty cities found Minneapolis to have the best park system in the United States.[14]

N

| Parks |
| Water |
| Major Roads |

Columbia
Park

Theodore
Wirth
Park

Loring
Park

Cedar
Lake

Lake
of the
Isles

Lake
Calhoun

Mississippi River

Lake
Harriet

Lake
Hiawatha

Lake
Nokomis

Minneapolis Park System

Lake Calhoun, Minneapolis (2009). During the summer the park provides a setting for beach volleyball, jogging, cycling, and numerous other activities—all with the downtown skyline as a backdrop. (Alexander Garvin)

Minneapolis's parks are the product of an inspired initial vision, exceptionally scenic topography, continuing citizen support, and determined leadership, particularly from Theodore Wirth, who served as superintendent of the city's parks for thirty years beginning in 1906. The system began in 1883, when the city's Board of Trade unanimously adopted a resolution calling for acquisition of property to create "not only the finest and most beautiful system of public parks and boulevards of any city in America, but which, when secured and located as they can now be at a comparatively small expense, will, in the near future, add many millions to the real estate value of our city."[5]

It is noteworthy that, much as was the case when New York's Central Park, London's Regent's Park, and scores of other successful parks opened to the public, Minneapolis benefitted from an understanding that the entire city could benefit from large investments in individual parks. That understanding helped to persuade the Minnesota State Legislature to authorize a referendum that established an independent, citizen-elected park board with the power to issue bonds, levy taxes, condemn property, and develop parks *without* the approval of property owners, taxpayers, or the city council. No other parks agency in the United States has such broad powers, but because its nine members have to face the voters every four years, the Park and Recreation Board remains particularly responsive to citizen demands. The city collects an annual tax of $85 per $1,000 real estate tax assessment from privately owned property in the city that goes directly to the

Park and Recreation Board and must be devoted exclusively to parks, guarantee-ing the board's independence. As a result of this history and the board's current broad powers and secure funding structure, Minneapolis has the best-located, best-designed, best-maintained, and best-managed park system in America.

In creating the system, the board sought advice from Frederick Law Olm-sted and from H. W. S. Cleveland, who also prepared a master plan for the park network and designed many of its earliest facilities. In 1883 Cleveland recom-mended buying land before it became too expensive and connecting "picturesque pleasure grounds on the river shores, with the parks and parkways (around) the lakes."[16] Olmsted, in an 1886 letter to the commissioners, urged them to include parkways that "if judiciously designed, are likely to become the stems of systems of streets which will be the framework of the permanent residence quarters of our cities of the future . . . making enjoyment of natural scenery available" to their residents.[17] The letter reinforced Cleveland's prior recommendations for an "extended system of boulevards."[18] Together, they persuaded the board to create a park system, rather than only independent recreational facilities.

The park system began with several topographical gems such as the Mis-sissippi River Valley, Minnehaha Falls, and spectacular lakes fed by charming creeks, but also benefits from active improvement of its existing landholdings

Minnehaha Parkway, Minneapolis (2009). Everybody in the city lives within walking distance of a park. (Alexander Garvin)

and the purchase of additional property. Theodore Wirth made the most dramatic improvements to the system's 1,497 acres (606 ha) of water. The flat-water areas within its boundaries range from small lagoons (approximately 2 acres [0.8 ha] in size) to 424.5-acre (171-ha) Lake Calhoun. When these properties were initially acquired, they regularly flooded adjacent properties during heavy rainfalls and snow melts. At Wirth's direction the city dredged and deepened lakes and filled in, regraded, and re-landscaped lowlands. In all cases his objectives were not merely to prevent flooding. He also sought to maximize natural scenic attractions and promote recreational activities. Indeed, even today, the board continues to acquire additional lands to supplement the huge array of recreational facilities throughout the system. As a result the Minneapolis park system offers some of the nation's most extraordinary opportunities for swimming, fishing, ice-skating, sailing, canoeing, kayaking, and rowing.

Lake Calhoun, Minneapolis (1922). Until the lake was dredged it regularly inundated surrounding properties. (from *Minneapolis Park System 1883-1944*, by Theodore Wirth, Minneapolis Parks Legacy Society, Minneapolis, 2006)

Opposite page-top:
Lake Harriett, Minneapolis (2013). The seventeen lakes in the park system provide the widest range of recreational opportunities. (Alexander Garvin)

Opposite page-bottom:
North Commons Park, Minneapolis (2013). (Alexander Garvin)

The park system that the Minneapolis park board has spent nearly a century and a half creating provided precisely what Olmsted said it would: "the framework of the permanent residence quarters" in which residents "take pride and pleasure."[19] This framework of parks, parkways, *and* residential districts provides a connective tissue for the entire city, so properties in these neighbor-

hoods, unlike those of many other midwestern cities, have been continuously and happily occupied for decades, while also continuing to increase in value.

No resident of Minneapolis lives farther than six blocks from a park. So, as in London, green space is integral to the life of every neighborhood. The difference is that the prevalence of large lakes, jogging-cycling trails, golf courses, and playing fields allows everybody in Minneapolis to take part in active recreational activity summer and winter. Moreover, this extraordinary system serves a population of about 400,000, which is less than 5 percent of London's population.

Perhaps as a result of this abundance of outdoor recreation space, in 2014 the American College of Sports Medicine rated Minneapolis the second healthiest metropolitan area in the United States.[20] Furthermore, without its extraordinary park system, the evolution of Minneapolis would probably have differed little from such Rust Belt cities as Pittsburgh, Buffalo, Cincinnati, and St. Paul, which declined in population between 1950 and 2010 by about 51 percent, 50 percent, 34 percent, and 39 percent, respectively. Minneapolis's population declined only 26 percent. Though it is difficult to draw an empirical line between Minneapolis's investment in its park system and the rate of decline in the size of its population, the city's abundant, high-quality public realm has certainly transformed everyday life in Minneapolis and helped it to retain residents who in other cities may be more likely to move to the suburbs for easier access to green space and opportunities for recreation.

Calle de Argumosa, Madrid (2013). With vehicular traffic under control, street life in Madrid has become even more active. (Alexander Garvin)

The Madrid Miracle—In downtown Madrid a once hopeless snarl of humans and machines has, thanks to investments in and regulation of public roadways, undergone a dramatic turnaround, providing a safe, attractive environment and an improved state of mind for all its inhabitants. The new Madrid that has emerged, as we will see, arose from both helter-skelter development and periods of inspired planning. Despite, or perhaps because of this haphazard blend, the city now boasts one of the safest and easiest to use street networks in Europe.

Yet, while Madrid's street network has been evolving since the sixteenth century and has always played a major role in the day-to-day life of its residents, that role began to significantly change and improve only fifteen years ago. At that time the city's streets and sidewalks could be characterized with a single word: chaos. Many of its roadways had been built to handle carriages and carts rather than trucks and buses, and for years they were clogged with traffic. Drivers and pedestrians routinely did whatever they needed—or wanted—to get where they had to go, making illegal turns, going the wrong way on one-way streets, disregarding street lights and traffic signs, blasting their horns, parking anywhere they pleased, and at times even driving up on the sidewalk and endangering pedestrians. As a result, in 2000 Madrid's public realm was an utter mess, negatively affecting personal well-being, the environment, and urban life.

Now let's move ahead fifteen years in time, to the present. As of today Madrid's street network has been sufficiently transformed to drastically reshape and improve its daily life. A visitor who travelled there in 1985, let us say, and then returned in 2015 might remark that Madrid seems a totally altered city—changed, they will gladly tell you, for the better.

Notwithstanding decades of well-intentioned planning, at the end of the twentieth century the old avenues of the downtown city district had become a chaotic muddle, their jumble of narrow, winding streets and alleys enduring a daily blitz of truck traffic, buses, taxis, private automobiles, motorcycles, bicycles, and pedestrians. At that time, it was common for quarter-mile-long lines of cars to be stalled on a street because a lone driver had triple parked. Delivery vans and cars routinely parked on the sidewalks, and pedestrian jaywalking was common. Even if every person in Madrid had respected its regulations—which they decidedly did not—the carrying capacity of its existing street network was simply inadequate to handle the human and vehicular crush. The city's broad boulevards, regional highway network, and subway system had, it is true, been designed to handle large volumes of traffic, but, because of the density of development and the huge number of commuters and tourists that came to Madrid

Key:
1- Parque Madrid Río,
2- Royal Alcázar Palace,
3- Plaza Mayor,
4- Barrio de las Letras,
5- Paseo del Prado,
6- Passeo de la Castellana,
7- Calle Serrano,
8- Parque del Retiro,
9- Salamanca district.
(Cortez Crosby, Owen
Howlett, Alexander Garvin)

every day, the network could not handle the congestion that now threatened to engulf and paralyze this great metropolis.

Thus, despite the continuing expansion of Madrid's subway system, the city's traffic had become utterly unmanageable and, for the people living there, unbearable. Something had to be done to improve the functioning of this metropolitan city, which by 2010 had a population of nearly 6.5 million people, half of whom lived within the city limits.[21]

Finally, without an official decision to do so, Madrid's streets began to change and, slowly, surely, miraculously, to improve. The transformation began with the retrofitting of avenues and squares to include separately defined territories—one for pedestrians, one for vehicles, one for businesses. The city also constructed extensive underground parking and regulated what (and where) parking was permitted on all its main streets. Madrid's public realm now had a place for everything, and everything had its place: pedestrians, moving vehicles, parked cars, delivery vans, buses, taxis, motorcycles, playgrounds for children, benches for pedestrians, trees, flowers, kiosks selling magazines, shops, cafés, restaurants, and bus shelters. All began to integrate and work together to improve the street surroundings.

Calle Cruz, Barrio de las Letras, Madrid (2011). Bollards protect pedestrians using the sidewalk and in some spots are set back to provide a place for delivery vehicles to unload. (Alexander Garvin)

Calle Mayor, Madrid (2013). Separate areas are set aside for pedestrians; cyclists; moving vehicles; parked cars, bicycles, and motorcycles; and even braille-marked pedestrian crossings. (Alexander Garvin)

As a result of the physical changes to the public realm and improved management of vehicular traffic, the people walking the streets and sidewalks of Madrid began causing fewer problems for themselves and each other. For example, on some streets in the Barrio de las Letras (Writers' Quarter) established in the seventeenth century, the city eliminated curbs separating streets from sidewalks and repaved the sidewalks with granite. More importantly, they placed bollards on certain streets to keep vehicles from parking on the sidewalks and from blocking the flow of motor vehicles. These additions freed up areas that were now set aside exclusively for pedestrians. On other streets the city omitted bollards, instead designing the territory exclusively for truck pickups and deliveries to nearby stores. Still other locations on the street were allocated for temporary stopping by cars to unload passengers and belongings. The city reconfigured even major thoroughfares such as the Calle Mayor to include crosswalks with stop signs requiring motor vehicles to give way to pedestrians, plus special paving to help blind people identify where to cross. The city also widened its sidewalks, planted lines of trees, colored bicycle lanes to make clear that other vehicles and pedestrians were not welcome, and set aside sections of the street for temporary parking.

Calle Serrano, Salamanca district, Madrid (2013). (Alexander Garvin)

Perhaps the most impressive example of the organizing and civilizing of Madrid's streets can be seen today in the high-income Salamanca district of the city. As a result of Carlos Maria de Castro's 1860 *Plan de Ensanche*, the streets here were already wide enough for the city to retrofit them with interventions such as specific parking areas set aside for cars, delivery vans, taxis, and motorcycles. On-street parking within the neighborhood is restricted to residents with permits. Some of Salamanca's north-south and east-west streets are wide enough to accommodate several lanes of traffic in each direction. One of the most impressive of these, Calle Serrano, a particularly luxurious shopping street, provides shoppers with an underground parking garage that stretches for many blocks. On Calle Serrano's side streets, the city has installed special drive-down ramps, making it easy for motorists to enter the underground areas and park their cars. The drive-up ramps then discharge onto the street itself for ease of exit, along with stairs and elevators for pedestrian access, a bike lane protected by parked cars, and benches for people to sit and enjoy. As a result, there is less traffic on city streets, fewer drivers from outside the neighborhood bringing their cars to the neighborhood, and more room for residents of the neighborhood to stroll and more places for them to sit down.

Calle de Claudio Coello, Salamanca district, Madrid (2013). The intersection is funneled down to make pedestrian crossing easy and provide room for seating, landscaping, lighting and signage. (Alexander Garvin)

Calle de la Torrecilla del Leal, Madrid (2013). The billboard above proudly announces in French: "We are an example of (successfully) living together." (Alexander Garvin)

Many narrow, local and one-way streets of the new Madrid roadways include one moving lane plus ample parking for specific vehicles. The traffic funnels down at each intersection where a large pedestrian area provides benches and plantings. The mix of land uses and activities throughout the entire neighborhood, the moderate density of the predominantly six- to eight-story buildings, and the prevalence of underground parking make these uses possible.

The revitalized public realm of Madrid has greatly improved the way of life for everybody on its streets, visitors and residents alike. In the Lavapiés neighborhood, for example, one of the more heterogeneous areas of the city that includes enclaves of Turks, Arabs, Africans, and a variety of other immigrants, there is room for people to meet, shop, have lunch, park their bikes, sit on a bench, pick up a date, and pursue their plans without disturbing others. Previously, much of this space accommodated passing traffic. There is even a billboard in this area that proclaims in French: *"Nous sommes un exemple de vie un commun"* ("We are an example of [successfully] living together."). Its authors are making a statement that their counterparts in Paris, New York, or Copenhagen would easily recognize as evidence of a burgeoning civil society.

The latest roadway to be added to Madrid's revitalized public realm, Parque Madrid Río, is as much a street as it is a park. Created between 2006 and 2010, this six-mile-long (10-km) parklike street and street-like park has changed the way of life for millions of residents in metropolitan Madrid. Spanish architecture firms of Burgos & Garrido, Porras La Costa, and Rubio & Álvarez-Sala, in cooperation with the Dutch landscape architecture firm West 8 (see chapter 10), conceived its design. It was constructed on top of the western side of the city's M30 inner loop highway, initially built between 1970 and 1979. At the time, the city was engaged in canalizing the Manzanaras River in an effort to control storm runoff.

Because Madrid Río rested on top of a concrete platform covering two highway ribbons that flanked the river, however, there was little room for soil. The horticultural solution was to plant a continuous corridor with eight thousand hardy Spanish pines that required minimal soil and water, and could thrive in rocky conditions. The city also erected numerous bridges to reconnect the two sides of the city that the highway had divided three decades earlier. In many places the park ribbon was widened or actually integrated into the adjacent pre-existing parks. Today there are children's small playgrounds everywhere on this street, along with attractive fountains and flower beds. In addition, the old slaughterhouse district located nearby has been restored as a creative arts center.

With guidance from some of the designers who were responsible for Parque Madrid Río, in July 2013, I spent a Saturday morning cycling its entire length. During my ride, the serene mood and cheerful disposition of the people riding, jogging, strolling, sitting in the sun, and using its play equipment impressed me deeply. I started my trip at 9:00 a.m. when the path was nearly empty, but by midday Madrid Río was too crowded for easy cycling. It seemed clear to me that everyone in the park that day had adopted a new lifestyle that would have been impossible without the changes that the city had planned fifteen years earlier. At that time people living in the buildings lining the Madrid Río looked out on highway traffic jams and went to sleep with truck noise reverberating in their heads. Now the street is remarkably quiet for a major artery, and the residential view includes a vista of trees and flowers. This new pedestrian artery, moreover, is merely one part of a street system that in less than two decades has completely transformed the mood and efficiency of the city.

In addition to the park, bridges, and tunnels, Madrid relocated a six-mile-long (10-km) portion of the M30 highway underground at a cost of more than 3.7 billion EUR (~$4 billion).[22] At the time the project began, Spain was in the midst of an economic boom and the national budget was in surplus. Yet, despite the nation's post-2008 economic woes, the positive impact Madrid Río has had on Madrid's daily life makes it appear to be an incredibly good investment.

Most residents of Madrid today truly enjoy spending time on its refurbished streets. Some sit on benches reading the newspaper or sending text messages. Others take their constitutionals or window shop. Bars, restaurants, and cafés have set out tables and chairs on the sidewalks, encouraging pedestrians to hang out and enjoy an hour of people-watching. Informal business negotiations and political debates are as likely to take place here as discussions about Cervantes or the merchandise offered in the local boutiques. The same was true of the streets of Paris in 1941 when Oscar Hammerstein wrote: "The last time I saw Paris, her heart was warm and gay. I heard the laughter of her heart in every street café . . ." and thought "of happy hours, and people who shared them."[23] Hammerstein could easily have written the same lyrics about Paris in 2015—and about Madrid as well.

All this, of course, is not to say that Madrid's renovations have made its people problem-free or that life for everyone here is a bed of roses. Nevertheless, thousands and thousands of people now spend many happy hours walking, riding, shopping, and basking on Madrid's welcoming thoroughfares, just as they do on the very best boulevards of London, Rome, Vienna, and New York. In other words, the formerly congested metropolis has become a reborn urban center that lies among the ranks of the world's great cities.

The Key to Greatness

The initial investment in the exceptional public realm of London and Minneapolis and its dedicated management by property owners and taxpayers who had a financial stake in that public realm allowed them to appeal to and hold residents who might have otherwise moved elsewhere. Madrid's public realm remained adequate until it was inundated by motor vehicles. By making major investments in its improvement and management, Madrid enhanced and enriched daily life significantly enough to compel the attention of people who had not previously thought of life in Madrid as exceptional. London, Minneapolis, and Madrid demonstrate that as long as cities continue to improve their public realm they will continue to attract and retain the people who make them great.

What are the most promising *new* actions, you must be wondering, that a city can take to make itself more livable, welcoming, and accessible and to provide a framework for development and for nurturing a civil society? The next and final chapter of this book details new approaches to the physical improvement and maintenance of the public realm and provides examples for what already great cities can do better and for those that are on their way to being great.

Parque Madrid Río, Madrid (2013). This park is built on top of a six-mile-long section of the highway ring encircling the city. (Alexander Garvin)

Lower Manhattan
skyline (2013)
(Alexander Garvin)

Creating a Public Realm for
the Twenty-First Century

The great twentieth-century architect Le Corbusier wrote that "New York is not a finished or completed city. It gushes up. On my next trip it will be different."[1] Few cities "gush up" in the way that New York does; but virtually all of them will be different the next time you visit because people keep adjusting cities to meet the demands of their culture, economy, and changing personal needs. In fact, the only cities that are "finished" are the ones that have been abandoned, often because they were too rigidly designed to change in response to market conditions.

When Le Corbusier wrote about the gushing up of New York he was referring to the city's privately owned real estate. Indeed, when people think of New York, they picture the Manhattan skyline, which is privately owned. As this book demonstrates, however, privately owned real estate is, in great measure, shaped by investments in the public realm; thus any investment in a city's publicly owned streets, squares, and parks contributes to its "greatness."

The question that every city faces is, *What is the size and shape of the public realm that will satisfy the needs of the present and accommodate future generations?* In 1922 Le Corbusier provided his answer: the *City of Tomorrow*—a flat, green plain crisscrossed by elevated highways that divided the city into districts that contained the necessary residential and office towers, public buildings, and

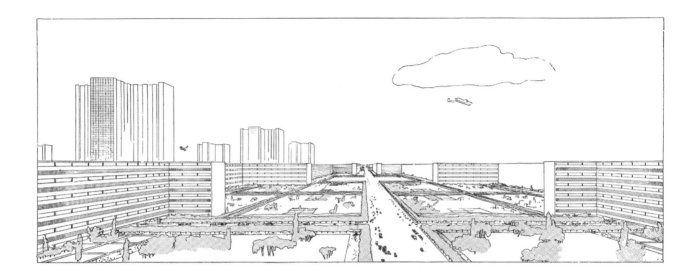

The City of Tomorrow (1922). Le Corbusier's City of Tomorrow is a finished city with no place for residents to adjust it to their needs or the needs of future generations. (from *The Complete Works of Le Corbusier* Volume 1, 1910–1929, Birkhauser Publishers, Boston, 1999)

government services. The buildings were all of the most advanced design and provided their occupants with comfortable rooms in which to eat, sleep, play, and do business—something ordinarily available only to the wealthy at the time. The resulting city of three million inhabitants consisted of carefully designed buildings, motorways, and open territory between buildings that guaranteed every citizen plenty of light and air—but, other than the green ground plane, some trees, and elevated highways, the *public realm* he depicted included almost nothing else.

The abstract green space that permeated Le Corbusier's *City of Tomorrow* provided few if any of the attractions that draw people into cities. Perhaps this is why most of the images with which Le Corbusier illustrated his proposals were devoid of people. The people were there, but because there was nothing for them to do within the public realm, they had no alternative to remaining within their apartments in the sky. The City of Tomorrow was not only devoid of people, it was a finished city without a framework for future development. It should come as no surprise, therefore, that Le Corbusier's vision has largely been discarded in favor of other more people-friendly proposals for the future. There are many twenty-first-century examples of cities at work improving their public realm. I have chosen to present five of them below that demonstrate particularly effective ways for already great cities to improve the public realm.

The Patient Search for a Better Tomorrow

As the previous chapters discuss, for there to be people in cities, there must something to attract them, a way for them to get to their desired destinations, areas in which they can gather together, interact, and do business with one another, and places for rest, recreation and amusement—*a great public realm*. Furthermore, a great public realm provides a framework for future development that allows cities to grow while retaining their character. This public realm is what our predecessors spent so much time, effort, and money creating, and what we keep reconfiguring to meet contemporary needs. In maintaining this public realm, however, those of us living in the twenty-first century cannot rely entirely on past solutions. We need approaches that will be appropriate for the foreseeable future and for the future we cannot foresee.

In an already built-up city with a full complement of streets, squares, and parks, adding to and altering the public realm is not easy: usually it involves major expenditures, substantial dislocation, political controversy, and often legal altercations. This dislocation and controversy, however, can be minimized by

- · reconfiguring the public realm that already exists,
- · inserting carefully conceived additions to the public realm that involve little or no impact on private property,
- · converting obsolete property into an actively used public realm,
- · retrofitting the public realm to accommodate further growth, and,
- · only when necessary, reconceiving entire cities, as was done in Bilbao at the end of the twentieth century.

Several examples in this chapter illustrate how a city can transform its public realm with minimal disruption and maximum benefit to urban life. First, the evolution of the Place de la République in Paris, particularly at the start of the twenty-first century, provides a vivid illustration of how a city can reconfigure the public realm at relatively low cost and with minimal dislocation. Second, the work now under way on Post Oak Boulevard in the Uptown section of Houston, Texas, illustrates how cities can insert new transit service and an improved pedestrian environment to decongest a district and accommodate substantial additional private development. Third, the emerging Brooklyn Bridge Park demonstrates how obsolete and abandoned properties can be converted into actively used recreational facilities. Next, the transformation of abandoned railroad rights-of-way into an "emerald necklace" of trails and parks that is currently under way in Atlanta, Georgia, provides a model for transforming obsolete and decaying infrastructure that people considered a liability into an asset that connects neighborhoods, removes private automobiles from congested highways, and generates billions of dollars of new private investment. And finally, where more small-scale strategies are insufficient to reverse urban decline, massive public realm investments, such as those now being made along the waterfront in Toronto, Canada, will reconceive entire cities.

Place de la République, Paris.
(1770, 1811, 1867, 2014).
(Owen Howlett, Alexander Garvin)

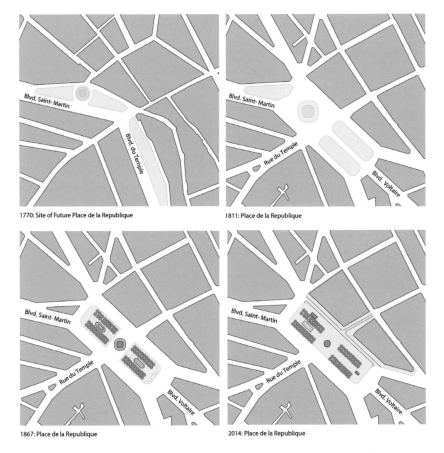

1770: Site of Future Place de la Republique

1811: Place de la Republique

1867: Place de la Republique

2014: Place de la Republique

Place de La République, Paris—At first there was no square at all at the location that is now the Place de la République—just a continuation of the Boulevard Saint-Martin, one of the Grands Boulevards created when Paris demolished the wall of Charles V (see chapter 6). The street was widened in 1809, which brought additional vehicles carrying consumers and products from all over the city.

The most important changes to the area came during the Second Empire, when Haussmann pierced four new avenues through the city, thereby creating a huge traffic juncture at the site that connected the surrounding neighborhoods with the rest of Paris. The 8.3-acre (3.4-ha) square that emerged was largely devoted to circulation.[2] It officially opened in 1867 and was renamed a dozen years later as Place de la République, in honor of the newly established Third Republic. The increase in traffic also brought additional customers. New businesses opened in buildings around the square, and when a huge sculpture of Madame République, a woman (sometimes called Marianne) representing the Republic of France, replaced the fountain at the center of the square in 1883, even more people came to the area.

At first horse-drawn vehicles circled around the statue. They were replaced in the early twentieth century, however, by an even greater number of cars, trucks, and buses, and by subway commuters using the five Metro lines that converged there. At this point, conditions in the square had become dire: the limited space available to pedestrians was crowded and unpleasant; amenities for cyclists were

Huge volumes of traffic used to swirl around the sculpture of Mme. de la Republique and the two public plazas, making it difficult for pedestrians to get to these traffic-free islands in Paris.

Opposite page—top: Place de la République, Paris (2014). The toy lending library is just one of the attractions that brings people to the square. (Alexander Garvin)

Place de la République, Paris (2013). The square now has a popular café and a shallow water feature in which children like to wade. (Alexander Garvin)

nonexistent; pedestrian crossings were inconvenient; street furniture was inadequate; motor vehicles occupied too much space (60 percent); and noise levels during the day were among the highest recorded in Paris. Everybody favored change. Consequently, during the start of the twenty-first century, the city government initiated a planning process to rectify the situation. It began in 2008 with meetings that involved area residents, businesses, consumers, government agencies, elected officials, and a wide range of metropolitan interests.[3]

The city asked five teams of landscape architects, architects, and planners to propose redevelopment schemes that would solve the above problems, which had been identified in the planning process. In 2009, after nine months of interaction with technicians and the public, a jury of stakeholders, designers, and public officials selected the proposal of a design team led by the planning and architecture firm of Trévelo & Viger-Kohler with assistance from the landscape architecture firms of Martha Schwartz Partners and Areal. The final design, approved in 2011, was the result of two years of work and ongoing consultations with the public. The plan called for the transformation of the Place de la République into the largest pedestrian precinct in Paris.[4]

Two years later, when the completely redesigned square reopened, it had been smoothed out into a very gently sloping hilltop at the intersection of twelve streets, some of which converged before arriving at the square. The balance between pedestrians and vehicles, however, had been reversed. Now, 60 percent of Place de la République is devoted to pedestrians. Cars neither swirl around the statue representing the French Republic, nor race along the street on the north side of the square, which has been set aside for pedestrians. Instead, the traf-

fic roundabout circling Mme. République between the two flanking rectangles has become a single pedestrian precinct paved with large, prefabricated concrete slabs. The statue of Mme. République still anchors the square, but has ceased to be its main attraction. In addition to pre-existing subway entrances, visitors now make use of four large tree-lined sitting areas, a café, a podium for public presentations, a toy lending library, over 150 new trees, and, during summer months, a shallow sheet of water that is popular with local children.

Place de la République, Paris (2014). Skateboarding is another popular activity that now takes place in the remodeled square. (Alexander Garvin)

I last visited the Place de la République on a sunny day at the end of March 2015. Coming from the Boulevard Saint-Martin I saw the usual heavy traffic. When I crossed the street and entered the square, however, I left Paris traffic behind and entered into a very different city. Older people were sitting on stylish benches protected from the sun by shade trees. A couple of cyclists went past me as I made my way past the café and Mme. République to the eastern end of the square, where I discovered the toy lending library. I sat down nearby to watch the small children playing with their borrowed toys. When I had been there nine months earlier, I was distracted by a commotion behind me—about fifty African demonstrators with colorful flags were there to rally support for Biafra. This time my attention was diverted to three teenagers who were trying to show off their skateboarding skills.

Place de la République, Paris (2014). Demonstration of Biaffrans. (Alexander Garvin)

The new public realm for the Place de la République succeeds along a number of the principles laid out in this book: It is easy to get to and to move around in; in its new form it has plenty of attractions that draw people there and places where they can gather to interact with one another; there is something for everybody—small children and teenagers, pedestrians and cyclists, older people resting, and politically active demonstrators; and they all can do what they came for without interfering with so many others who are there for quite different reasons.

The renovations to the Place de la République have made the environment safer and healthier. More people can enjoy the square at the same time as others are going about their business. The mix of people and activities that take place there every day are evidence of an increasingly integrated civil society.

The transformation of this aging section of Paris has been accomplished without the massive relocation, demolition, and reconstruction that were an integral part of the downtown redevelopment projects recommended by Le Corbusier and implemented in countless American cities. Instead, the city of Paris successfully invested in small-scale adjustments to the public realm, all of which allowed it to retain market demand in this vibrant section of the city.

As lovely and heavily used as the Place de la République has become, however, it has done little to increase private market activity in the buildings surrounding the square or lining the streets carrying traffic passing through this section of Paris. The explanation for the meager private market reaction is that public officials responsible for renovating the square concerned themselves with its redesign without much consideration for anything other than pedestrian and vehicular traffic and the activities that took place on the square itself.

Nevertheless, the renovation of the Place de la République demonstrates how (as a result of clever redesign and with virtually no dislocation) a city can recoup large amounts of roadway from noisy traffic and transform it for use by people of every age, reorganize existing pedestrian areas so that they can be used by more people, and add facilities that attract people from the surrounding area and beyond. The Place de la République provides a twenty-first-century approach to the improvement of densely packed, intensively used urban areas. Every city can use the same techniques to alter its own public realm and continue on its path to greatness.

Post Oak Boulevard in the Uptown District of Houston—Paris did not experience any appreciable growth during the twenty-first century. Thus, the changes to the Place de la République were intended to better serve the needs of the existing population of the district. On the other hand, planning in Houston, Texas, has always focused on attracting further development and encouraging growth. The city's downtown has accommodated exponential growth without the massive relocation of businesses, jobs, and people that were required for the typical American downtown redevelopment project.

Uptown Houston (1961). When the interstate highways were being built, a decade before the Galleria opened, one of the country lanes passing through the rapidly suburbanizing Houston countryside was called South Post Oak Road. (Uptown Houston)

Uptown Houston (1978). By 1978 Uptown included the Galleria shopping center, glass towers, and upscale retail stores all fronting onto what was by then called Post Oak Boulevard. (Uptown Houston)

Like Place de la République, the Uptown district of Houston has undergone waves of investment in its public realm—but in far less time, with a more distinctive aesthetic, and with an emphasis on private real estate development that more closely resembles that of the Haussmann era than that of early twenty-first-century Paris. The actions that enabled the growth of the Uptown Houston district included construction of interstate highways; several stages of reconfiguration of its main traffic artery, Post Oak Boulevard; installation of unique street furniture designed to create a brand for the district; and massive private real estate development, including air-conditioned shopping malls, office towers, and multistory residential condominiums. Furthermore, the city has augmented these developments by broadening the territory devoted to Post Oak Boulevard, widening sidewalks, installing additional trees, and planning a landscaped bus corridor.

Post Oak Boulevard, Houston (2015). By 2015 Uptown Houston had grown to be America's seventeenth largest office district. (Alexander Garvin)

At the end of World War II, Uptown did not exist; it was unincorporated Texas territory. Even in 1955, only a few streets east of what was then called South Post Oak Road were within Houston's city limits.[5] Today, however, Uptown includes more than 27 million square feet of office space, 7 million square feet of retailing, and more than 7,800 hotel rooms and 20,000 apartments.[6] It is the seventeenth largest business district in the United States, with 180,000 people living within a 3-mile (4.8-km) radius of the district.[7]

The primary reason for the emergence of the Uptown District is the rapid growth of Houston itself, which went from the fourteenth largest city in the country with a population of 596,000 in 1950 to the fourth largest in 2010 with a population of 2.1 million. One reason the city was able to absorb this rapid growth was investment in a 600-mile (957-km) network of major highways that consists of three highway loops and a dozen radials connecting those loops with downtown Houston.[8]

Construction of the second highway ring, the 42-mile-long (68-km) interstate highway I-610, proceeded in stages between the 1950s and 1973.[9] This loop attracted real estate investment to its intersections with the major radial arterials leading from the downtown business district. Once they had become successful destinations, further private real estate investment spread out in either

The Galleria on Post Oak Boulevard, Houston (1974). The opening of this mixed-use development with retail facilities, hotels, office buildings, and a skating rink triggered substantial additional development in Uptown Houston. (Alexander Garvin)

direction from those intersections. Initially the city's growth could have emerged anywhere along the second loop.

The growth that emerged along Post Oak Boulevard on the west side of Houston, between Allen Parkway and interstate highway I-69, was the product of the particularly convenient access to downtown that those roads offered. Without developer Gerald Hines's vision and entrepreneurial skill, however, that growth might not have coalesced into the district we now call "Uptown." And without the major public realm investments made by the Uptown Development Authority after its establishment in 1999, it would resemble other sprawling commercial areas in suburban Houston and would *not* now be on the verge of surpassing downtown Denver, Pittsburgh, or Baltimore, currently the nation's thirteenth, fourteenth, and fifteenth largest business districts, respectively, in size and prominence.

During the ten years before he founded his own real estate firm, Gerald Hines gravitated from engineering to developing small office buildings and warehouses. In 1962 when the Uptown section of the I-610 loop opened, Hines, like many other Houston real estate developers, believed it was an area of the city in which to invest. The following year Joske's (now Dillard's) department store opened on the block between I-610 and South Post Oak Road, facing Westheimer Road, and Sakowitz,

Post Oak Boulevard, Houston (2007). A third of a century later Post Oak Boulevard had matured as a mixed-use district. (Alexander Garvin)

a more upscale department store, opened across the street. Hines identified this intersection (now Post Oak Boulevard and Westheimer Road) as the area's most desirable corner and decided to assemble a large enough property there to create the air-conditioned shopping mall that would become the Galleria.

It took Hines five years and involvement with six times as much property as he needed to assemble the 33 acres (13 ha) he ultimately required for the project.[10] Besides putting together the site, however, Hines needed a prime tenant, but he would not settle for just any retailer. Instead, he sought out Neiman Marcus, the very best, high-end department store in Texas. Neiman Marcus already had purchased 25 acres (10 ha) on Westheimer, on the other side of the I-610 loop. Hines persuaded the Marcus family to give up its site and become part of the new Galleria by giving them free land on which to erect the department store and at his expense also building the parking facilities they wanted.[11]

Galleria, Houston (2007).
(Alexander Garvin)

Post Oak Boulevard, Houston (1995). By the end of the twentieth century high-rise residential condominiums and office buildings vied for pride of place with the Galleria and a variety of low-scale retail strips. (Alexander Garvin)

Hines succeeded in attracting his anchor tenant, but assembling the property for the Galleria had been so complex, time-consuming, and expensive that the land cost could not be supported by retail outlets alone. Consequently, the Galleria became a high-density, mixed-use complex that included a hotel, two office towers, an air-conditioned mall with a skating rink at the bottom, and structured parking for seven thousand cars.[12]

Since then, the project has expanded several times. Galleria I, which opened in 1970, triggered Galleria II (1976) with a Marshall Field's department store addition (1979), Galleria III (1986), and Galleria IV (2003). By 2014 this mini-city included 2.4 million square feet (222,967 m²) containing 400 stores and restaurants; Neiman Marcus, Saks Fifth Avenue, Nordstrom, and two Macy's department stores; two hotels; three towers with 1.1 million square feet (102,193 m²) of office space; nearly 14,000 parking spaces; three banks; and a wide selection of recreational opportunities from ice-skating to swimming.[13] During 2014, the Galleria, now owned by Simon Property Group, grossed $1.4 billion in spending, which was more than the annual budget of Minneapolis in 2014. The project will, no doubt, continue to morph in response to changes in ownership and market demand.

Later, Hines added two other iconic projects to Post Oak Boulevard: Post Oak Central, built between 1973 and 1982, and Williams Tower (formerly Transco Tower), completed in 1983. Both were designed by Johnson/Burgee Architects, with whom Hines worked on buildings in downtown Houston and New York City, and both provided prestigious office space that attracted major corporations to Uptown. Post Oak Central is a 17-acre (6.9-ha) complex of three 24-story glass buildings with 1.3 million square feet (120,774 m²) of office space, 90,000 square feet of retailing, and parking for 4,200 cars.[14] At 900 feet, the 64-story Williams Tower is the tallest office building outside downtown Houston. Moreover, its real contribution is as an iconic beacon on the skyline.

As the Galleria grew, other nearby developers invested in towers, such as the 400-apartment Four Leaf Towers housing complex and the 1.8 million-square-foot (167,225 m²) office space in the Four Oaks Place office complex, both designed by Cesar Pelli & Associates.[15] From the beginning, however, most developers did what most suburban property owners do: they lined Post Oak Boulevard with parking lots and built low-rise strips of retail stores or hotels behind the parking.

As a result of all the development, traffic increased sufficiently to make property owners and businesses worry that competition from outlying, less-heavily trafficked developments would lure customers away. To address these concerns, in 1975 they formed a voluntary organization, the City Post Oak Association, to take actions that would be in their mutual benefit.[16] By the mid-1980s, this organization had evolved into an agency public-private partnership formally responsible for "traffic operations, public maintenance and beautification, infrastructure improvement, economic development, marketing and communications."[17] In sum, the association sought to coordinate investment in and maintenance of the public realm, a term with which I doubt they were familiar at that time.

The device they selected was similar to the business improvement districts (BIDs) that were already in operation in New Orleans, Denver, and New York. In 1987, they persuaded the Texas Legislature to create the Uptown Houston District (Harris County Improvement District #1). Unlike most BIDs, which are chartered by city government, Uptown Houston is a political subdivision of the State of Texas. Its governance is similar to a BID in that it consists of a board of directors made up of landowners, long-term tenants, or agents of landowners. Also similar

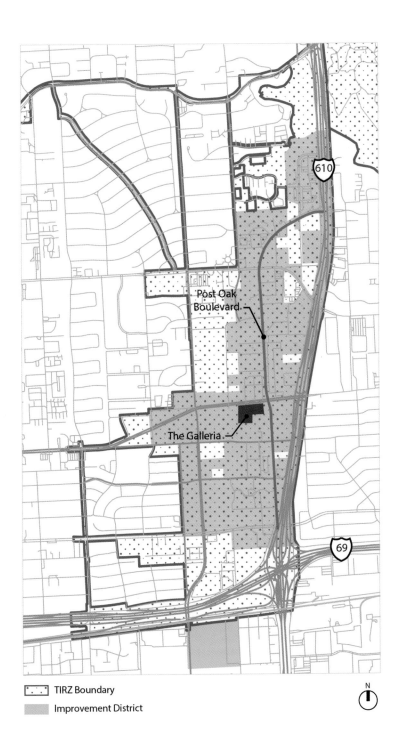

Post Oak
Boulevard

The Galleria

Houston's Tax Increment
Reinvestment Zone (TIRZ)
discussed later in this chapter
and the Uptown Houston
improvement district. (Owen
Howlett, Alexander Garvin)

TIRZ Boundary

Improvement District

N

to most BIDs, its revenue comes from an *ad valorum* tax levied on all real estate—in this case, $0.14 per $100 of assessed value—which can be used for operating expenses or pledged as debt service on bonds issued by the organization and used to finance capital improvements.

Post Oak Boulevard, Houston (2007). Live oak trees are growing in and will soon provide shade for large sections of Post Oak Boulevard. (Alexander Garvin)

To spur further private investment along Post Oak Boulevard, in 1993 the board allocated proceeds of its initial $11 million bond issue to finance utility relocation, relighting, and dramatic streetscape additions (stainless steel arches in particular). Industrial designer Henry Beer, a partner in the firm Communication Arts, Inc., which is now part of Stantec, Inc., conceived of the design. The board allocated money to improvements to the rights-of-way and infrastructure, to planting live oak trees along the boulevard, and to establishing places for floral displays. The most cost-effective expenditures, however, were the unique stainless steel arches erected at critical intersections and the enormous stainless steel hanging rings with lettering that spells out the names of street intersections. The money spent on Uptown's dazzling stainless steel street furniture (bus shelters, street lamps, traffic signals, and trash receptacles) gave Post Oak Boulevard a distinctive appearance and helped to brand Uptown as a very special place indeed.

Twelve years later, two complementary agencies, the Uptown Development Authority (UDA) and the Tax Increment Reinvestment Zone, began to administer capital construction and finance Uptown development projects, respectively. Between its establishment in 1999 and 2014, the Tax Increment Reinvestment Zone has raised $127 million in *ad valorum* taxes and UDA has spent $130 million on districtwide pedestrian improvements, traffic signals, transit shelters, rights-of-way reconstruction, and other street improvements for Post Oak Boulevard, San Felipe Street, and other arteries.[18] Furthermore, the Uptown District spends its annual operating budget of approximately $5 million largely on traffic operations, public maintenance and beautification, infrastructure improvements, communications, and marketing.[19]

In 2015, the UDA and the Texas Department of Transportation began a three-component transformation of the district's principal axis. The reconceived Post Oak Boulevard will extend from the transit center at the north end south to a second transit center, which will be built at its other terminus. The project also includes: (i) a new elevated two-lane bus way erected along the I-610 highway starting at the north transit center and terminating at grade where the northern end of the boulevard begins and (ii) complete reconstruction of Post Oak Boulevard. Buses coming and going from elsewhere in Houston will pick up or collect passengers whose destination is the Uptown corridor. There, Post Oak passengers will transfer from or to new buses traveling in either direction along the dedicated elevated busway or the entirely new Post Oak Boulevard.

The $192.5 million cost of reconstructing Post Oak Boulevard and creating its accompanying transit centers will be split between Uptown ($76.5 million) and the federal government ($45 million). The $45 million cost of the West Loop/Northwest Transit Center will be split between Uptown ($20 million) and the Texas Department of Transportation ($25 million), and the $27 million Bellaire/Uptown Transit Center will be split between Uptown ($9.1 million) and the federal government ($16.9 million).

Once Post Oak Boulevard has been reconstructed, property owners are likely to want to replace the low-rise commercial buildings fronting onto open parking lots that will have become underperforming assets with the more profitable uses for their property: lively, diverse, interesting, mixed-use, multistory buildings opening onto the new tree-lined sidewalks used by their potential customers.

Post Oak Boulevard, Houston (2014). The district is branded by the highly polished stainless steel arches at street intersections (shown in the distance). (Alexander Garvin)

Building a better tomorrow by adjusting and readjusting the public realm worked for the Place de la République in Paris, as it has during the past six decades for Post Oak Boulevard. In Paris those readjustments were made to retain existing businesses and residents. In Houston, however, the improvements to the public realm have continued to be made in a successful effort to attract and retain a sizable portion of the growing demand for retail, office, and residential space in one of the fastest growing cities in America. But it is an approach that is difficult to use in cities experiencing problems caused by changes in the global economy. Those situations require major changes to the public realm, such as are currently under way along the Brooklyn waterfront, the Atlanta BeltLine, and in Toronto, Canada.

Brooklyn Bridge Park—Intelligently conceived squares, like the Place de la République, and streets, like Post Oak Boulevard, can attract and retain market demand. So can parks. This is difficult in cities where most existing property is already in use. But parks do not have to be created on open land; they can also be the product of the adaptive reuse of empty buildings, as happened in New York City,

Post Oak Boulevard as it will look
after the combination of roadway,
sidewalk, transit lane, and trees
is enlarged and reorganized.
(Uptown Houston)

when the city and state governments decided to convert abandoned East River piers into the new Brooklyn Bridge Park. The process of creating this park, which grew out of the community activism of the 1980s, took off after the Port Authority of New York and New Jersey announced plans to close the piers in the 1990s. Local leaders formed the Downtown Brooklyn Waterfront Local Development Corporation. Thereafter, plans for the park finally took shape in 2002 when the Brooklyn Bridge Park Development Corporation (BBPDC) began to design and then build a 1.3-mile-long (2.1-km) facility on the East River, opposite the Lower Manhattan financial district. The area north of the Brooklyn Bridge consists of a series of smaller landscaped spaces with views of the Brooklyn and Manhattan Bridges. These sites include playgrounds, a carousel, and other places for recreation—all connected to streets leading into DUMBO (Down Under the Manhattan Bridge Overpass) at one end, a neighborhood where old warehouses and lofts have been adapted for use as residences and small businesses. In addition to this land, the BBPDC took possession of six large abandoned Brooklyn piers from the port authority, which it has since transformed into an amazing collection of places for active recreation.

Brooklyn Bridge Park (2015).
(Brooklyn Bridge Park
Conservancy, Owen Howlett)

Creating Brooklyn Bridge Park required a significant balancing act:

- Community residents demanded recreational opportunities for the widest range of Brooklyn residents.
- Government officials had to ensure that $390 million in government investments would be wisely spent.
- Designers had to restore the piles supporting the piers, reinforce the shoreline, accommodate the dimensional requirements of all the field sports, and provide appropriate settings for regular public events.
- Park officials had to combine everything into a new park that would be connected with Brooklyn-wide bicycle, jogging, and pedestrian networks.

The facilities that emerged are the product of design ideas from the landscape architecture firm of Michael Van Valkenburgh Associates, Inc., the determined leadership of Regina Myer, president of the BBPDC, and continuing input from community groups and city officials.

Brooklyn Bridge Park (2014). The berm along the eastern edge of the park shields it from the noise and exhaust fumes of Furman Street and the cantilevered highway above. (Alexander Garvin)

Among the many design problems that the Brooklyn Bridge Park had to deal with were the vehicular traffic that traveled along the service road on its inland side and noise from the six lanes of traffic speeding by on the cantilevered highway overhead, the Brooklyn-Queens Expressway. In response, BBPDC built a grass-covered berm that hides the service road, planted trees and bushes to absorb some of the noise and pollution from the highway, and established a protected path that runs along the park side of a landscaped buffer.

In addition, the site's abandoned piers presented an unusual design challenge. Although park-goers might enjoy the piers' river breezes and their spectacular views of the Lower Manhattan skyline, it would have been prohibitively expensive to reinforce the supporting structures sufficiently to bear the weight of the soil, trees, and bushes that are key components of a traditional park. Recognizing this limitation, BBPDC developed four of the piers as absolutely flat hardscapes with surfaces appropriate for beach volleyball, soccer, playground equipment, and any of the many other active forms of recreation popular with Brooklyn residents, some of whom travel long distances to make use of the park's facilities. Though most piers may not accommodate the typical elements of a green park, they do provide recreational facilities that are in great demand throughout Brooklyn, so they have been inundated with people ever since they opened in 2014.

One reason Brooklyn Bridge Park is so successful is that it keeps adding facilities and programming events that appeal to great numbers of people, including a carousel, performance lawns, a pop-up pool, and more than one place where visitors can have a bite to eat or enjoy a cold drink. Three of the six piers at Brooklyn Bridge Park can be used simultaneously for different forms of active recreation within the same pier.

Brooklyn Bridge Park (2014). There are places for people of all ages to enjoy, while others are busy using nearby facilities. (Alexander Garvin)

Pier 6 includes several separate spots for swings, a slide mountain, beach volleyball, and a string of lawns surrounded by wildflowers that bloom at different times of the year and provide an amazing contrast to the spectacular views of Lower Manhattan. Pier 5 accommodates three open-air athletic fields, two playgrounds, a fishing station, and a picnic area. Its three synthetic turf playing fields can be used for soccer, lacrosse, cricket, rugby, and flag football. The lightweight semitransparent roof covering part of Pier 2 provides shade that allows basketball, handball, shuffleboard, roller skating, and bocce games to take place while others use picnic tables or enjoy fitness and playground equipment. Pier 4 Beach combines a beach with marina facilities for private boats. Among the events scheduled during the year are gypsy punk, electro-jamz, and African dance parties; concerts, outdoor movies, opera, plays, and other cultural events; and fitness classes, training for kayaking, hip hop aerobics, and other recreational happenings.

One of the Brooklyn Bridge Park Corporation's innovations is the use of direct earnings from real estate transactions to finance park operations. Five park-owned properties along the inland edge of the project area have been leased to private owners for 99 years. The leases require the lessees to pay sizable amounts of money when the lease is signed plus annual rental payments to the BBPDC. Generally, annual lease outlays and payments in lieu of real estate taxes pay for

Brooklyn Bridge Park (2014). The recreational opportunities on Piers 2 and 5 provide something for everybody. (Alexander Garvin)

park maintenance and operations and capital maintenance, which is projected to be approximately $16 million per year when the park is completed in 2017. The city and state governments are paying for the rest of the park's $390 million development cost, along with $85 million from the port authority.

Ten years ago, there was no Brooklyn Bridge Park. There were, however, six unused piers on the water side of a service road. Those piers, like so many remnants of the economic life of another era, can be found along the waterfronts of cities around the world. Brooklyn Bridge Park illustrates that transforming these leftovers into popular additions to a city's public realm requires

- understanding specific uses that are appropriate to their physical characteristics (e.g., active sports that require the broad flat surfaces of open waterfront piers, or marinas that can be fitted in between these piers),
- providing sites for the greatest possible variety of activities that will attract as many diverse users as possible,
- connecting all these places with a series of walks for the various park users to enjoy,
- working with as many community organizations as possible to program activities that will bring people to the many facilities that can accommodate their activities at different times of the day and seasons of the year, and
- making sure that there are plenty of easy-to-use connections to surrounding neighborhoods.

Atlanta's BeltLine Emerald Necklace—Development of the Atlanta BeltLine, like Brooklyn Bridge Park, converted property previously used for shipping freight into an actively used part of the city's public realm. Like the Brooklyn Bridge Park, even before completion it attracted thousands of citizens. The BeltLine, however, also has provided a public realm framework that has already triggered a widespread and sustained private market reaction and will change daily life in Atlanta.

The Atlanta City Council approved the BeltLine in 2005. When it is completed, this "Emerald Necklace" will have transformed three separate decaying freight rail lines that encircled the city into a 23-mile-long (37-km) recreational facility connecting 46 Atlanta neighborhoods, 20 new or expanded parks occupying 1,300 acres (526 ha), 32 playing fields, 6 playgrounds, 3 swimming pools,

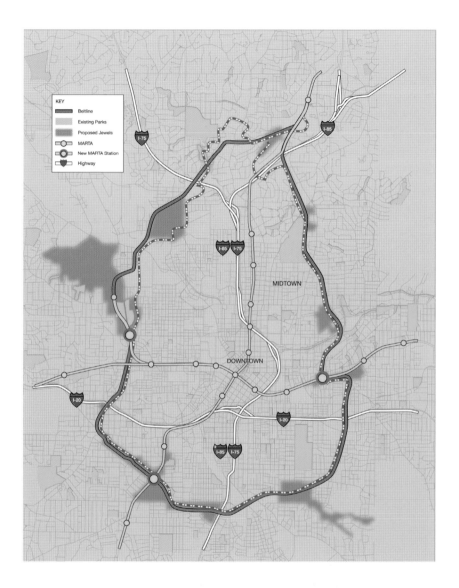

Atlanta BeltLine Emerald Necklace proposal (2004). Inspired by Olmsted's Boston Emerald Necklace, Alex Garvin & Associates (now AGA Public Realm Strategists) proposed expanding four parks, adding nine new parks, and tying them together with a 23-mile-long (37-km) landscaped trail. (Alexander Garvin)

and 3 different legs of the Metropolitan Atlanta Rapid Transit Authority subway system.[20] Indeed, people think of the already completed portions of the BeltLine as a year-round living room.[21]

The Atlanta BeltLine was not initially conceived primarily as a recreational facility. Its first incarnation, in a 1999 Georgia Tech master's thesis, reimagined the rail lines that would ultimately become the BeltLine as a transit corridor.

In 2004, however, the Trust for Public Land commissioned my firm to analyze Atlanta's green space challenges and opportunities.[22] I thought the BeltLine provided an opportunity for Atlanta to add much-needed public parkland, recreational trails, and eventually also to accommodate public transit. At the end of 2004 we released a detailed plan for what I conceived of as an Emerald Necklace, inspired by Olmsted's work in Boston (see chapter 7). [23]

The following year, Mayor Shirley Franklin created the Atlanta BeltLine Partnership to promote the proposed combination of park, trail, and transit. The city council followed by approving the BeltLine Redevelopment Plan, a tax increment financing scheme to pay for it, and Atlanta BeltLine, Inc., to implement the project.

BeltLine, Atlanta (2015). When the initial segments of the BeltLine opened so many people of every age, income, and ethnicity turned out that it began changing the way of life of the people who lived or worked near the trail. (Alexander Garvin)

BeltLine, Atlanta (2014). New housing construction started appearing all over the East Side, one of the first sections of the trail to be completed. (Alexander Garvin)

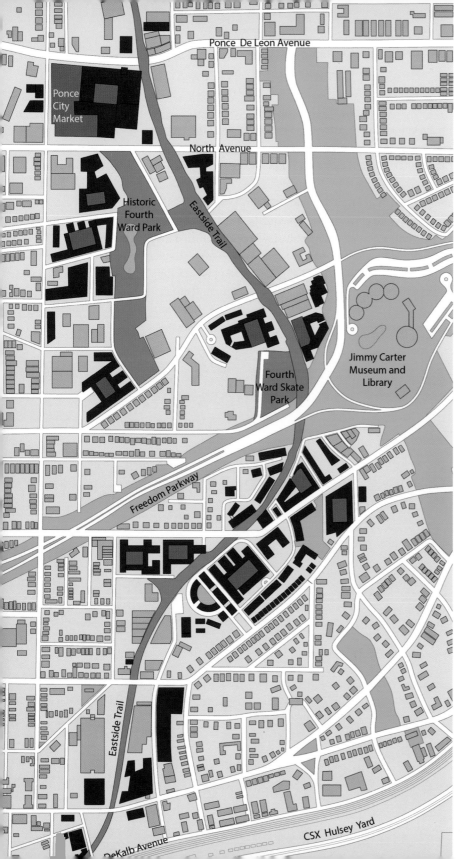

BeltLine, Atlanta (2013). One of the earliest sections of the BeltLine to be completed was on the city's East Side, where the private market reaction (black) to public investment (green) resulted in more than $1 billion in new construction and rehabilitation. (Owen Howlett, Alexander Garvin)

Just a few years into its construction, however, the project's major achievement is already evident in the extraordinary continuing private market reaction that has taken place along its edges. Between 2005 and 2013, private real estate development completed or under way within a half-mile of the Eastside Trail alone represents an investment of approximately $775 million.[24] Construction has accelerated since then. In late 2015, the Jamestown Properties will complete its Ponce City Market project, a 2.1 million-square-foot (195,096 m²) mixed-use renovation of what had been the Sears Roebuck and Company distribution center for the southeastern United States between 1926 and 1987. The project includes 259 condominium apartments, 300,000 square feet (27,871 m²) of offices, and 550,000 square feet (51,097 m²) of retail stores. In years to come, private development along the BeltLine will only grow in importance.

BeltLine, Atlanta (2014). The new Historic Fourth Ward Park became the setting for a wave of new construction. (Alexander Garvin)

BeltLine, Atlanta (2014). Whole neighborhoods are changing as a result of park and housing construction. (Alexander Garvin)

Daily life is changing for people who live along already developed sections of the BeltLine. The park corridor is becoming the place where residents of every ethnicity, income level, and social class encounter one another, cycle, skate, jog, or just wander. Furthermore, as more and more of the BeltLine opens for public use, it will have greater and greater impact on city residents.

Ponce Street Market, Atlanta (2014). This $200 million renovation includes retail and restaurant space, office space, apartments, and parking for 1,300 cars in a building that was once the distribution center for Sears Roebuck and Company in the southeast United States. (John Clifford, S9 Architecture)

If the city had not invested in the BeltLine, this additional investment would have taken place in areas without the supporting open space or eventual transit capacity—increasing dependence on private automobiles and peak-hour highway congestion. Instead, Atlanta is demonstrating how to achieve better balanced, less congested urbanization and create a park system that will supplant the city's interstate highways as the focus of daily life for hundreds of thousands of Atlantans. Still more important, the BeltLine demonstrates how cities in the twenty-first century can repurpose neglected, obsolete property, in the process creating a public realm that not only alters daily life, but can pay for itself with tax revenues generated by private real estate development that would otherwise not have occurred.

Waterfront Toronto—By the second half of the twentieth century, shipping, maritime-related industrial activity, and large-scale manufacturing had begun to move away from major port cities such as New York, London, and Amsterdam. Moreover, as they entered the twenty-first century, port cities also faced what Amsterdam had dealt with for a thousand years: a rising water table and the possibility of disruptive flooding. Consequently, their continued prosperity depended on reconceiving the city's relationship to declining waterfront districts.

Toronto waterfront (1983), just as redevelopment was getting under way. (City of Toronto, Owen Howlett)

Toronto accomplished this, perhaps surprisingly, by reorganizing and redesigning the public realm along all 29 miles (46.7 km) of its shoreline along Lake Ontario. Its efforts began with the 2.2 miles (nearly 3.5 km) of waterfront-related maritime, manufacturing, and warehousing separated from downtown by railroad tracks and the multilane Gardiner Expressway. It was an area that had been hemorrhaging blue-collar jobs for years.

Implementing significant changes to property on the edge of the central business district of Canada's largest city required overcoming major environmental, governmental, entrepreneurial, and financial obstacles. Moreover, the properties along the lakeshore were in scattered ownership, under supervision of different government agencies, and subject to a past era's zoning and other regulations. In response to these difficulties, the city devised entirely new institutions created specifically to redevelop the area.

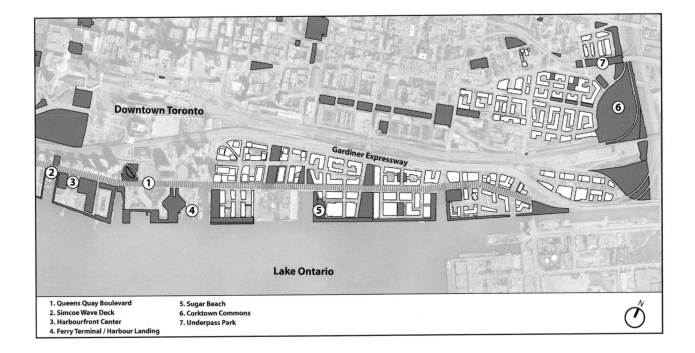

1. Queens Quay Boulevard
2. Simcoe Wave Deck
3. Harbourfront Center
4. Ferry Terminal / Harbour Landing
5. Sugar Beach
6. Corktown Commons
7. Underpass Park

The amount of money required to revive the lakefront was even more daunting than the many physical, governmental, and environmental obstacles. Environmental remediation, regrading of the land, and other costs needed to reuse the property would cost more than $4 billion—a sum far in excess of what any private property owner could raise, even if assembling it under a single titleholder was feasible. In fact, $4 billion was just the necessary public financing. Reuse of most of the rest of the site would entail an additional $34 billion in private equity investment.[25] Such huge sums of money were unavailable in the budget of any single existing government agency.

In 1971, the *Toronto Star* began the move of non-port-related uses to the waterfront. A year later the government of Canada made the next move. It acquired 100 acres (40 ha) of property on the Toronto shore of Lake Ontario west of York Street, south of the Gardiner Expressway, and across from Union Station (which is the very epicenter of the business district).[26] Four years later the Canadian government established the federal Harbourfront Corporation to develop the property. The corporation's first project was an adaptive reuse of the 750,000-square-foot (69,677 m²) Queen's Quay Terminal. In 1983 it converted this 57-year-old,

Completed redevelopment of Waterfront Toronto (as projected in 2016). (1) Queens Quay Boulevard (2) Simcoe Wave Deck (3) Harbourfront Center (4) Ferry Terminal/ Harbour Landing (5) Sugar Beach (6) Corktown Common (7) Underpass Park (Trevor Gardner, Waterfront Toronto)

10-story cold storage warehouse into a 14-story mixed-use condominium that included office, residential, arts, and retail tenants.

Harbourfront Centre, Toronto (2014). Once government redevelopment efforts began, new private construction followed suit. (Alexander Garvin)

By the end of the twentieth century, however, it had become obvious that this nationally chartered agency could not handle the complete redevelopment of the Toronto waterfront without the direct involvement and cooperation of provincial and city government agencies. That realization coincided with Canada's decision to compete for the 2008 Summer Olympic Games. What better location than the shore of Lake Ontario for an Olympic Village or for the other competition venues that did not exist at that time in Toronto? What more cost-effective justification for enhancing the city's tourist industry than preparing for the 500,000 people per day who would come to Olympic events?

Consequently, in 1999, the prime minister of Canada, the premier of the province of Ontario, and the mayor of Toronto created the Toronto Waterfront Revitalization Task Force to propose a mechanism for dealing with the undeveloped, misused, and derelict lands of Toronto's Central Waterfront. The task force recommended establishment of Waterfront Toronto (initially called the Toronto Waterfront Revitalization Corporation), jointly funded by the three levels of government, to oversee and lead waterfront renewal.[27] A year later the federal government, the province, and the city announced their commitment to spend $1.5 billion to revitalize the Toronto waterfront. Although Canada ultimately lost its Olympic bid to China, it went forward with Waterfront Toronto and appropriated the necessary funds in 2001.

Waterfront Toronto has been working ever since with the City of Toronto, Harbourfront Center, the port authority, and all the other waterfront stakeholders to

- · assemble substantial amounts of waterfront property for private development under the direction of a single agency acting as *master developer*,
- · identify and require necessary actions by private developers to deal with existing and future environmental hazards (e.g., managing storm water, cleaning up contaminated soils, eliminating the risk of flooding, and naturalizing appropriate areas),
- · invest in a manner that encourages private development,
- · package territory for private development of offices for expanding businesses, new housing construction, and supporting public facilities,
- · make the water's edge an accessible, public amenity,
- · hire fine designers to devise a welcoming layout for the public realm, and
- · re-enforce the connections with downtown.

Waterfront Toronto has been successful because it adopted a strategy that consisted of making it easy to get to the waterfront, improving circulation within its territory, and providing attractive destinations with plenty of room for people to gather and do things together. This strategy was embodied in Waterfront Toronto's 2006 Central Waterfront Public Realm International

Design Competition, won by Netherlands landscape architecture firm West 8, Inc., working with DTAH of Toronto.

Together with the staff of Waterfront Toronto, they devised a public realm framework that included numerous green lawns, benches for people to lounge in the sun, and lots of places to have fun. People can rent kayaks, take a sailboat onto Lake Ontario, wander for hours along paths that go through the parks; attend impromptu and organized concerts, theater performances, and festivals; and even go dancing along the shore. All these activities take place in facilities connected along the lakeshore by promenades and along downtown by Queens Quay, a new boulevard that opened in 2015. Unsurprisingly, this combination of public facilities and arteries has become the framework around which developers erect new office buildings, apartment houses, hotels, retail stores, cafés, and restaurants.

Perhaps the most remarkable of the new parks is Corktown Common, an 18-acre (7.3-ha) park designed by the landscape architecture firm Michael Van Valkenburgh Associates, Inc., which opened in 2013.[28] Eight years earlier, when Christopher Glaisek became vice president for planning and design of Waterfront Toronto, the city planned to decontaminate the area and create a huge, raised, flat space that, like a dike, would hold back floodwaters should the Don River overflow its banks.[29] Glaisek agreed with many local representatives who wanted the berm to be more than just functional, and persuaded government authorities that, in

Corktown Common, Waterfront Toronto (2014). The design of this park is based on decontaminating polluted land, creating functional wetlands, and blocking floodwaters. (Alexander Garvin)

addition to blocking floodwaters and remediating contaminated land, it should (i) recreate some of the area as functional wetlands, (ii) build up the rest of it into relatively low hills that would allow creation of real parkland with large trees that would remain above floodwaters, and (iii) simultaneously function as the centerpiece of the new neighborhood and a recreational amenity for residents and workers who would move into the new housing planned for the area.

Like other parks, Corktown Common includes hundreds of trees and shrubs, open lawns that accommodate athletic fields, playgrounds, benches, and picnic tables. What makes it unique, however, is the carefully designed marsh at the base of the hill, which acts simultaneously as a storm water management facility and a place where children can come to learn about and enjoy aquatic plants, birds, frogs, ducks, and other wildlife.

Corktown Common, Waterfront Toronto (2014). The park is a major asset for residents of the new apartment buildings being built nearby. (Alexander Garvin)

Opposite page–top: Simcoe Wave Deck, Waterfront Toronto (2014). Decks serve imaginative functions as backless chairs, gathering places, and popular recreational destinations. (Alexander Garvin)

Opposite page–bottom: Sugar Beach, Waterfront Toronto (2014). When the new park opened in in 2010, it included a sand beach with 36 sturdy metal umbrellas painted bright pink and 150 Adirondack-style wooden chairs, a paved performance plaza, and a tree-lined promenade. (Alexander Garvin)

Below: Underpass Park, Waterfront Toronto (2014). Planners have found inventive ways to transform leftover space into useable recreational facilities. (Alexander Garvin)

Waterfront Toronto includes a number of other remarkable recreational destinations. One is Underpass Park, the children's playground erected under the off-ramps of the elevated Don Valley Parkway. Among the other structures that attract children who want to play are three undulating, wooden "wave decks" designed by West 8, Inc. Although the wave decks are really wider promenades that replaced narrow sidewalks, they also function as backless chairs from which to watch the waterfront, gathering places for small groups to eat lunch or photograph themselves, and popular recreational destinations.

The public realm of Waterfront Toronto also offers numerous places that simultaneously increase the livability of the environment and the personal well-being of Toronto residents. For example, Sugar Beach, one of two sand beaches with colorful umbrellas located along this lakefront, was designed by Claude Cormier + Associés. It was created by tearing up and decontaminating two acres (0.8 ha) of an industrial parking lot and transforming it into a recreational facility.[30]

Perhaps the most important component of the public realm of Waterfront Toronto is the straight, 2.2-mile-long (3.5-km) completely refashioned Queens Quay Boulevard, which opened in 2015. Designed by the West 8, Inc./DTAH team,

Promenade at Sugar Beach, Waterfront Toronto (2014). (Alexander Garvin)

Queens Quay Boulevard, Toronto (2015). Within a few weeks of opening in the summer of 2015, the 2.2-mile-long (3.5-km) completely refashioned boulevard had become a major destination for people in downtown Toronto. (Alexander Garvin)

it runs along the entire north side of the project and includes widened, tree-lined sidewalks paved with red and white granite cobblestones, the Martin Goodman bicycle and jogging trail, and only two lanes of vehicular traffic.[31] Christopher Glaisek believed that the waterfront pubic realm was very fragmented and needed a powerful and coherent identity to tie the pieces together as part of a larger system. The Queens Quay revitalization was the result of a sustained effort to change perceptions and win local support for rebalancing the street for modern demands, by eliminating two lanes of vehicular traffic to provide space for pedestrians, cyclists, and a double allée of trees, as well as converting the remaining two lanes to a slower speed local street. Within three months of opening, Queens Quay saw an increase from 45 bicycles an hour to 500 bicycles an hour at peak times, transforming it into the most heavily used recreational bicycling facility in Toronto almost overnight.

Simultaneously with the completion of Queens Quay, the city announced Harbour Landing, the project that will become the centerpiece of the new Toronto. It is located at the intersection of Queens Quay with Yonge and Bay Streets, the primary routes between downtown Toronto and the ferries that take people to the islands in Lake Ontario. As its designers, KPMB Architects, West 8, and Greenberg Consultants, explain, it will fuse together a new ferry terminal with additional parkland at the critical juncture of the two east-west corridors and their intersection with the Yonge-Bay route downtown. Underground there will be parking; at grade there will be the ferry terminal; on its roof there will be an undulating green park; in combination with the rest of the public realm the park will provide promenades, boat slips, play areas, viewing decks, and a lift bridge that will similarly fuse shipping, ferry and water taxi service, sightseeing vessels, and recreational boating. Thus, Harbour Landing will provide a place for anything one might wish to do along the waterfront.

As of 2015, the corporation expected 66,000 new residents on property it controls and as many as 20,000 on adjacent land; 51,000 new jobs; nearly 3 million square feet (278,709 m2) of retail stores, restaurants, and galleries; a variety of new community facilities (including schools and day care centers); and 432 acres (175 ha) of parkland (35 percent of the territory in manages).[32]

Harbour Landing, Waterfront Toronto (2015). This undulating green park includes the Jack Layton Ferry Terminal, a belowground parking garage, promenades, and boat slips. (Ken Greenberg, Greenberg Consulting)

What Makes a City Great

Toronto's waterfront will never be finished. Tomorrow and the day after tomorrow, people will be asking if such-and-such is already there and wondering what will be coming next. Its greatness, like that of any city, lies in the ability of its public realm to keep changing in response to the demands of its current occupants, keep stimulating an evolving private market reaction, keep providing a framework for further development, and keep accommodating the evolving needs of future generations. But how should cities be thinking about improvements that will produce an even better public realm and, thereby, an even greater city?

Too many people think, as did Le Corbusier, in terms of "finished" cities. Some erroneously believe that most of the city's territory is already occupied, so there is no room for anything new. Others think that most of what is already in place should not or cannot be changed. In fact, the projects described in this chapter demonstrate how wrong those assumptions are. These projects present various techniques for improving the public realm in already great cities—without doing damage to people's daily lives.

The changes that Paris made to the Place de la République, like the changes Houston is making to Post Oak Boulevard, increase access to the public realm, improve circulation within it, and provide additional room for the people using it. They demonstrate that cities should be continuously examining existing components of the public realm, determining what can be done to increase their effectiveness, and then making the necessary alterations. The projects featured in this chapter also demonstrate that intelligent investments in a public realm framework will attract enough additional people to provide a much larger market for the privately owned properties around it. This additional market will turn existing properties into underperforming assets that their owners replace with buildings containing many more businesses paying substantially more rent.

Projects like the Atlanta BeltLine and the Brooklyn Bridge Park demonstrate that cities should be looking at underutilized and abandoned property that can be transformed into an entirely new public realm and that, in turn, will transform daily life throughout the city.

Waterfront Toronto has done both: reclaim underutilized and abandoned property and make better use of the already existing public realm. These are the most promising paths to a great public realm—one that will attract and retain people, who ultimately make cities great. I hope that this book will inspire you to go out and do just that.

Queens Quay
Boulevard,
Toronto (2015).
(Alexander Garvin)

NOTES

Preface

1 F. Scott Fitzgerald, "My Lost City," *The Crack-UP* (New York: New Directions, 1945), 30.

2 Warren Hoge, "Bilbao's Cinderella Story," *New York Times*, August 8, 1999.

3 Jörg Plöger, *Bilbao City Report*, Centre for Analysis of Social Exclusion (London: London School of Economics, 2007).

4 Basque Statistics Office.

5 Interview with Pablo Otaolo, director of the Zorrotzaurre Urbanistica and former director general of Bilbao Ría 2000, June 5, 2013; interview with First Deputy Mayor Ibon Areso, June 6, 2013; interview with Juan Ignacio Vidarte, director general of Guggenheim, Bilbao, June 6, 2013.

6 I am deeply indebted to Pablo Otaolo, who first explained to me the strategy and actions behind the revitalization of Bilbao, and who has directed much of the redevelopment program.

7 Areso interview.

8 Plöger, 28.

9 Instituto Nacional de Estadistica (Spanish Statistical Office), Madrid, 2013.

Acknowledgments

1 Jane Jacobs, *The Death and Life of Great American Cities* (New York: Random House, 1961), 6.

2 Charles E. Beveridge et al. (ed.), *The Papers of Frederick Law Olmsted*, Volumes I–IX and Supplementary Series (Baltimore: The Johns Hopkins Press).

3 Pierre Pinon, *Atlas du Paris haussmannien: La ville en heritage du Second Empire a nos jours* (Paris: Editions Parigramme, 2002).

Chapter 1

1 Alexander Garvin, *The American City: What Works, What Doesn't*, 3rd ed. (New York: McGraw-Hill Education, 2013), 96–98.

2 Alexander Garvin, *The Planning Game: Lessons from Great Cities* (New York: W. W. Norton & Company, 2013), 182–188.

Chapter 2

1 Jane Jacobs, *The Death and Life of Great American Cities* (New York: Random House, 1961), 14.

2 Ibid., 150.

3 The World Commission on Environment and Development, *Our Common Future* (Oxford: Oxford University Press, 1987), 8.

Chapter 3

1 Robert F. Gatje, *Great Public Squares: An Architect's Selection* (New York: W. W. Norton & Company, 2010), 50–55; Michael Webb, *The City Square: A Historical Evolution* (New York, The Whitney Library of Design, 1990), 32–36.

2 For a discussion of the origin and evolution of Oglethorpe's plan of Savannah, see Thomas D. Wilson, *The Oglethorpe Plan: Enlightenment Design in Savannah and Beyond* (Charlottesville: University of Virginia Press, 2012).

3 Gerald T. Hart, "Office Building Expansion," *Downtown Denver—A Guide to Central City Development* (Washington, D.C.: Urban Land Institute, 1965), 26.

4 Alexander Garvin, *The American City: What Works, What Doesn't*, 3rd ed. (New York, McGraw-Hill Education, 2013), 176–177.

5 Ibid., 219–228; Howard Kozloff and James Schroder, "Business Improvement Districts (BIDS): Changing the Faces of Cities," *The Next American City* 11 (Summer 2006), http://americancity.org/magazine/article/web-exclusive-kozloff/; and O. Houstoun Jr., "Business Improvement Districts," (Washington, D.C.: Urban Land Institute, April 2003).

6 Leo Adde, *Nine Cities: The Anatomy of Downtown Renewal* (Washington, D.C.: Urban Land Institute, 1969), 188.

7 Harvey M. Rubenstein, *Pedestrian Malls, Streetscapes, and Urban Spaces* (New York: John Wiley & Sons, Inc., 1992), 186.

8 Robert Schwab, "16th Street Mall Tops Area Tourist Draws," *Denver Post*, June 22, 2000.

9 *Denver Post*, September 6, 2015, http://www.denverpost.com/editorials/ci_28759582/time-reset-denvers-16th-street-mall.

10 Allan B. Jacobs, Elizabeth Macdonald, and Yodan Rofé, *The Boulevard Book: History, Evolution, Design of Multiway Boulevards* (Cambridge, Mass.: MIT Press, 2002), 83.

11 Gatje, *Great Public Squares*, 150–157.

12 Garvin, *The American City*, 371–375.

13 Hultin, Johansson, Martelius, and Waern, *The Complete Guide to Architecture in Stockholm* (Stockholm: Arkitektur Forlag AB, 2009), 7.

14 Robert A. M. Stern, "Introduction," in Shirley Johnston, *Palm Beach Houses* (New York: Rizzoli International Publishers, 1991), 8–23.

Chapter 4

1 Frederick Law Olmsted, "Public Parks and the Enlargement of Towns," in Charles E. Beveridge and Carolyn Hoffman, eds., *The Papers of Frederick Law Olmsted*, Supplementary Series, Volume I, (Baltimore: The Johns Hopkins Press, 1997), 186.

2 Jan Gehl, *Life Between Buildings: Using Public Space* (Copenhagen: The Danish Architectural Press, 2001), 11.

3 Edmond Texier, quoted in Patrice de Moncan, *Les Grands Boulevards de Paris: De la Bastille a la Madeleine* (Biarritz, France: Les Editions du Mecene, 1997), 166.

4 Olmsted, Vaux, and Co., Report to the Chicago South Park Commission, March 1871, reproduced in Beveridge and Hoffman, *Papers of Frederick Law Olmsted*, 217.

5 Galen Cranz, 7–8.

6 Michael Webb, *The City Square: A Historical Evolution* (New York: The Whitney Library of Design, 1990), 9.

7 Alta Macadam, *Rome* (New York: W. W. Norton, 2003), 182–184.

8 Franklin Toker, *Pittsburgh: An Urban Portrait* (Pittsburgh: University of Pittsburgh Press, 1994), 29–31; http://marketsquarepgh.com.

9 David Brownlee, personal communication, May 5, 2014.

10 For a discussion of the role and history of business improvement districts, see Alexander Garvin, *The American City: What Works, What Doesn't*, 3rd ed. (New York, McGraw-Hill Education, 2013), 219–228.

11 Project for Public Places, Downtown Pittsburgh Partnership, and the Urban Redevelopment Authority of Pittsburgh, *Pittsburgh Market Square: A Vision and Action Plan*, Pittsburgh, November 2006.

12 http://www.downtownpittsburgh.com/play/market-square.

13 Interview with Douglas Blonsky, president and CEO of The Central Park Conservancy, July 1, 2014.

14 Morrison H. Heckscher, *Creating Central Park* (New York: Metropolitan Museum of Art, 2008), 21.

15 Roy Rosenzweig and Elizabeth Blackmar, *The Park and The People: A History of Central Park* (Ithaca, N.Y.: Cornell University Press, 1992), 150, 160–161.

16 Frederick Law Olmsted, Letter to William Robinson, dated May 17, 1872, reprinted in David Schuyler and Jane Turner Censer, eds., *The Papers of Frederick Law Olmsted*, Volume VI, (Baltimore: The Johns Hopkins University Press, 1992), 551.

17 Blonsky interview.

18 Allan B. Jacobs, *Great Streets* (Cambridge, Mass.: MIT Press, 1995), 37.

19 Ibid., 96.

20 http://www.cityofchicago.org/city/en/depts/cdot/supp_info/make_way_for_people.html.

21 http://www.streetsblog.org/2008/04/18/sadik-khan-were-putting-the-square-back-in-madison-square/.

22 http://www.nyc.gov/html/dot/html/pedestrians/public-plazas.shtml.

23 "Corona Plaza Receives $800K Leadership Gift," *Queens Gazette*, December 4, 2013.

24 Jane Jacobs, *The Death and Life of Great American Cities* (New York: Random House, 1961), 150.

Chapter 5

1 Richard Florida, *The Rise of the Creative Class* (New York: Basic Books, 2002), 5.

2 Ibid., 16.

3 For a detailed account of the history of Third Street, see Alexander Garvin, *The Planning Game: Lessons from Great Cities* (New York, W. W. Norton & Company, 2013), 58–63.

4 For a discussion of the role and history of business improvement districts, see Alexander Garvin, *The American City: What Works, What Doesn't*, 3rd ed. (New York, McGraw-Hill Education, 2013), 219–228.

5 Joan DeJean, *How Paris Became Paris: The Invention of the Modern City* (New York: Bloomsbury, 2014), 46.

6 Robert F. Gatje, *Great Public Squares: An Architect's Selection* (New York: W. W. Norton & Company, 2010), 137.

7 Hilary Ballon, *The Paris of Henri IV: Architecture and Urbanism* (New York: The Architectural History Foundation and the MIT Press), 1991, 68–71.

8 Geometrically clipped linden trees were planted on the square's perimeter in 1682, but lasted for only a century. Replacements, planted at the start of the twentieth century, also did not survive.

9 John Summerson, *Georgian London* (London: Barrie & Jenkins, 1988), 166–180.

10 Steen Eiler Rasmussen, *London, the Unique City* (Cambridge, Mass.: MIT Press, 1967), 271–291; Ben Weinreb and Christopher Hibbert, eds., *The London Encyclopaedia* (London: Macmillan London Limited, 1993), 660–66.

11 Garvin, *The Planning Game*, 81–84.

12 Georges-Eugène Haussmann, *Memoires du Baron Haussmann* (1890; repr., Boston: Elibron Classics, 2006): Tome III, 496–497 (translation by the author).

13 Adolphe Alphand, *Les Promenades de Paris* (1873; repr., Paris: Connnaissance et Memoires, 2002), 237.

14 The avenue connecting the Arch of Triumph to the Bois de Boulogne was called Avenue de l'Impératrice until 1870, when it was renamed Avenue Général-Uhrich. In 1875 it became Avenue du Bois de Boulogne. In 1929 it was renamed again in honor of World War I hero Marechal Ferdinand Foch.

15 Tertius Chandler and Gerald Fox, *3000 Years of Urban Growth* (New York: Academic Press, 1974), 150.

16 Garvin, *Planning Game*, 70–71.

17 Jean Des Cars and Pierre Pinon, *Paris–Haussmann* (Paris: Editions Du Pavillion de l'Arsenal, 1991), 95–99.

18 Haussmann: Tome II, 87.

19 Eugene Sue, *Les Mysteres de Paris* (Paris: Robert Laffont, 1998), 31–33, quoted in Michel Carmona, *Haussmann: His Life and Times, and the Making of Modern Paris* (Chicago: Ivan R Dee, 2002); Haussmann: Tome II (Part 1), 487.

20 Garvin, *Planning Game*, 97–121.

21 Walter Moody, *What of the City?* (Chicago: A. C. McClurg & Co., 1919), 374.

22 http://www.wienerlinien.at/media/files/2011/wl_annual_report.

23 Roberto Brambilla and Gianni Longo, *For Pedestrians Only: Planning, Design, and Management of Traffic-Free Zones* (New York: Whitney Library of Design, 1977), 114–117.

24 Garvin, *American City*, 584–587.

25 Christopher Gray, "An Enduring Strip of Green in an Ever-Evolving City," *New York Times*, April 22, 2007.

26 Alexander Garvin, *Public Parks: The Key to Livable Communities* (New York: W. W. Norton, 2010), 160–164.

27 Ibid., 158–159.

28 William J. Thompson, *The Rebirth of New York City's Bryant Park* (Washington, D.C.: Spacemaker Press, 1997), 8.

29 William H. Whyte, *The Social Life of Small Urban Spaces* (Washington, D.C.: The Conservation Foundation, 1980), especially 58.

30 Garvin, *Public Parks*, 51–52.

Chapter 6

1 Kevin Lynch, *The Image of the City* (Cambridge, Mass.: MIT Press, 1960), 46–49.

2 Douglas Allen, "Learning from Atlanta," in Harley F. Etienne and Barbara Faga, eds., *Planning Atlanta* (Chicago: Planners Press, American Planning Association 2014), 15.

3 Ibid.

4 Antun Travirka, *Dubrovnik* (Zadar, Croatia: Forum, 1999), 14, 54–59.

5 Edmund Bacon, *Design of Cities* (New York: Viking Press, 1967), 117.

6 W. Bruce Lincoln, *Sunlight at Midnight: St. Petersburg and the Rise of Modern Russia* (New York: Basic Books, 2002), 17–20.

7 Ibid., 32–33.

8 Nikolai Gogol, "Nevsky Prospekt," in Leonard J. Kent, ed., *The Complete Tales of Nikolai Gogol*, Volume 1, (Chicago: University of Chicago Press, 1985), 207.

9 Joan DeJean, *How Paris Became Paris: The Invention of the Modern City* (New York: Bloomsbury, 2014), 96.

10 Bernard Rouleau, *Paris Histoire d'un Espace* (Paris: Editions du Sieuil, 1997), 227.

11 Patrice de Moncan, *Les Grands Boulevards de Paris: De la Bastille a la Madeleine* (Biarritz, France: Les Editions du Mecene, 1997), 7.

12 DeJean, *How Paris Became Paris*, 109.

13 Ibid., 97.

14 They included (and still do) the Boulevards des Capucines, des Italiens, Montmartre, Poissonniere, Bonne Nouvelle, Saint-Denis, Saint-Martin, Filles du Calvaire, Temple, and Beaumarchais, which extended from the Madeleine to the Bastille.

15 DeJean, *How Paris Became Paris*, 97.

16 Pierre Pinon, *Atlas du Paris haussmannien: La ville en heritage du Second Empire a nos jours* (Paris, Editions Parigramme), 24–39.

17 Alexander Garvin, *The Planning Game: Lessons from Great Cities* (New York, W. W. Norton & Company, 2013), 86–93.

18 Interview with Eugenie Ladner Birch, Lawrence C. Nussdorf Professor of Urban Research and Education, University of Pennsylvania, December 23, 2013.

19 Caroline Brooke, *Moscow: A Cultural History* (Oxford: Oxford University Press, 2006), 13.

20 Timothy J. Colton, *Moscow: Governing the Socialist Metropolis* (Cambridge, Mass.: Belknap Press of Harvard University Press, 1995), 272–280.

21 Ivan Lykoshin and Irina Cheredina, *Segey Chernyshev, Architect of the New Moscow* (Berlin: DOM Publishers, 2013), 159.

22 I am indebted to Olga Zinovieva for clarifying the differences among Moscow's major arteries and, in particular, for confirming that the trees that lined Tverskaya Ulitsa and the New Arbat were removed at the end of the twentieth century.

23 Colton, *Moscow*, 147.

24 Hilary Ballon, ed., *The Greatest Grid: The Master Plan of Manhattan, 1811–2011* (New York: Museum of the City of New York and Columbia University Press, 2012).

25 Marion Clawson, *The Land System of the United States* (Lincoln, Neb.: University of Nebraska Press, 1968), 44–53.

26 Sam Roberts, "City of Angles," *New York Times*, July 2, 2006.

27 Alexander Garvin, *The American City: What Works, What Doesn't*, 3rd ed. (New York, McGraw-Hill Education, 2013), 495–504.

28 Ibid., 495–504, 505–507.

29 City of New York Temporary Commission on City Finances, An Historical and Comparative Analysis of Expenditures in the City of New York, New York City, October 1976, 28.

30 Interviews with Daniel Biederman, president of the Thirty-Fourth Street Partnership, November 18, 2013 and December 18, 2013.

31 Howard Kozloff, "34th Street Partnership," in O. Houstoun Jr., "Business Improvement Districts," (Washington, D.C.: Urban Land Institute, April 2003), 176–184.

32 Statistics for Thirty-Fourth Street were provided by Maureen Devenny, research assistant, and Anne Kumer, archivist, Thirty-Fourth Street Partnership, December 18, 2013.

Chapter 7

1 Fredrick Law Olmsted, quoted by Charles E. Beveridge in "Planning the Niagara Reservation," in *The Distinctive Charms of Niagara Scenery: Frederick Law Olmsted and the Niagara Reservation* (Niagara University, 1985), 21.

2 Fredrick Law Olmsted, "Paper on the (Back Bay) Problem and its Solution read before the Boston Society of Architects" (1886), reprinted in Beveridge and Hoffman, eds., *Papers of Frederick Law Olmsted*, Supplementary Series, Vol. I, 441–442.

3 Ibid., 437–452.

4 Frederick Law Olmsted, "Notes on the Plan of Franklin Park and Related Matters" (1886), reprinted in Charles E. Beveridge, Carolyn F. Hoffman, and Kenneth Hawkins, eds., *The Papers of Frederick Law Olmsted*, Volume VII, (Baltimore: The Johns Hopkins University Press, 2007), 468.

5 E. W. Howe, city engineer, "The Back Bay Park," from the proceedings of the Boston Society of Civil Engineers, (1881), 126.

6 Fredrick Law Olmsted, "Paper on the (Back Bay) Problem and its Solution," 441–442.

7 Frederick Law Olmsted, "Suggestions for the Improvement of Muddy River" (December 1880), reprinted in Beveridge, Hoffman, and Hawkins, eds., *The Papers of Frederick Law Olmsted*, Volume VII, 517.

8 Alexander Garvin, *Public Parks: The Key to Livable Communities* (New York: W. W. Norton, 2010), 142–147.

9 Alexander Garvin, *The Planning Game: Lessons from Great Cities* (New York, W. W. Norton & Company, 2013), 132–163.

10 Robert Moses, "The Building of Jones Beach" (a tape-recorded talk delivered on February 26, 1974, at a meeting of the Freeport Historical Society), published in Joann P. Krieg, ed., *Robert Moses: Single-Minded Genius* (Interlaken, NY: Heart of the Lakes Publishing, 1989), 135.

11 http://www.nysparks.com/parks/10/details.aspx.

12 Cleveland Rodgers, *Robert Moses: Builder for Democracy* (New York: Henry Holt and Company, 1952), 55; John Hane, *Jones Beach: An Illustrated History* (Guilford, Conn.: The Globe Press, 2007), 14–17.

13 Robert Moses, *Public Works: A Dangerous Trade* (New York, McGraw-Hill Inc., 1970), 97–98.

14 Tom Lewis, *Divided Highways: Building the Interstate Highways, Transforming American Life* (New York: Viking Penguin, 1997), 37.

15 New York State Department of Motor Vehicles.

16 Hane, *Jones Beach*, 3.

17 Owen D. Gutfreund, "Rebuilding New York in the Auto Age: Robert Moses and His Highways," in Hilary Ballon and Kenneth T. Jackson, eds., *Robert Moses and the Modern City: The Transformation of New York* (New York: W. W. Norton & Company, 2007), 90.

18 Robert Moses, "New Highways for a Better New York," *New York Times*, November 11, 1945.

19 "To Add 2000 Acres to State Parks," *New York Times*, November 30, 1925.

20 NYC highways were built by borough presidents. As chair of the Triborough Bridge and Tunnel Authority, Moses was responsible for the bridges and tunnels that connected them. In addition, as NYC parks commissioner, the agency he administered built and managed the city's many parkways.

21 Carl Abbott, *Portland: Planning, Politics, and Growth in a Twentieth-Century City* (Lincoln, Neb.: University of Nebraska Press, 1983), 211–214.

22 Alexander Garvin, *The American City: What Works, What Doesn't*, 3rd ed. (New York, McGraw-Hill Education, 2013), 598–600: 1 Robert F. Gatje, *Great Public Squares: An Architect's Selection* (New York: W. W. Norton & Company, 2010), 216.

23 Garvin, *Public Parks*, 81–82.

24 Interview with Bram Gunther, chief of forestry, horticulture, and natural resources, NYC Department of Parks and Recreation, January 9, 2014.

25 Dan L. Perlman and Jeffrey C. Milder, *Practical Ecology for Planners, Developers, and Citizens* (Washington, D.C.: Lincoln Institute of Land Policy, 2004), 49.

26 John W. Reps, *The Making of Urban America: A History of City Planning in the United States* (Princeton, N.J.: Princeton University Press, 1965), 304.

27 Terence Young, *Building San Francisco's Parks 1850–1930* (Baltimore: Johns Hopkins Press, 2004), 171–172.

28 http://www.tfl.gov.uk/assets/downloads/congestion-charging-low-emission-factsheet.

29 http://www.tfl.gov.uk/assets/downloads/corporate/central-london-peak-count-supplementary-report.pdf.

30 https://www.stadt-zuerich.ch/portal/en/index/portraet_der_stadt_zuerich/zahlen_u_fakten.html.

31 Samuel I. Schwartz with William Rosen, *Street Smart: The Rise of Cities and the Fall of Cars* (New York: Public Affairs, 2015), 174–181.

32 Ibid., 178.

33 Ibid., 176–177.

34 Ibid., 175.

35 Lois Wille, *Forever Open, Clear and Free: The Struggle for Chicago's Lakefront* (Chicago: The University of Chicago Press, 1972), 3.

36 Dennis McClendon, *The Plan of Chicago: A Regional Legacy* (Chicago: Chicago CartoGraphics), 2008.

37 Garvin, *Public Parks*, 120–135.

38 Daniel Burnham and Edward Bennett, *Plan of Chicago* (1909; repr., New York: Da Capo Press, 1970), 50.

39 Lewis F. Fisher, *Crown Jewel of Texas: The Story of the San Antonio River* (San Antonio: Maverick Publishing Company, 1997), 31–35.

40 Ibid., 41–42.

41 http://www.thesanantonioriverwalk.com/history/history-of-the-river-walk.

42 Clare A. Gunn, David J. Reed, and Robert E. Cough, *Cultural Benefits from Metropolitan River Recreation—San Antonio Prototype* (College Station, Tx.: Texas A & M University, 1972) and http://www.thesanantonio riverwalk.com/history/history-of-the-river-walk.

43 Garvin, *Public Parks*, 65–67.

44 http://communitylink.com/san-antonio-texas/2011/02/17/hospitalitytourism/.

45 https://www.sara-tx.org/public_resources/library/documents/SARA-fact_sheets/SARIP-ENG.pdf.

46 NYC Planning Commission, *Capital Needs and Priorities for the City of New York* (New York: NYC Department of City Planning, March 1, 1978), 3.

47 Alexander Garvin, Parks, *Recreation, and Open Space: A Twenty-First Century Agenda*, Planning Advisory Service Report 497/498 (Chicago: American Planning Association, 2000), 40–42.

48 New York City is divided into fifty-nine community districts, whose fifty board members participate in the annual budget-making process.

49 Interview with Douglas Blonsky, president and CEO of The Central Park Conservancy, July 1, 2014.

Chapter 8

1 Mike Lydon and Anthony Garcia, *Tactical Urbanism: Short-Term Action for Long-Term Change* (Washington, D.C.: Island Press, 2015).

2 Neville Braybrooke, *London Green* (London: Victor Gollancz Ltd, 1959), 49.

3 Ibid., 54–55.

4 Ben Weinreb and Christopher Hibbert, eds., *The London Encylopaedia* (London: Macmillan London Limited, 1993), 414, 660–664.

5 Alexander Garvin, *The American City: What Works, What Doesn't*, 3rd ed. (New York, McGraw-Hill Education, 2013), 220–228.

6 Michael Kimmelman, "In Istanbul's Heart, Leader's Obsession, Perhaps Achilles' Heel," *New York Times*, June 7, 2013.

7 City of Copenhagen, *Copenhagen Bicycle Account 2012* (in Danish), 2013.

8 Jan Gehl, Lars Gemzoe, Sia Kirknaes, and Britt Sondergaard, *New City Life* (Copenhagen: The Danish Architectural Press, 2006), 24.

9 City of Copenhagen, *Copenhagen Bicycle Account 2010* (in Danish), 2011.

10 http://www.smartgrowthamerica.org/complete-streets/complete-streets-fundamentals/complete-streets -faq.

11 Lesley Bain, Barbara Gray, and Dave Rodgers, *Living Streets: Strategies for Crafting Public Space* (Hoboken, N.J.: John Wiley & Sons Inc., 2012), 99.

12 W. Bruce Lincoln, *Sunlight at Midnight: St. Petersburg and the Rise of Modern Russia* (New York, Basic Books, 2002), 113–114.

13 Maria Teresa, *City Squares of the World* (Verscelli, Italy: White Star Publishers, 2000), 122.

14 Ibid., 190–191.

15 Ibid., 248.

16 Michael Webb, *The City Square: A Historical Evolution* (New York: The Whitney Library of Design, 1990), 168.

17 Caroline Brooke, *Moscow: A Cultural History* (Oxford, UK: Oxford University Press, 2006), 33–58.

18 Ibid., 33.

19 Times Square Alliance, http://www.timessquarenyc.org/index.aspx.

20 David Freeland, *Automats, Taxi Dances, and Vaudeville: Excavating Manhattan's Lost Places of Leisure* (New York: New York University Press, 2009), 70–127.

21 Edwin G. Burrows and Mike Wallace, *Gotham: A History of New York City to 1898* (New York: Oxford University Press, 1999), 1149.

22 Ric Burns and James Sanders, *New York: An Illustrated History* (New York: Alfred A. Knopf, 2003), 347–351.

23 David Freeland, *Automats*, 166.

24 Garvin, *The American City*, 511–513.

25 Lynne B. Sagalyn, *Times Square Roulette: Remaking the City Icon* (Cambridge, Mass: MIT Press, 2001).

26 Times Square Alliance, *Twenty Years: Twenty Principles* (New York: Times Square Alliance, 2013), 6. (http://www.timessquarenyc.org/)

27 Interview with Tim Tompkins, president, Times Square Alliance, March 26, 2014.

28 Samuel I. Schwartz with William Rosen, *Street Smart: The Rise of Cities and the Fall of Cars* (New York: Public Affairs, 2015), 138, 166.

29 Andrew Tangel and Josh Dawsey, "At Times Square, Fewer Traffic Injuries," *Wall Street Journal*, New York, August 25, 2015.

30 Times Square Alliance, personal communication. (http://www.timessquarenyc.org/)

31 Ibid.

32 Ibid.

33 Police Commissioner William J. Bratton, "Policing 'Awful but Lawful' Times Square Panhandling," *Wall Street Journal*, New York, September 5–6, 2015, p. A11.

Chapter 9

1 Todd Longstaffe-Gowan, author of *The London Square: Gardens in the Midst of Town* (New Haven, Ct.: Yale University Press, 2012), writes that he does not subscribe to the common belief that there are over six hundred squares in Greater London. See 13–15.

2 Todd Longstaffe-Gowan, author of *The London Square: Gardens in the Midst of Town* (New Haven, Ct.: Yale University Press, 2012), 219.

3 Robert Thorne, *Covent Garden Market: Its History and Restoration* (London: The Architectural Press, 1980), 2–5.

4 Steen Eiler Rasmussen, *London: The Unique City* (Cambridge, Mass.: MIT Press, 1967), 166.

5 For further discussion of the business aspects of long-term leases in use in London, see Rasmussen, *London*, 191–195, and John Summerson, Georgian London (London: Barrie & Jenkins, 1988), 51–56.

6 Summerson, *Georgian London*, 80–81; Longstaffe-Gowan, *London Square*, 50–53.

7 London Parks and Gardens Trust, *Open Gardens Squares Weekend* (London: National Trust, 2013), 56.

8 Longstaffe-Gowan, *London Square*, 76, 159–161.

9 Charles Dickens, "Leicester Square," Household Words, London, 1958, 67.

10 Longstaffe-Gowan, *London Square*, 161–163.

11 http://minneapolisparks.org/.

12 Peter Harnick, *2014 City Parks Facts* (Washington, D.C., The Trust for Public Land).

13 Alexander Garvin, *The American City: What Works, What Doesn't*, 3rd ed. (New York, McGraw-Hill Education, 2013), 75–78.

14 Harnick, *2014 City Parks Facts*.

15 Theodore Wirth, *Minneapolis Park System 1883–1944* (Minneapolis: Minneapolis Board of Park Commissioners, 1945), 19.

16 Parkscore.tpl.org.

17 Minneapolis Park and Recreation Board, https://www.minneapolisparks.org/.

18 H. W. S. Cleveland, "Suggestions for a System of Parks and Parkways for the City of Minneapolis," reproduced in Wirth, *Minneapolis Park System*, 28–34.

19 Frederick Law Olmsted, "Letter to the Park Commissioners of Minneapolis," reproduced in Wirth, *Minneapolis Park System*, 34–39.

20 American College of Sports Medicine. Actively Moving America to Better Health: Health and Community Fitness Status of the 50 Largest Metropolitan Areas. 2014. http://americanfitnessindex.org/docs/reports/acsm_2014AFI_report_final.pdf.

21 Michael Kimmelman, "In Madrid's Heart, Park Blooms Where a Freeway Once Blighted," *New York Times*, December 26, 2011.

22 Ibid.

23 "The Last Time I Saw Paris," from the film *Lady Be Good* (1941), music by Jerome Kern, lyrics by Oscar Hammerstein II.

Chapter 10

1 Le Corbusier, *When The Cathedrals Were White* (New York: McGraw-Hill Book Company, 1964), 45.

2 Patrice de Moncan, *Les Grand Boulevards de Paris de la Bastille a la Madeleine* (Paris: Les Editions du Mecene, 1997), 134–135.

3 http://www.placedelarepublique.paris.fr/.

4 Tim Waterman, "At Liberty," *Landscape Architecture Magazine*, April, 2014, 114–126.

5 http://houstorian.wordpress.com/old-houston-maps/.

6 Bob Ethington, director of research and economic development, "The Boulevard" project liaison, Uptown Houston District, personal communication.

7 http://www.uptown-houston.com/images/uploads/FactBook.pdf.

8 Samuel I. Schwartz with William Rosen, *Street Smart: The Rise of Cities and the Fall of Cars* (New York: Public Affairs, 2015), 171.

9 http://www.houstontx.gov/planning/Demographics/Loop610Website/index.html.

10 Lisa Gray, "The Galleria," in *Hines* (Bainbridge Island: Fenwick, 2007), 67.

11 Ibid., 68.

12 Carla C. Sobala (compiler), *Houston Today* (Washington, D.C.: Urban Land Institute, 1974), 105.

13 http://www.simon.com/mall/the-galleria/about.

14 Stephen Fox, *Houston Architectural Guide* (Houston: The American Institute of Architects/Houston Chapter and Herring Press), 1990, 233.

15 Urban Land Institute Editorial Staff, *Houston Metropolitan Area... Today 1982* (Washington, D.C.: Urban Land Institute, 1982), 63–64.

16 Interview with John Breeding, Uptown Houston District president and Uptown TIRZ/UDA administrator, August 22, 2014.

17 City Post Oak Association was a volunteer group that eventually became the Uptown Houston District, a legally established government entity. http://www.uptown-houston.com/images/uploads/FactBook.pdf.

18 Interview with Bob Ethington, director of research and economic development, Uptown Houston District, August 27, 2014.

19 Ibid.

20 Alex Garvin & Associates, Inc., *The BeltLine Emerald Necklace: Atlanta's New Public Realm* (New York: Trust for Public Land, 2004), 22–28; Atlanta BeltLine, Inc., Annual Report 2012 (Atlanta, 2013), 29; The Atlanta Belt-Line 2030 Strategic Implementation Plan Draft Final Report (Atlanta, August 7, 2013).

21 As of 2015: Of the 33 miles of planned trails, 6.75 miles (18%) have been completed and 13.5 miles have been designed. Of the 1,300 acres of additional green space, 202 acres (16%) had been designed and created.

22 http://www.tpl.org.

23 Garvin & Associates, *BeltLine Emerald Necklace*, 32–45.

24 Atlanta BeltLine, Inc., Atlanta BeltLine 2030 Strategic Implementation Plan Draft Final Report, 71.

25 Waterfront Toronto, The New Blue Edge: Revitalizing Our Waterfront for Everyone (Toronto, undated).

26 http://www.harbourfrontcentre.com/whoweare/history.cfm.

27 City of Toronto, Our Toronto Waterfront: The Wave of the Future! (November 1999); Our Toronto Waterfront: Gateway to the New Canada [aka Waterfront Task Force Report or Fung Report] (March 2000).

28 http://www.friendsofcorktowncommon.com/sample-page/about-the-park/.

29 City of Toronto, The Toronto Waterfront Scan and Environmental Improvement Strategy Study (Toronto, March 2003).

30 http://www.waterfrontoronto.ca/explore_projects2/east_bayfront/canadas_sugar_beach, 08.16.2014.

31 http://west8.com/projects/toronto_central_waterfront/.

32 Christopher Glaisek, personal communication, January 10, 2015.

INDEX